NLN PAX RN & PN Exam Prep 2019-2020

A Study Guide for the Pre-Admission Exam for Registered Nurses and Practical Nurses, Including 400 Test Questions and Answers (National League for Nursing)

Copyright 2019 by PAX Nursing Test Prep Team - All rights reserved.

This book is geared toward providing precise and reliable information about the topic. This publication is sold with the idea that the publisher is not required to render any accounting, officially or otherwise, or any other qualified services. If further advice is necessary, contacting a legal and/or financial professional is recommended.

-From a Declaration of Principles that was accepted and approved equally by a Committee of the American Bar Association and a Committee of Publishers' Associations.

In no way is it legal to reproduce, duplicate, or transmit any part of this document, either by electronic means, or in printed format. Recording this publication is strictly prohibited, and any storage of this document is not allowed unless with written permission from the publisher. All rights reserved.

The information provided herein is stated to be truthful and consistent, in that any liability, in terms of inattention or otherwise, by any usage or abuse of any policies, processes, or directions contained within, is the solitary and utter responsibility of the recipient reader. Under no circumstances will any legal responsibility or blame be held against the publisher for any reparation, damages, or monetary loss due to the information herein, either directly or indirectly.

Respective authors own all copyrights not held by the publisher.

The information herein is offered for informational purposes solely and is universally presented as such. The information herein is also presented without a contract or any type of guarantee assurance.

The trademarks presented are done so without any consent, and this publication of the trademarks is without permission or backing by the trademark owners. All trademarks and brands within this book are for clarification purposes only and are the property of the owners themselves, and not affiliated otherwise with this document.

Table of Contents

Chapter 1: Role of the RN and PN in the Health Sector 7

Integrity in Testing 7

Marketability of the Licensed Practical Nurse 7

Employment Settings for Licensed Practical Nurses (LPNs) 8

PNs in Hospitals 8

PNs in Rehabilitation Centers 8

PNs in Nursing Homes 8

PNs in Home-based Care 9

PNs in a Medical Office 9

PNs in a School Setup 10

Fields of Practice for Licensed Practical Nurses 10

Pediatric Unit and the Neo-natal 10

Neuro–ICU, Trauma, and Burn Unit 11

Burn Unit, Cardiac ICU, and Emergency Room 11

Rehabilitation and Gerontology 11

Finding a Job after Training 12

How to Find a Job as a Licensed Practical Nurse 12

Make a Good Impression 13

Be Psychologically Prepared for a Math Test 13

Chapter 2: The PAX RN and PN Exam 14

Areas Tested in the PAX RN & PN 14

The English Proficiency Section of the NLN PAX 14

The Mathematics Section of the NLN PAX *15*

The Science Section of the NLN PAX *15*

Retaking the NLN PAX RN & PN Exam 15

The Validity of the RN & PN Exam Results 15

How to Register for PAX-RN & PN 16

What You Need on Exam Day 16

Cost of the NLN RN or PN Exam 16

Chapter 3: How to Effectively Tackle Reading Comprehension 17

Main Types of Reading Questions 17

The School Uniform Debate *19*

About Cocoa *20*

Important Tips on Tackling Questions About the Main Idea *21*

Definition According to Context *23*

Chapter 4: Importance of Math & Science in Healthcare 25

Importance of Math in Healthcare 25

Importance of Science in Nursing 25

Why Nurses Must Study Science *26*

Why Nurses Need to be Creative and Perceptive *27*

Practice Test 1 - Questions 29

English Proficiency Section of the NLN-PAX 29

Science Section of the NLN PAX 53

Mathematics Section of the NLN PAX 91

Practice Test 1 - Answers 111

English Proficiency Section of the NLN-PAX 111

Science Section of the NLN PAX 129

Mathematics Section of the NLN PAX 167

Practice Test 2 - Questions **191**

English Proficiency Section of the NLN-PAX 191

Science Section of the NLN PAX 214

Mathematics Section of the NLN PAX 246

Practice Test 2 – Answers.. **259**

English Proficiency Section of the NLN-PAX 259

Science Section of the NLN PAX 277

Mathematics Section of the NLN PAX 307

Chapter 1: Role of the RN and PN in the Health Sector

Many countries have created a tremendous opportunity for nurses who are trained but not to the level of registered nurses. These professionals are known as practical nurses. Still, some of them wish to further their training and become registered nurses over time.

The staff at the National League for Nursing (NLN) appreciate what the faculty and their students need, and so it has created a professional team to promote the profession. The team comprises of school specialists, curriculum developers, testing specialists, and even managers in charge of relations. The members of this team are geared toward providing the best services to the consumers.

Since its inception, the NLN has helped nurses build and extend their career by offering the exam system and provision of related services. From the time a person is preparing for admission to a college of nursing and through the assessment, it is the NLN's systems that help the prospective nurses find their way. All the profits the organization makes are plowed back into the improvement of the products and services offered by NLN for the excellence of nursing training.

Integrity in Testing

NLN is committed to keeping the exams credible, and the center for assessment and evaluation does follow the gold standard when conducting testing, as published by a group of professional bodies including the American Educational Research Association. There is inclusivity as far as setting nursing exams is concerned, and the people involved are from diverse sections of the health industry. Some are distinguished nurse educators and other experts charged with reviewing the test products. Inclusivity also extends to ethnicity, culture, and gender, as well as physical locations.

Marketability of the Licensed Practical Nurse

The licensed practical nurse is in high demand, and they are not only needed in hospitals and doctors' clinics but also in other institutions providing healthcare. Nursing homes are some of the places that engage the services of practical nurses. As for duties, practical nurses are often in charge of routine patient care, observation, and monitoring of patients' health status, provide assistance to physicians and registered nurses, and communicate with both the patients and their families.

Nevertheless, a huge proportion of practical nurses render their services away from the traditional settings of healthcare. In fact, a good number of practical nurses are employed by individual families, where they provide care to patients privately without being supervised by any health institution. There are other practical nurses who are engaged by business owners or business institutions as providers of basic healthcare to the personnel. They are also made available by these institutions so that employees and other people associated with the business have the ability to consult on matters related to their health.

Employment Settings for Licensed Practical Nurses (LPNs)

There is a whole range of places practical nurses can work. One of the main employers is the hospital setting.

PNs in Hospitals

While working in a hospital environment, practical nurses offer their services to the severely ill in-patients and to the patients who are fresh from surgery. LPNs are supervised by a registered nurse as they perform their duties, and they normally liaise together to ensure the patients' health is best enhanced. A great number of community hospitals are consumers of services offered by PNs, and often hire them on a long-term basis. Nevertheless, the greatest employers for PNs are the larger teaching hospitals. The PN's schedule of work often varies depending on the facility, although it is normal to have 12hr working shifts. Those working on such terms are given weekends off. Moreover, the working shifts are normally managed on a rotational basis.

PNs in Rehabilitation Centers

There are institutions, though not often as large as hospitals, where patients reside as they go through different forms of rehabilitation. Such centers provide health care to recuperating patients as they regain the different skills they lost due to sickness or surgery.

While at the rehabilitation centers, patients are treated by therapists with varying specialized skills including physical therapists, occupational therapists, and speech therapists as per the individual's needs. PNs assist these specialists as an RN works alongside them. For instance, if a patient who has undergone hip replacement surgery and has no complications to warrant staying in the hospital, he could be taken to a rehabilitation center to receive therapy that will help him regain strength in his muscles. He may also need to be trained to learn how to move around with clutches or to walk on different types of floors.

PNs in Nursing Homes

Patients who have been taken into nursing homes are different from those in rehabilitation centers in that the rehabilitation center is a point of transition for the patients with the hope they are going to improve the skills that are wanting and be able to be independent. In short, patients who are admitted in rehabilitation centers have hopes of leaving after a period of time, in fact, often after a predictable length of time. By contrast, patients in nursing homes have no hope of leaving the institution unless to a similar institution. Whatever problems they have are not expected to be cured any time soon, and so they require the assistance of PNs on a continued basis.

Some patients will have gone through different institutions of care before finally arriving at a nursing home. For example, a person who has suffered a stroke will probably be admitted to the hospital, but after he is stable, the hospital will release him with a recommendation that he attends a rehabilitation center. The reason such a patient is sent to a rehabilitation center is to help him regain speech if necessary and even to re-learn how to walk.

After such a patient has gained all that is possible and progress can be seen to have reached a plateau and cannot return home, he is transferred to a nursing home for continuous long-term support. Although institutions like the nursing home have their PNs working 12hr shifts, there are some who have 8hr shifts.

PNs in Home-based Care

Some patients are able to live well at home as long as they have support from members of their family or from healthcare providers or both. Individual patients require to be supported differently depending on their health needs. It is not surprising to see a patient who requires the services of an LPN for most of each day just to give the family time to catch up on their sleep if they are the ones that attend to the patient during the night. Other home-based patients require the services of a practical nurse that ensures the patient's medical plan is executed as recommended by the physician.

If the patient needs to be educated on matters related to his health, it is the LPN who is charged with the responsibility to teach him accordingly. The work shift for home-based nurses does not have to be the same as health institutions – sometimes the hours can be long and other times they may be just a couple in a day. For this category of patients, sometimes the arrangement involves visits by the nurse for a pre-agreed number of hours that could be as few as one or two hours.

PNs in a Medical Office

Health practitioners sometimes engage the services of LPNs in their medical offices where patients visit to have medical checkups or other health-related services. In such settings, the practical nurse helps the doctor by taking the patients' vital signs, their history pertaining to past treatments and their weight. If need be, the LPN ensures the patient is properly scheduled for upcoming tests or other procedures. In such a work setup, the nurse' work schedule depends on the clinic's hours of operation. A lot pertaining to the hours the nurse is required depends on the doctor in charge, and this means the nurse should anticipate weekend engagements once in a while.

PNs in a School Setup

Many schools have become used to engaging the services of practical nurses, and their services are mainly to deal with the minor health issues of students as they periodically arise. Nurses of different levels are often required not only by elementary schools where pupils are young in age but also in high school and colleges. With the services of a PN, the student can manage to wait for the parents to take him for further treatment or to recuperate in a more comfortable environment at home.

For more mature students, like those in college, the practical nurse provides them with care until they are ready to drive home. If more advanced care is required, the PN can accompany such patients to an emergency care unit or to a hospital. For the nurses' work schedule, it depends on the school's daily program and the periods when students are on campus.

Fields of Practice for Licensed Practical Nurses

Once you have trained to be a practical nurse, it is advisable that you work in different setups to gain experience because each environment is unique just as every LPN has her unique strengths. Nurses who have experience in a wide range of areas are bound to be more marketable.

Pediatric Unit and the Neo-natal

One of the areas where nurses are in high demand is the pediatric unit. This is an area that deals with young children including newborns who have health problems. Another area is the labor unit. In this department, the nurses take care of women during different stages of pregnancy, and they are also at their service soon after delivery and a couple of days thereafter. After delivery, the nursing support extends to the newborn as well.

The neo-natal unit needs nursing support for the newly born babies who are unwell or born prematurely. Oncology is another area where nursing services are in high demand. In oncology, the patients being treated and supported have been diagnosed with cancer, and they require different levels of support depending on how unwell they feel before and after chemotherapy and other treatments. Practical nurses can deal with patients who are experiencing nausea or pain. Some higher level nurses have also specialized in oncology to provide support for physicians.

Neuro–ICU, Trauma, and Burn Unit

The neuro unit is the sector where patients with brain surgery or serious trauma to the head recuperate. The nurses in this area specialize in conducting a neurological evaluation of patients, and they also learn the best way to monitor the patient who is either getting better or worse. Other nurses work in trauma centers where patients usually need close care. Sometimes the patients are victims of motor vehicle accidents, collapsed buildings, and other types of serious incidents that cause injury. Not only do the practical nurses offer such patients support on arrival alongside the registered nurses, but they also continue to offer them support after their major treatment, which is often surgery.

Burn Unit, Cardiac ICU, and Emergency Room

The burn unit is where burn victims are admitted as they receive treatment and seek to recover. Usually, the burns of such patients are extensive and could cover a large proportion of the body. Practical nurses in this unit specialize in dressing and changing burn wounds, managing pain and monitoring the patients for sepsis. At all times, practical nurses are ready to receive instructions from senior medical personnel including the registered nurses.

Nurses working in the ICU can learn a lot about handling vulnerable patients and those whose health condition is very delicate. For example, a patient who has just left the theater after heart surgery is likely to be taken to the ICU to be closely monitored.

Practical nurses working in the emergency room, or the ER, support patients who have all of a sudden become incapacitated or unstable, or those who have just been a victim of an accident of one kind or another. In the ER, the nurses join other personnel to render the necessary support for the patients to become stable. It is after that kind of support that these patients are taken to the ICU or the relevant ward to receive advanced treatment.

Rehabilitation and Gerontology

A practical nurse specializing in rehabilitation supports patients undergoing physical, occupational, or speech therapy. With skilled nurses on standby and scheduled to assist with therapy on a regular basis, many patients improve much faster than they would without such support. Nurses who hone their skills of gerontology become competent in handling patients who are advanced in age. Such are some of the patients requiring support on a continuous basis. It is because of such areas of specialization that the careers of PNs and RNs are continuing to grow and have better prospects for employment.

Finding a Job after Training

It is reassuring to know there are job opportunities available as you aspire to qualify as either a licensed practical nurse or a registered nurse. After passing your PAX NLN exam, the next thing should be to decide the area in which you want to specialize. Once you are certain of the area of your inclination, visit the web and seek institutions offering related services and then submit your application.

If, for example, you would like to work with patients suffering burns, look for hospitals or other medical institutions that have a burn unit. For better guidance, understand that burn units are normally found in hospitals whose designation is a Level Three Trauma Center. Once you identify such a hospital, visit its official website and investigate the careers offered. Once you click on that link, you will be able to search for available jobs. At this juncture, you should click only on the link showing a job you would like to have – in this case, a job that will lead you to support burn victims.

To utilize your opportunity, only click on a link if it leads you to an LPN job that is available. Make sure you understand the job description, the number of hours you are expected to work, the possibility of working shifts, and the salary offered. Take the opportunity also to compare LPN jobs in different institutions, and make note of which one has better terms for you.

How to Find a Job as a Licensed Practical Nurse

You do not have to know someone in a health institution to get employment after passing the RN and LPN exam. All you need is to have the diligence to go online and submit your application. Being diligent, you will have some important documents on hand as you apply so that the information you provide is not only correct but complete. The information you are likely to require in completing your job application includes your history of employment. When providing this information, you need to name the institution or institutions where you have worked, the applicable addresses and phone numbers, and the name of your supervisor and his or her direct telephone number.

Provide your history of education: the name, the physical address, and the phone number of the high school(s) you attended, and the post-secondary schools and nursing school you attended. Sometimes the organization that has advertised jobs demands that you provide your grades before they will respond to you. Be ready to communicate with the LPN school you attended and ask for a transcript with grades.

Have information on your licensing ready. The application form may require the date and the state where you sat the nursing exam. Do not doubt the credibility of the job advertisement if you are not asked for details of your nursing licensing as some employers opt to have the Human Resource department check that directly online. You need to take a moment to go online to determine what you need to do to have your nursing licensing accepted in another state if you are looking to relocate.

Make a Good Impression

Irrespective of the fact that you are applying for an LPN job online, you need to fill in your details in a manner that makes a good impression. Everything you key in should be correctly spelled and you should only use grammatical language. Do not leave spaces blank if you have the information or if you can halt and search for it. Remember that you are applying for a nursing job where an error of commission or omission can cause terrible harm to somebody else.

Be Psychologically Prepared for a Math Test

Even when you are already licensed as a nurse, you may still be required by some hospitals to sit a math test to determine if they will or will not hire you. The questions usually cover simple ratios and conversion of IV drip, and terminologies used in the field of medicine.

When you sit the math test, inquire of the people in charge of the test what the pass mark is and work toward attaining that. In the event the paper is not timed, take time to answer the questions thoroughly. Sometimes the test may be part of your job application process or a follow-up to your application. Whatever it is, ensure you concentrate and do your best. Then review the details of your application before clicking the 'send' button.

Chapter 2: The PAX RN and PN Exam

PAX RN & PN stands for the pre-admission exam for candidates seeking to enroll in either the registered nursing or the practical nursing program. The exam these candidates sit is set and regulated by the National League for Nursing, or NLN. This exam is set at 3hrs and is standardized for all aspiring nurses in the US.

The NLN comprises of faculty nurses as well as leaders within the sector for the education of nurses, and its operations are national. Not only does this organization ensure the exam provided in preparation for entry into nursing programs is standardized, but it also offers development for faculty and opportunities for them to network. It also seeks grants required for research and originates initiatives for public policy.

Whether you aspire to join a nursing program for practical or vocational training, or to join a program for registered nursing, this guide will be very helpful to you. It contains the kind of questions the NLN includes in the exam for these two categories of candidates. In short, those preparing for NLN PAX-RN will benefit as much as those preparing for NLN PAX-PN. It is essential to have a guide to help you prepare for the exam in an organized way, but do not be anxious as some of the skills tested will not be entirely new to you. There are some you have already come across in high school courses.

Areas Tested in the PAX RN & PN

The PAX exam is computerized, and you will be part of a group as you sit the exam that is administered under the supervision of an invigilator.

The NLN tests candidates' skills in mathematics and science, and in written English. In order for you to pass the exam, you do not need to have prior knowledge or experience in nursing. The exam actually seeks to establish if you have the potential for successful training as a nurse.

You will find the questions in the format of multiple-choice, with every question having four answer options to choose from. For the 3hrs allowed for the exam, you are advised to allocate an hour for each of the three sections.

The English Proficiency Section of the NLN PAX

In the section testing your skills in English, you will be assessed on your competence in comprehension, knowledge of words, and your ability to think critically. Among the questions are those where you need to state the meaning of particular words as used within given sentences and other words based on passages that are fairly short.

When it comes to honing your verbal skills, there is not much else you can do but read widely and do practice exercises such as those found in guides such as this one. The reason is that no one can predict the vocabulary you will be tested on. Nevertheless, it is helpful to appreciate the importance of defining every word in the context of the sentence or the passage in which it appears. You could enhance your range of vocabulary by doing crosswords and different word puzzles.

The Mathematics Section of the NLN PAX

In the section with math questions, you are tested on how well you can reason from a mathematical perspective, how well you are able to solve operations of a basic nature, and how competent you are in computing fractions and decimals, geometry and algebra, unit conversions and such other fundamentals of math.

For you to prepare for this math section, you need to practice basic arithmetic, algebra, and analyzing data, among other things. Some types of questions include percentages and decimals as well as fractions. Note that you are normally not allowed to enter the exam room with a calculator, but if one is required in the exam, some centers provide them or you are allowed to use the one on your computer.

The Science Section of the NLN PAX

In the science section of the exam, you can anticipate biology questions including some anatomy and physiology; chemistry and physics questions; and questions on health science including ecology.

Retaking the NLN PAX RN & PN Exam

You are allowed to retake the exam after 90 days, which is 3 months, and there is no limit to the number of times you can take the exam. For you to be deemed to have passed the exam, you are required to score a minimum of 74% in one sitting.

The Validity of the RN & PN Exam Results

It should be remembered that the exam is meant to be the key to a school of nursing. As such, different schools have different requirements regarding how old the RN or PN results are. While some nursing schools consider only those applicants whose scores are less than a year old from the date you sat the exam, others accept results that are up to two years from the time of the exam.

Nevertheless, it is worth noting that exam results may not be available after 3 years have passed, and so you may need to retake the exam if you want to attend a school of nursing after the end of this period. For those who present multiple results, schools will often take the highest score achieved when considering you for admission.

Sometimes schools of nursing also check the candidate's GPA score, and some will accept you with a score of 2.5, others demand their students to have passed with a minimum of 3.0. Needless to say, if your target school is among the most popular you need to have a high GPA score.

For the document bearing your results to be considered official, it has to have the stamp of your exam center, and sometimes it is simply embossed.

How to Register for PAX-RN & PN

When you decide to register for the exam, all you need to do is visit the NLN exam portal online and schedule the appointment. To accomplish this, you need to click on the button indicated 'Schedule an Exam'. However, you must ensure the date you want to be scheduled is a week or seven days in the future. Simply put, exam scheduling should be done a week in advance.

What You Need on Exam Day

When you present yourself for the NLN RN or PN exam, ensure you have a photo identification that is valid, with not only your photo but also your signature. You must also remember your login credentials to be able to access the NLN exam portal.

Cost of the NLN RN or PN Exam

The cost of the exam is around $65 and even if rises it is unlikely to go beyond $100. Refunds are not given by the NLN, and so you must sit the exam once you have registered and paid for it, otherwise you forfeit the amount paid. Be ready to pay for the exam again if you still want to sit the PAX-RN or PN exam.

Chapter 3: How to Effectively Tackle Reading Comprehension

For reading comprehension, many students begin by reading through the questions then going back to the passage in search of the answers. They fail to understand that this is not only a time-consuming technique but also a very dangerous one. You need to first read the passage to understand the questions and what the provided answer choices mean. When you read the questions before understanding the passage, you only create room for confusion which leads to wasting time.

Main Types of Reading Questions

You will encounter questions which ask for the main idea, the importance of a passage, or what the central idea of the passage is. Specific detail questions are those that require you to explain ideas which have been clearly stated in the passage.

Some questions will be on word meanings as per the context. Other questions will test you on how well you can draw inferences by asking you to explain what a certain statement means. There are also questions that are designed to test whether you are able to recognize the authors' emotional state through their attitude or tone. There will be technique questions which test you on recognizing the authors' writing style and organizational technique.

Does your mind easily wander when you are reading long passages? Are reading comprehension exams difficult for you because you are a slow reader and it takes you longer to understand the passages? There is no better way for you to prepare for reading comprehension than to read. Reading habitually will not only help you concentrate on lengthy passages in the exam but also increase your reading speed and improve your ability to understand. Remember that reading quickly does not mean that you hastily go through a passage; take your time when reading, understand and make sure that you recognize important ideas.

When sitting for standardized tests, you need to have a good plan in place that will help you successfully tackle the reading comprehension segment. Here are a few steps that you can apply.

- Timing is everything. Make sure that you allocate each section a reasonable time of about 4 to 5 minutes, which is enough time for you to read one section.

- Thoroughly go through the guidelines given for every section. Make sure that you also listen to any verbal instructions that might be added because they may help to clarify any confusing or unclear guidelines given on the paper.

- Read the passage very carefully as you underline important events or characters on your test sheet or you can also use a rough sheet to do this. Using the margins of your paper to draft a simple list is also another option that is embraced by many students. Underline or write down one-worded summaries of important numbers, key ideas, characters, and significant events to help you focus your thinking and to retain information. Do not however allow yourself to get carried away no matter how captivating the passage might be. Continue to read swiftly and remember that the main objective when highlighting all those points was to get the information which will provide answers to the questions.

At this point, you know what the passage is about, you have a rough idea of what the key ideas are, and you have highlighted the main points.

- Read the questions carefully as well as all the given choices. Often, tests are set in such a way that the questions can easily confuse you and so it is important to maintain a clear and focused mind. Avoid choosing an answer until you have read and understood all the choices given. Bear in mind that the answers will mostly be centered on a few conclusions or facts from your passage.

- Now that you have gone through the various choice answers that have been provided, revisit your passage and look for the appropriate information. If the choices have unique or big words it will be easier for you to identify them in the passage.

- Review the choices again and finally mark the answer you think is correct.

You need to familiarize yourself with the various kinds of standardized comprehension tests for you to succeed. You will generally find questions that will test you on facts found in the passage, a few others will be inference questions that deal with the anticipated consequences of the said actions. From time to time, you will also come across application questions that are designed to make you think beyond what you read to connect the information from the passage.

There are different ways that you can choose to answer your questions. You can decide to answer them just as they follow in the paper which is what some students find easier to do since they feel that marking the questions, then putting them in their respective categories is time-consuming. You can also decide to tackle the easy questions first and then tackle the difficult ones. If you decide to tackle the questions according to their level of difficulty, start by handling the questions based on facts first because it is easy to spot the answer from what you read in the passage.

The next set of questions might be the inference questions that might require you to read the question a couple of times. Tackle the application questions last because they will take up a lot of your time. Do as many practice exams as you can.

When you are reading a standardized test passage, you may find it boring and sometimes difficult. It may become even more difficult to identify the topic, main idea and the supporting details from the passage. Often times, those tasked with creating the tests use passages that are not interesting or those with unfamiliar information.

The topic, also known as the subject of the passage is the overall idea that is being communicated and it can be explained in a simple phrase or a single word. In some cases, when a passage has been taken from a larger text, the examiners give a brief description of that passage. Pay close attention to the given description since it might be carrying the topic but if that is not the case then read the passage carefully and identify what it is about. Below is an example of a short passage that you can read and identify the topic. Once you have identified the topic, it is easier to go to the next step.

The School Uniform Debate

The intense debate on school uniforms has been going on for years with some arguing that children should be allowed to express themselves and their individuality through what they wear to school. There are however some academic and social challenges that come with such a demand. Not all students are privileged enough to have the kind of clothes that they want. Some, on the other hand, can afford to dress well and this may cause bullying in schools as the less privileged are oppressed. When attention is shifted from school work to an individual and to dressing, then the whole concept of school is lost. It is, therefore, necessary to retain school uniform.

From this short passage, can you tell what the topic is? If you have read it keenly, you will find that the topic is school uniforms. Once you know the topic, you can now move on to the main idea. Basically, the writer will communicate what you should learn from the passage in one distinct statement which is the main idea. You will almost always find this main idea written as a thesis statement. When you want to find out what your main idea is in a whole passage, all you have to do is get the thesis statement which you will either find at the beginning or the in the last paragraph as it is always used to summarize the conclusion. For a passage of one paragraph, you will find your main idea as a topic sentence which will most likely be the very first sentence or the last one.

There is also a simple method that you can use to find the main idea whether it is in a paragraph or a whole passage. The first thing you need to identify is the topic and once you have that you should then figure out what information the author wants you to know about that topic. The next step is to create a sentence of your own to summarize the author's point and then match it with sentences in the text. The sentence that is similar to yours is the main idea.

Regarding the sample one-paragraph passage, the 'school uniform' is the topic. To get the topic sentence or main idea, you need to know what the author is saying about school uniforms. The summary of this topic clearly states that it is necessary to retain school uniforms. The topic sentence shows that school uniforms are important and so the main idea is that school uniforms are necessary. As you can see, every sentence is supporting the main idea.

Supporting details will always give answers concerning the main idea. They always answer the questions where, what, why, how, when, how much, or how many. From the short passage, you can tell that several sentences answer these questions. The main idea is school uniforms are necessary; our question becomes why are school uniforms necessary? The answer is because not all children can afford nice clothes and they might face bullying from kids who are dressed smarter than they are. The supporting detail is that attention will be shifted from studying to how attire will affect school work.

In cases where the topic sentence does not give you the main idea, you can create your own main idea. It may sound like a daunting task but it is quite easy to do. Since paragraphs are based on ideas, all you are required to do is establish the topic then look for those supporting details that relate to one another. Think about what the interaction between these supporting details means and there you will come up with your main idea. For example, from the sentence below, you can easily create the main idea by looking at the supporting details used.

About Cocoa

Cocoa is an ingredient in chocolate which makes chocolate a good snack. There are many varieties of chocolate which include dark chocolate, milk chocolate, white chocolate, and semi-sweet chocolate.

To find the main idea from these sentences, you need to first establish the topic which is chocolate. The next thing you should ask is why, what, where, when and how. These questions will be answered by the supporting details which inform us that chocolate is a good snack because it comes from cocoa, it is sweet, and there are a variety of flavors. Now determine how these details relate to each other and what message the author is sending. The main idea will then emerge that chocolate is a good snack because of its healthy property and because of its sweetness.

Important Tips on Tackling Questions About the Main Idea

When answering questions that are based on the main idea, there are some helpful tips. It is best to tackle the main idea based questions last because the answers take longer to find compared to other questions. For example, the answers to all the other types of questions in standardized tests such as the SAT are arranged in such a way that you can easily identify them in a flowing manner from the passage. You are likely to come across terms such as generalization, theme, or purpose in main idea questions so look for such terms. You can decide to lightly read through the questions then underline the topic sentences as you read the passage.

Always remember that answer choices that are either too broad or too wordy are often incorrect. As mentioned earlier, it is also important to first create your own answer before going to the choices and then check to see what answer closely mirrors yours in the given choices.

We draw conclusions and inferences all the time without even knowing that we are doing so. We also make educated guesses based on the clues given by the author in a passage. These hints are known as context clues.

There are times when reading that you can correctly guess what would happen next. You did not just magically think of an event and it luckily happened as you imagined it. You simply used the context clues that had appeared in the story and you made informed assumptions to predict the next event. Look at this short paragraph below and see if you can come up with correct conclusions.

Jean likes spending time with children. The best part of her work is that she gets to work with the children every week from Monday to Friday. Jean gets tired sometimes because her work is quite involved but she is proud that she can influence young minds. You will often find Jean carrying books and a long ruler.

From the short passage, what do you think is Jean's occupation? Is she a musician, a pediatrician, a therapist, or a teacher? The correct answer is a teacher. Drawing inferences is not always easy but this is just a simple example to show you how the principle of drawing inferences works. You were not directly told that Jean is a teacher but the context clues led you to that conclusion. In this case, the context clues were that Jean spends the entire week with the children, she is able to influence their minds and that she carries books and a long ruler.

However, you need to be careful when drawing inferences. Sometimes you may have some personal knowledge or experience about the topic that is discussed in the passage and so you may find yourself drawing inferences from your own understanding and not from the passage and this is wrong. You must draw inferences strictly from what the author has provided to avoid making incorrect inferences.

Let us look at this example.

Becky is your favorite aunt and she is a kind, funny and smart lady. When you come across a passage with a character whose name is Becky, you should not immediately assume that she is kind, smart and funny like your aunt. It could be that the character Becky in the passage is a merciless and mean old lady who is always grumpy. When you draw a conclusion based on what you know about your aunt, you will draw the wrong conclusion. Below is another example.

Candy Crush is a very interesting game that you can play on your phone whenever you want to engage your mind in something fun and mind-involving. Since the game was introduced a few years ago, many people have downloaded it to their computers and phones. It is known that a large population of young people has this game application on their phones for quick and easy access. Candy Crush was invented by a young boy in school who was looking for something engaging to do and he did not know that it would grow to such a remarkable extent. Today, the founder of candy crush is worth billions because of this creative game.

Candy Crush is not the only game application that is available in the market. There are other games that have since been invented such as Temple run, Subway surfers, and Sudoku that have also gained a lot of popularity since their invention.

What do you think is the reason why other game applications like Temple run, Subway surfers, and Sudoku were created? Is it because the other students were asked to create their own game applications? Did other gamers see the potential in creating more games after the success of Candy Crush? Did the founder of Candy Crush recruit other people who made more game applications to provide competition? Is it because the game was not as interesting as many would have wanted it to be?

The correct answer is that other creators saw the success of Candy Crush and decided to create more games. From that paragraph, what context clues led you to make this conclusion? There is a sentence that says that 'there are other games that have since been invented' which means that Candy Crush was created before all the other games came on the market. We also see that the founder of Candy Crush is now worth billions which tells us that many other game developers would want to create similar games and become as successful.

Now let us look at the other alternative answers provided. If you decide to go with the answer that states that the other students were asked to create their own game applications, you have no supporting evidence for this. We do not know anything about the school, the students, or any other creations that originated from the school. In fact, we do not even know the name of the school. The answer is wrong because it lacks supporting evidence. If you decide to go with the answer that many users did not find the game as interesting as they expected it to be, then it could be that you are choosing this answer based on your personal experience or a negative review that you have heard from your peers or other people.

Remember that you should always base your answers on what you have learned from the passage even when your own knowledge on the subject is factual. If you choose the founder recruited people to make other game applications so that there would be competition, you are making conclusions based on the fact that he has made a lot of money from the application and he can now afford to employ people to create more applications. This is a strategy that can be used in an actual situation but you need to use only context clues from the passage.

In summary, remember that all you have to do is use the information that you have been given in the passage to draw conclusions and inferences. Do not be intimidated by this process and remember drawing inferences is a skill that you have been practicing for a long time even without your knowledge.

Definition According to Context

You will often come across questions that will require you to choose the definition of a word according to how it has been used in the passage. There are a few tips that you can use to be able to answer 'definition in context' questions. We have countless words in the English language and it is not practical to know the meaning of all the English words. Context provides helpful clues that can help us know what a certain word means.

Here is a basic example of how you can derive the meaning of a word from the context clues.

In some poor countries, children and adults do not get enough food to attain their nutritional requirement and so they are malnourished.

You might not know what the word 'malnourished' means but the context clues can guide you to understand that when a person does not get enough food the body does not get the right nutrients needed to function. From this, we can then understand that the word malnourished means lacking the essential nutrients. The context clues have led us to the correct meaning of an unfamiliar term. Below is another example.

The world is developing at a fast rate and technology is one of the major factors contributing to this growth. Children as young as three are able to use devices such as phones and laptops to learn and play games. These tech-savvy children will become the inventors of tomorrow as they continue to be exposed to advanced technology throughout their lives.

What information can you get from these sentences? You have learned that young children are exposed to technology and that they are able to operate certain devices with ease. From this clue, we can establish that the term tech-savvy is related to knowing or being good at technology.

Here are two more examples.

Sandra bought some ice cream at the mall and ate a bit of it but the sun was so hot that the ice cream started to melt. Afraid that it would ruin her dress, she wrapped it up and discarded it.

What do you think the word 'discard' means? Is the correct answer to return, throw away, or eat? We know that Sandra had already begun to enjoy her ice cream before it started to melt and so she could not return it because it was already hers. We are also informed that she wrapped it up before discarding it which means that she could not eat it after wrapping it. She did not want to ruin her dress and so she had to throw the ice cream away. Therefore the meaning of the word discard is to throw away.

Billy was very good at soccer until Ben hit him with a bat on the knee which made Billy loathe Ben.

What does 'loathe' mean? Is it like, care for, hate, or respect? Billy used to play soccer until his knee was hurt by Ben. He cannot enjoy the sport anymore and Ben is to blame. It is only natural that what Billy feels toward Ben is hate, so loathe means hate.

Chapter 4: Importance of Math & Science in Healthcare

Some people may assume that medical and nursing students do not need to study mathematics. The reality is that all professionals in the medical field need to have some background in mathematics.

Importance of Math in Healthcare

All professionals in the medical field need some background in mathematics.

To record the success rate of various treatments or the rate of an epidemic on a statistical graph, you need to have sufficient knowledge as to how to record and interpret a graph and this can only be possible if you have some mathematics background. For nurses or doctors to administer medication or write prescriptions, they need to know math. Prescriptions usually contain the type of medication as well as the dosage.

When it comes to the field of medicine, every calculation must be accurate and there is no room for error because the lives of people are involved. Numbers play a key role in the medical field because they provide crucial information to doctors, nurses, and patients.

For medical companies to identify, treat, and avoid medical conditions, they need to get reliable information and data. Understanding and utilizing scientific calculations and the various health care tools enhance efficient delivery of service. When medical services are delivered effectively, there is a lower risk of medical errors that may lead to tragedies and medical malpractices.

Importance of Science in Nursing

During your stay in the hospital, a nurse will be attending to your every need. The impact is not only felt by the patients who interact with the nurses but also the patient's family. You are likely to remember a nurse who was caring and helpful even long after you have left the hospital.

The caring and serving nature of nursing makes it a profession that is highly regarded and respected and it is no wonder that for years it has remained a most respected career. You may think that nursing is all about caring for the sick and comforting grieving families but there is another element to nursing that you may not be familiar with and that is the science aspect of it.

As you may know, the healthcare industry is based on many scientific findings. For you to become a nurse, you have to study for a number of years to learn about the complexities of a human body. For you to be able to grasp all the scientific knowledge that is involved in nursing you need to be attentive and sharp minded. Nursing is a profession that requires you to combine caring and the scientific aspects of the career.

As a nurse, you not only have to be in touch with your emotional side but also use your knowledge. You are faced with situations that require you to make correct judgments and determine what care solution best suits your patients, and to do this, you need to apply critical thinking. Providing treatment demands that you apply your scientific knowledge.

Nursing is a science and also an art so you cannot be a successful nurse if you do not utilize both aspects. As Stephanie Sargent, a registered nurse and vice president of product development at a consulting firm dealing with healthcare quality said, "Even if you have all the knowledge in medical sciences and technology yet you do not know how to use your emotional intelligence, you will provide poor care for your patients". She further stated that if you are a caring nurse but have no idea how to use equipment such as the ventilator, then you will still encounter difficulties.

Why Nurses Must Study Science

According to Amos Restad, a DNP student and nursing instructor, nursing is legitimately a scientific discipline that is based on theory, evidence, and ongoing research. He continues to explain that nurses do their work on the basis of evidence in a bid to improve the quality of care they provide.

When studying nursing, you will come across complex scientific concepts and theories as well as practical methodologies, all intended to help you understand the intricate human body. According to Jonathan Steele, a registered nurse and the Water Cures executive director, nurses are actually scientists because they study and acquire expert knowledge on one or several of the physical or natural sciences, which is basically what a scientist does. He continued to say that nurses work with physical sciences, which encompass nursing and medical sciences together. The care provided by doctors is only effective when the nurses play their part in facilitating care.

For you to practice nursing, you must pass the science courses of chemistry, anatomy, physiology, and microbiology. Behavioral sciences of sociology and psychology are also courses you need to pass in order to practice nursing.

Apart from understanding these complex sciences, you are also required to be familiar with the technology that is used in the healthcare system. Stephanie Sargent explains that nursing has evolved from what it was hundreds of years ago. Technology is now a key contributor to the healthcare system and you must know how to use it as it is used everywhere from traction devices, infusion pumps, fall alarms, ventilators, and to store health records.

You can only offer effective services if you have the knowledge needed to utilize the important scientific concepts, evidence-based practices, as well as technical skills that are available. However, Restad states that even if you are knowledgeable of the many protocols, facts, theories, and algorithms in nursing but you do not apply the human aspect of nursing, you will not be successful in your practice. If nursing was only about having the required knowledge then robots would qualify to be nurses. The human aspect of it is what makes nursing what it is.

Why Nurses Need to be Creative and Perceptive

As a nurse, you learn a lot about the human body during training, but how you apply this knowledge is what displays the beauty of nursing. When you have the expertise and knowledge but you lack the required art of applying it, then the knowledge is not very helpful. There are different ways to be creative and perceptive: how you relate to a patient and their family which leads to trust; how you are able to understand a patient's feelings; and your ability to communicate effectively. Sometimes it can even be how you are able to interpret some unsaid clues.

Nurses need emotional intelligence too, and according to Sargent, emotional intelligence is the art of being able to read the energy in a room, something that is not taught in any nursing school. If you are able to read the feelings of the people around you and to interact with those people based on your interpretation, then you have emotional intelligence. People with this ability are able to relate with others well and move faster up the career ladder.

Some nurses develop an intuition to recognize situations. Steele narrated an event that occurred when he was a hospice caregiver. He noticed that one of his patients was entering the last phase of his illness and would soon die, and so he called the patient's family to have their last visit. Steele said that how he was able to recognize this is not something that can be taught in class and that this kind of competence can only be achieved through experience.

Sometimes the art of nursing can be seen in how a nurse improvises according to the situation. Steele gave another example of how his friend started to have chest pains and the nearest hospital was one hour away. Steele gave his friend some water and a little salt as a substitute for a saline IV. His friend felt better almost immediately thanks to Steele's creativity.

Restad explains that nurses' ability to balance duties is also an important art. When you are responsible for two patients and one is seriously ill, you must know how to take care of both of them without one patient feeling like more attention is being paid to the other. You are required to offer effective care to both your patients according to their needs.

Nursing is basically about taking the nursing skills and scientific concepts gained and applying them to real medical situations. This art of applying what you know is what makes nursing a holistic profession. It is easy to acquire nursing skills or learn how to use medical equipment, but combining all these skills and knowledge and adding a human touch to it is what nursing is about.

Practice Test 1 – Questions

English Proficiency Section of the NLN-PAX

Identify the answer choice that has a similar meaning as the word or description given in the question.

(1) The adjective 'corrupted' means:

(A) Adulterated — make impure, degrade, taint, lessen quality by adding something

(B) Infuriated — to make angry + impatient, provoke, enrage, incense

(C) Harbored — to keep a thought in one's mind secretly, cling to, give home/shelter to

(D) Inculcated (instill an idea, habit, etc by persistent instruction)

(2) The noun 'eagerness' means:

(A) Alacrity — cheerful readyness, willing, enthusiastic, zeal, keenness

(B) Marital — relating to marriage, wedding, spouses

(C) Happiness

(D) Detonator

(3) A verb that means 'making less harsh' is:

(A) Suspend

(B) Alleviate

(C) Action

(D) Ingrate — "ungrate"; like an ungrateful person, ungrateful

(4) A verb that means to sanctify is:

(A) Train

(B) Brand

(C) Bless

(D) Negate

(5) A noun used to refer to someone who donates money or a gift to a charitable organization is:

(A) Teach

(B) Benefactor

(C) Captain

(D) Source

(6) The meaning of the adjective 'hidden' is:

(A) Carriage

(B) Covert

(C) Accustomed

(D) Hide

(7) The verb 'straightforward' means the same as:

(A) Illegal

(B) Candid

(C) True

(D) Lawful

✓ (8) The verb 'fearless' means:

(A) Extraordinary

(B) Feeble - *lacking physical strength, faint, lacking strength/character*

— (C) Dauntless

(D) Strong

× (9) An appropriate verb to describe the act of removing a leader from a high position is:

(A) Drop

(B) Sack

2 (C) Depose - *remove from office suddenly + forcefully; overthrow, dethrone*

— (D) Suspend - *temporarily prevent from continuing or being in force or effect*

× (10) To make someone strong in morals or matters of religion can be described using the verb _____.

(A) Deceive

— (B) Sanctify - *set apart, declare holy, consecrate, free of sin, binded by sanction*

(C) Edify - *instruct or improve someone morally or intellectually*

(D) Pacify - *to put an end to anger, bringing peace to something*

(11) People are said to be headstrong when _____.

(A) They do not listen

(B) They are stubborn

(C) They are willing

(D) They do not believe

(12) Being oblique means _____.

(A) Being direct

(B) Being indirect

(C) Being sharp

(D) Being straight

(13) The word 'temper' can be best described as to _____.

(A) exacerbate — make worse

(B) aggravate — make worse

(C) improve

(D) Intensify

(14) The meaning of 'cryptic' is _____.

(A) Building a house in the graveyard

(B) Hard to understand

(C) Represented in coded print

(D) Printed on a crucifix

(15) To curtail something is to _____.

(A) reduce its extent or cut it short

(B) serve something with cocktails

(C) increase the extent of something or to prolong it

(D) return something

(16) The verb 'heed' means _____.

(A) ignore

(B) listen (pay attention)

(C) advise

(D) pay

(17) To be oblivious of something is to be _____.

(A) happy about something

(B) unhappy about something

(C) close to something

(D) unaware of something

(18) A podium is a _____.

(A) politician

(B) platform that is raised

(C) a spoken speech

(D) a written speech

(19) To be boorish is to be _____.

(A) ill-tempered

(B) ill-mannered

(C) ugly looking

(D) foul smelling

(20) 'Heresy' is best defined as _____.

(A) the opinion that is at variance with the orthodox

(B) the opinion that is similar to the orthodox

(C) the opinion that is surprising

(D) being open to any opinion

(21) The word, 'respite' can be best defined as _____.

(A) great respect

(B) intermission

(C) short sleep

(D) a gadget of technology

Dr. Seuss – For Questions 22 - 25

The author, Theodor Seuss Geisel, has been popular for over a century. His date of birth was March 2, 1902. The birthday of this renowned 'Dr. Seuss' is now being celebrated through events dubbed 'Read Across America', to be held all through March. School children all over the US celebrate this birthday by designing hats, making presentations, and conducting circles of 'read aloud' that feature some famous books of Dr. Seuss.

Who is Dr. Seuss? Did he attend any school of medicine? What was the location of his office? It may surprise you to realize Theodor Seuss Geisel was actually not a doctor of medicine. He only adopted Dr. Seuss as a nickname after becoming popular as an author of children's books. He was given that nickname because people equated the goodness of his books to medicine. This nickname continued to be used many years afterward, and all over the globe, he is still referred to as Dr. Seuss.

Remember during your childhood days. Was there a time you wanted to have a taste of 'green eggs and ham'? Was there a time you attempted 'Hop on Pop'? Can you recall learning something about your environment just from one creature named 'The Lorax'? Obviously, you have memories of one of the author's characters who are among the most famous; the Grinch who was green and stole Christmas. These are all stories that Dr. Seuss wrote that featured rhyming words as well as letters that were his signature. They also had words that he made up just so as to enhance his scheme of rhyme, although several of his book characters were his own creation, they appear completely real up to this day.

What about Dr. Seuss' 'signature' book titled 'The Cat in the Hut'? You obviously recall the cat and also 'Thing One' as well as 'Thing Two' from your childhood days. In the early years of the 1950s, did you realize it was feared children in the US were not enthusiastic about reading? Publishers back then thought the reason children were not passionate about reading was that children thought books were dull and not interesting. One publisher who was intelligent sent Dr. Seuss a book of words that he felt every child needed to learn at a young age. Dr. Seuss used those same words to write a story that became famous, 'The Cat in the Hat'. It is evident that for several decades his work has continued to influence children of tender age. It is for this reason that the doctor's birthday is celebrated every March.

(22) What is the meaning of 'passionate' as used in the passage?

(A) fast

(B) ardent

(C) lazy

(D) fast

(23) By equating the goodness of Dr. Seuss' books with that of medicine, the inference is that _____.

(A) People felt better after reading the books

(B) People found his books in doctors' clinics

(C) People did not need medicine after reading the books

(D) People felt like licking the books when they were ill.

(24) One publisher who sent Dr. Seuss a book with words is described as being intelligent because _____.

(A) He was literate

(B) He understood children were averse to reading

(C) He knew Mr. Geisel had the talent to write a bestselling book

(D) He knew Mr. Geisel had the talent to create a book which would interest young kids.

(25) The passage contains the theme _____.

(A) Dr. Seuss not being a real doctor

(B) Dr. Seuss influencing generations of young kids

(C) Dr. Seuss writing books that rhymed

(D) The appropriateness of reading a book on Dr. Seuss' birthday

Civil War in America – For Questions 26 - 29

The American Civil War started on April 12, 1861, and the initial shots were fired within Fort Sumter in the state of South Carolina. Interestingly, the first day of the war did not cause any fatalities, yet many Americans died later in that Civil War - more than in all other wars. The reason this war started was that eleven states in the south decided to secede and leave the Union, and they attempted to form a different government – The Confederate States of America.

What led to these states wanting secession? One major reason that led to the Civil War was a matter of slavery. The states in the south depended highly on the slaves they kept to enhance their lifestyle of farming and plantation. The states in the north had abolished slavery and could not understand why their counterparts in the south wanted to continue keeping slaves. In fact, the northern states were for the freedom of all slaves, and even the goal of President Lincoln was to bring slavery to an end while preserving the Union. On April 14, 1862, the president convinced Congress to declare they would fight Confederacy, and the result was four years of bloodshed as the northern states and the southern states fought each other.

From 1861 to 1863, it looked as though the southern states were going to win the war. Nevertheless, a very bloody 3-day war that took place at a Gettysburg field in Pennsylvania beginning on July 1, 1863, changed the outlook. As the three days of the most bloody American war ended, the war turned in favor of the northern states and they began to dominate the southern states. This domination continued until the war ended. The most memorable moment is likely to be the 'March to the Sea' led by General Sherman, where the Union Army traversed Georgia and North and South Carolina as they burned and destroyed everything in their path?

The Union Army later invaded Richmond in the state of Virginia, which served as the capital of the Confederate States, and in 1865 they captured the city. The Confederacy leader, Robert E. Lee, surrendered to the Union forces leader, General Ulysses S. Grant on April 9, 1865. Thus, the Civil War came to an end, leaving the Union intact.

(26) To secede means to _____.

(A) split

(B) succeed

(C) join an alliance or union

(D) to expand

(27) The following statement summarizes a fact contained in the passage.

(A) War was declared by Congress and thereafter the 'Battle of Fort Sumter' started.

(B) War was declared by Congress after the firing of shots at Fort Sumter.

(C) President Abraham Lincoln supported slavery.

(D) President Lincoln and the Congress were at Fort Sumter.

(28) The Confederacy finally surrendered when _____.

(A) the battle began at Gettysburg

(B) the battle began at Bull Run

(C) Richmond, the capital of the Confederate, was invaded

(D) the march led by General Sherman began

(29) In the context of the passage, 'abolish' means to _____.

(A) formerly bring to an end

(B) renew

(C) improve the conditions of

(D) condemn

Anne Frank – For Questions 30 - 33

When discussing history in class or during an English lesson, someone may have mentioned the term 'holocaust.' This term refers to an event that occurred between 1939 and 1945, whereby the Nazis eliminated the Jews, Catholics, homosexuals, Gypsies, and all other groups that they felt were beneath their Aryan race, a race that they believed to be superior. The Nazis held their captives in concentration camps that sometimes became Death Camps. Over a million children who were under sixteen years old died in the concentration camps and this was by far the saddest aspect of the event. Among the children that would face this cruel death under the Nazis, and just a couple of weeks until the end of the Second World War, was Anne Frank.

Anne Frank was born in June 1929 and led a pleasant life before the persecution of Jews by the Nazis. On her thirteenth birthday in June 1942, she received a simple gift that would later have an impact on millions of lives all around the globe. The gift she received was a tiny diary that was red in color and she called it kitty. It was later to become her most treasured possession during the time that she and her family took refuge from the Nazis inside a hidden annex at the top of her father's Amsterdam office building.

For two years and one month, Anne, her parents, her sister Margot, another family, and an elderly Jewish dentist took refuge from the Nazis in the small annex. They could not leave the annex, but with the help of Miep Gies and her husband who were both against the persecution of Jews by the Nazi's, they were able to have their food and supplies delivered to them. Young Anne used her little diary as an outlet to write about her time in hiding during those difficult times and to vent her frustrations.

Two years later, the Nazis learned of the annex hideout and Anne and her entire family were captured. To date, no one knows exactly who told the Nazis about Anne's family and the others hiding in the annex. Anne, her sister Margot, and her mother were separated from Anne's father, Otto Frank, and later their mother was also separated from them. In March 1945, Anne's sister, Margot Frank, succumbed to hunger in a concentration camp. Several days later, Anne Frank succumbed to typhus at the age of only 15 years. Otto Frank was the only survivor of the Holocaust of those who had sought refuge in the annex.

When the Second World War was over, Otto Frank went back to the annex and there he came across kitty. In it, Anne had written about how she felt and what she thought about the persecution she endured because she was a Jewish girl. In 1947, Otto Frank had kitty published and since then, it has continually remained in print. Today, over 55 languages have been used to publish the diary and over 24 million copies of this diary have been sold all over the world. Anne Frank's diary tells the story of a brave young girl who saw only the positive in everyone.

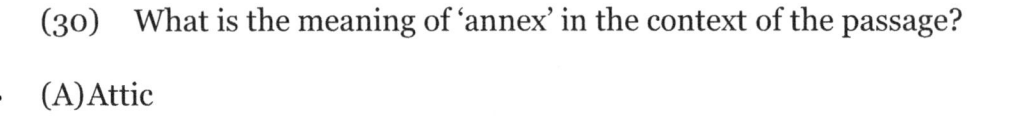

(30) What is the meaning of 'annex' in the context of the passage?

(A) Attic

(B) Basement

(C) Bedroom

(D) Kitchen

(31) What is the reason the diary that belonged to Anne is now translated into 55 languages?

(A) Because her father, Otto Frank, could speak several languages

(B) So that many people across the globe can learn about the horrors that took place during the infamous Holocaust.

(C) So that all people can understand the diary.

(D) Because the writer, Anne, happened to be Jewish yet her hiding place was Amsterdam and she passed away in Germany.

(32) What would you conclude is the meaning of 'typhus' from the way the deaths of Anne and even Margot have been described in the passage?

(A) Dying of starvation

(B) Some infection Anne got from the Germans

(C) Some illness Anne got while she was at the concentration camp

(D) Some poisonous gas the Germans used to eliminate Anne.

(33) What is the meaning of 'vent' as used in the passage?

(A) A spot where things can be plugged to penetrate the wall

(B) A place that Miep went to buy cheap provisions for Otto Frank's family

(C) A place for hiding that looks like an annex

(D) A way of Anne to express her inner thoughts

Tropical Fish – For Questions 34 - 37

Years ago, keeping tropical fish either in the office or in a home setting was a very popular trend. Today, however, it is no longer as popular as it was but it is still a relaxing and rewarding hobby. If you ask anyone who keeps tropical fish as a hobby they will tell you how relaxing and soothing it is to watch colorful fish in an aquarium living their lives.

There is some basic equipment that you should have if you want to keep tropical fish in your home. The first thing you need is a filter system to clean the aquarium and keep your fish healthy and alive. Filters come in different sizes and types and so you should choose yours depending on the aquarium's size as well as how stocked it is. Ideally, your filter should have a 3-5 times turnover rate every hour. What this simply means is that water inside the tanks needs to pass through this filter at least 3-5 times every hour.

Most tropical fish have a desired water temperature range of between 24 degrees to 26 degrees. It is important to have a heater that has a thermostat in order to regulate the water temperature. You also need to be keen when buying a heater because some can be submerged in water while others cannot.

You will also need lights and these come in various sizes, types, and strength. Light will not only help the plants inside the tank in the photosynthesis process but they will also enhance the appearance of your tank. If you are using plastic plants, still bear in mind that your fish require light, but in this case, you may need to use a light source with less strength.

The other item you need is a hood. This will keep out dirt, dust and other unwanted material from the tank. In some cases, the hood also helps prevent evaporation. Aquarium gravel is also important especially if you intend to put real plants in your aquarium and it also enhances the beauty of your aquarium.

(34)   The tone of the article is generally _____.

(A) Technical

(B) Informal

(C) An opinion

(D) Formal

(35)   Among the answer options provided, one of them cannot be deduced from the passage. Which is it?

(A) The size of filter you use should vary progressively as the size of the tank increases.

(B) Fewer people maintain aquariums at their place of work than in their homes.

(C) Use of gravel to nurture aquarium plants is advisable.

(D) Gravel makes an aquarium look more beautiful

(36) There is evidence provided in the passage that it is necessary to have aquarium lights. The evidence is _____.

(A) The plants in the aquarium need light.

(B) Both the plants and the fish in the aquarium need light.

(C) Light makes the aquarium look more appealing.

(D) Fish are able to swim better when the aquarium has light.

(37) Among the choices given below, one of them is just an opinion. Which is it?

(A) Use a filter that has a turnover rate of 3 – 5 times per hr.

(B) An aquarium's aesthetics is enhanced by gravel.

(C) A hood is used to stop dust and dirt and other unwanted objects from entering the tank.

(D) The ideal temperature of aquarium water depends on the species of tropical fish in the aquarium.

Helen Keller – For Questions 38 - 41

The name Helen Keller may sound familiar to you. Her fame is attributed to the fact that she could not hear or see and yet she learned how to read and speak and went on to attend a college and secure a degree. Helen's life is an interesting story, which she used to create her autobiography. Her autobiography was later adapted into a movie and stage play. The following is how Helen Keller overcame her disabilities and became the famous woman we now know her to be.

Helen was a normal child at birth but this changed. She was just a small child when she developed a high fever which lasted for a number of days and this sudden illness cost her both her sight and hearing. Since the tragedy happened when she was still very young, she had no memory of the time she could once hear or see. Helen's hearing disability meant that learning to talk would be an impossible task. Her blindness also made movement very difficult and so she spent her early six years in a dark and still world.

Can you imagine how sad her childhood was? Not being able to hear the voice of her mother or see how beautiful the farm was? She did not know where her bedroom was situated, who was bathing her, or who was hugging her. She also had no way to communicate or express what she was feeling.

At six years of age, her parents decided to hire a teacher called Anne Sullivan. She was partially blind but was able to read Braille and hear so this made her a suitable teacher for Helen. Initially, both Helen and Anne did not like each other. Anne found it difficult to teach Helen and described her not as a child, but as something wild. Whenever Anne attempted to help her, Helen would hit and bite her. Eventually, they both came to respect and love each other.

Helen was taught how to hear through placing her hand on a person's throat and feeling the produced sounds. Soon enough, she was able to feel people's words. After that, she learned how to read and understand Braille which is a method of printing designed especially for blind people. Finally, she learned how to talk but only Anne could understand what she was saying.

As Helen grew older, more people learned of her story and were amazed. She went on to college, wrote books that narrated her life, and gave public talks with Anne by her side to translate her message. Today, both Helen Keller and Anne Sullivan are famous and respected for the work they do.

(38)   Considering Helen Keller was both blind and deaf, her greatest childhood challenge was _____.

(A) Difficulty in communication

(B) Difficulty in walking

(C) Difficulty in playing

(D) Difficulty in eating

(39)   Soon Helen could tell what someone was saying by the feel of the person's vibrations as they spoke. Helen felt these vibrations through the person's _____.

(A) Lips

(B) Throat

(C) Nose

(D) Mouth

(40)   It is possible to deduce from the passage that Helen's teacher, Anne Sullivan, had a lot of patience because _____.

(A) at first, Helen would hit her and even bite her, yet she stayed to teach her

(B) she managed to teach Helen to read

(C) Helen could not hear properly

(D) she had dedicated her life to teaching

(41)   Although Helen Keller could finally speak, Anne Sullivan still found it necessary to translate what she said in public because _____.

(A) Helen used a language different from English

(B) the words Helen spoke were difficult for other people to comprehend

(C) Helen's voice was too soft for people far away to hear

(D) Helen's used sign language and her words were not verbal.

US First Ladies – For Question 42

Americans have always been interested in the wives of US presidents, and memories of several First Ladies have mostly revolved around the influence they had on their respective husbands. Of course, there have been some First Ladies who have made their mark in the history books as individuals.

There are two First Ladies who chose to send some signals as their husbands made speeches, and those were President Truman's wife, Bess Truman, and President Johnson's wife, Lady Bird Johnson. Whenever Lady Bird felt President Johnson was spending too much time talking, she would write a note and send it to be given to him at the podium. The note would read, 'It is time to stop', and her husband would take heed. As for Bess, there was a time she disliked something her husband was saying on TV, and she took upon herself to phone him and say, "If you cannot talk more politely than that in public, you come right home".

There are two presidents who were their wives' students, the 13th, and the 17th presidents. Abigail Fillmore was a teacher by profession and at one time Millard Fillmore, who later became the 13th president, was her pupil. Andrew Johnson was illiterate when he and Eliza got married, but she taught him to read and write.

First Lady Helen Taft made a name for herself by having the idea of planting the now famous Washington D.C.'s cherry trees. These trees blossom and attract visitors in their thousands to the US capital. Mrs. Taft was also instrumental in having the men in her family, as well as those serving at the White House, remain clean-shaven without a beard.

Soon following the unfortunate incident of President Woodrow suffering a stroke, Edith Wilson began to perform the presidential duties unofficially until the term of her husband ended. In the early years of the First World War, Mrs. Wilson made arrangements for sheep to be brought to the lawn of the White House to graze. The White House lawn remained mowed owing to the grazing of the sheep, and an auction that the First Lady sponsored received a good supply of wool from the sheep. Close to a hundred thousand dollars was raised for the benefit of the Red Cross.

In 1812 as the war raged, Dolly Madison ensured no one destroyed a painting portraying George Washington. She stayed behind so that she could rescue the portrait without caring that the guards themselves had departed, and in the meantime, the British were marching toward D.C. This painting was the sole item from the very first White House not to be burned.

Among the most famous presidents' wives was Eleanor Roosevelt, who was married to Franklin D. Roosevelt. During the time her husband was president, she remained active politically and socially. After the death of her husband, Eleanor's fame continued but this time because of the work she did within the UN for humanitarian efforts. Because of her, the lives of thousands of poor people across the globe were made better.

(42) The major idea in the passage is _____.

(A) All humanitarian work performed by First Ladies is crucial within the US government.

(B) The First Lady who was most influential among all was Dolly Madison.

(C) The president's wife who transformed the image of First Ladies was Eleanor Roosevelt.

(D) The presidents' wives are important in American culture.

(E) Among the major supporters of American presidents are the First Ladies.

Potatoes – For Question 43

Among the several vegetable varieties farmed across the globe, which one is everyone's favorite of the young and elderly? It is, without a doubt, the potato.

You may know the potato as 'taters', 'Kennebees', 'spuds', 'chips', 'shoestrings', or 'Idahoes'. Nevertheless, a potato is just a potato no matter the name you give it, and it is the most grown vegetable in the entire world. In fact, the average consumer of potatoes eats a minimum of 100 pounds of them every year.

That amount is just a small part of what is produced every year. Across the world, all the potatoes harvested total more than six billion bags with every one of those bags weighing 100 pounds. There are some potatoes produced that weigh as much as 4 pounds each. In America, the potatoes produced each year can fill about four hundred million bags. Although it may appear like this figure represents lots of 'taters', the US rates third among the potato growing countries of the world. Poland, for example, produces slightly more than eight hundred million bags every year, and Russia leads the producers with one and a half billion bags.

The very first potato crop was grown in South America by the Incas over four hundred years ago. The Incas have descendants in Chile and Ecuador, and they still grow this vegetable in the Andes Mountains, even at an altitude of 14,000 feet where most foods will not grow. In the early days, potatoes were shipped to the continent of Europe by the explorers from Spain and England, and later in the early 1600s, the crop found its way to the continent of North America.

There are different ways of consuming potatoes – they are sometimes baked, other times mashed, and other times they are roasted, and there are more ways than those three. However, people in the US prefer devouring potatoes as French fries. There is even a fast food chain that sells fries totaling one billion dollars every single year. Not surprisingly, this company is very particular about how its fries are made.

Before the fries can be released for consumption at the chain's popular eateries, they have to pass several different tests. Any potato failing a single test is rejected. For starters, the potatoes the chain uses are strictly Russet Burbank, an Idaho potato that has less water content than many other potato types whose content can be as high as 80%. After cutting the potato into shapes for 'shoestrings', they are partially fried in an undisclosed oil blend before receiving a spray of liquid sugar to brown them. They are then steam-fried over high degree heat and then flash frozen in preparation for shipping to various restaurants.

The measurement of every shoestring is taken before it can be shipped, and 40% of every batch must comprise shoestrings measuring 2 – 3 inches in length. Another 40% of the batch must comprise shoestrings longer than 3 inches, and the remaining 20% of that batch could be any size – probably even shorter than 2 inches.

So, with this information on the size as well as the value of potato crop farming, it is easy to appreciate the reason the largest proportion of the population admit this sector of food commerce is no place for 'small potatoes'.

(43) The major idea in the passage is _____.

(A) The world's potato revolution began in Ireland.

(B) The per capita consumption of potatoes in America is 50 pounds per year.

(C) People use potatoes to produce French fries.

(D) Potatoes are considered a very important vegetable in the US.

(E) Potatoes have been known by different names for a very long time.

Patents – For Question 44

Do you know the meaning of the word 'patent'? Does it sound like it could be connected to something you have? If so, ponder a while about some of the things considered commonplace, things you use on a day-to-day basis, or objects you consider part of your environment. Things like the radio, vehicles, the telephone, and thousands of other items that make our lives better today were once just ideas in people's minds. Were it not for the possibility of patenting those ideas in order to protect them, the originators might not have developed them to become worthwhile inventions to improve the quality of people's lives.

If there were no laws to protect patents, people would not have much incentive in inventing and innovating because after the details of the invention are known, there would be masses of imitators flooding the market that never took the risks or incurred expenses as the inventor. These imitators would offer their version of this product for sale and reap benefits from the efforts of the inventor. The progress in the field of technology that has led to America's greatness would wither fast without patent laws.

The basic principles governing the US patent structure originated in England. During the reign of England's Queen Elizabeth I, the expansion of the technology sector was enhanced by the move to grant exclusive privileges of manufacturing as well as selling to only those citizens responsible for inventing new processes or tools. This move did a lot to encourage creativity.

Later it was said by some critics that giving rights of monopoly to a single person was an infringement of other people's rights, but that argument was dismissed by England's Lord Chief Justice. He said that society was the beneficiary when such privileges were given to an inventor, as a patent was granted following an entirely new thing that the society did not enjoy before.

Another fundamental principle was introduced and made into law to benefit some powerful people within England who succeeded in obtaining a monopoly over ancient products such as salt; they had started to charge so much that people could barely tolerate it. There was such a public outcry that the government had no choice but to rule against such rights and monopolies and to declare that such rights could only be granted people who had introduced something entirely unique. These are the principles that served as the foundation of the modern US system of patenting.

In the days of the colonialists, the law of patenting was the prerogative of individual states. As a result, there was inconsistency and confusion as well as unfairness, and this led to the necessity of having a patent law that was uniform across all the states. Thus, a patent law to serve all states was incorporated into the US constitution. The signing of the very first patent law was on April 10, 1790, by George Washington, and within four months, a man by the name of Samuel Hopkins had been issued the first US patent for making a more advanced chemical method to make soap from potash.

A distinct bureau patent office was established in 1936, and it had eight members of staff at the beginning. The size of staff remained so only during the first year of the bureau's existence, as thereafter it has grown into a huge organization comprising of more than 2,500 employees who handle over 1,600 applications for patents and issue more than 1,000 patents every week.

Washington D.C.'s Patent Office is the biggest library of scientific and technical data in the world, and it is a treasure trove of information open to the public for inspection. Beyond being the custodian of over 3 million patents from the US, it also holds over 7 million patents from foreign countries together with volumes of technical literature in the thousands.

Abraham Lincoln had a patent for a device meant to elevate steam vessels across the shoals of rivers, and Mark Twain had one for a scrapbook that was self-pasting. Cornelius Vanderbilt, a millionaire, had a patent for inventing a kit for shining shoes.

A patent can be issued for any process that is new and useful, a machine, some manufacturing article, or composition like a chemical compound or combinations of different chemical compounds. It can also be issued for a plant variety that is distinct and new, and this is inclusive of particular mutants as well as hybrids.

This system of patenting has helped to improve the American worker's wages to a level not known before. The worker's output is greater and his wages are higher because of the computer, calculators, the drill press, and even the lathe. At the same time, prices are kept in check through inventions that have been patented because as efficiency increases in the manufacturing sector and competition is stimulated, the foundation of free enterprise as a system is enhanced.

The history of several decades has revealed there is little necessity to modify the existing patent configuration. The laws of patenting in the US have remained strong over time, the same as the US constitution from where the laws of patenting emerged. They promoted processes of a creative nature, helped to produce an immense benefit to society in general, and made it possible for US technology to surpass that of every other civilized country in the world.

(44) The major idea in the passage is _____.

(A) How free enterprise was encouraged by the system of patenting.

(B) How the US constitution offers protection to the established system of patenting.

(C) The influence England's system of patenting had on the American development of patenting.

(D) The importance of patents as inventors' tools.

(E) The protection patenting of inventions provides to inventors, free enterprise, and creative processes

The Beaver – For Question 45

There are many people who think it is alright to be as 'busy as a beaver', but what they do not realize is that although beavers may put a lot of effort into working, they actually do not accomplish a lot.

There is an expectation for beavers to be great at tree cutting, and while it is correct that one beaver is capable of gnawing through a tree at a very fast speed, for instance, a 6-inch birch takes the beaver just ten minutes; one might be surprised at what follows. A lot of times there is hardly anything useful the beaver does with the tree. There is an expert who established that for every five trees beavers cut one of them goes to waste.

For starters, beavers are poor at choosing their trees. Some beavers, it is said, worked as a group and managed to fell a 100-foot tall tree of the cottonwood type, only to realize there was no way they could move it.

Where woods are thick, sometimes a tree may not fall to the ground but instead gets trapped within other trees. Certainly, the beaver has no idea it would help to fell the trees preventing their tree from dropping to the ground, and so that good tree becomes sheer waste.

There are people who think beavers have the ability to influence the way a tree falls, but this is not true. There are times when, in fact, beavers have been pinned right under a tree as it falls. Whenever beavers embark on cutting a tree close to a stream, the tree often falls right into the nearby water, yet that was probably not the beaver's plan. The reality is that many of the trees happen to lean in the direction of the water.

What about the aspect of building dams? Most of the existing beaver dams are actually engineering wonders. The greatest ones are built very strongly with trees, mud, and even stones, with the bottom being wide and the top narrow. Beavers do not think about creating a dam over 200 feet in length. For example, there is a Montana beaver dam over 2,000 feet in length, and another one in New Hampshire, the biggest ever found anywhere, which stretches to 4,000 feet. The latter created a lake big enough to accommodate 40 homes for beavers.

Beavers create fine dams, but not always in suitable places. They have no capacity to plan. They even embark on building a dam where the stream is widest instead of locating a narrow part of the stream, and much of their hard work ends up going to waste.

One thing beavers ought to learn is that being busy is not sufficient. You need to be clear also about what you are doing. There was, for instance, a beaver in Oregon that was very active and it embarked on fixing a leak in a dam that was man-made. It despaired after five days of strenuous work. It had mistaken the lock through which boats passed to be a leak and that is what it had been trying to block.

(45)   The major idea of the passage is _____.

(A) Although it may be correct to say beavers are hard workers, the way these animals choose to work is not always the best in efficiency.

(B) Beavers are great at dam building.

(C) The biggest beaver dam was found in New Hampshire.

(D) Beavers are accomplished in cutting trees.

(E) Beavers are sometimes poor in surveying aquatic areas.

Science Section of the NLN PAX

(46) When animals and plants are found existing naturally in the same environment, the assemblage is referred to as _____.

(A) Population

(B) Society

(C) Community

(D) Biosphere

(47) A ban on wolf hunting was imposed some years ago, and thus their population soared and increased exponentially. In just a couple of generations the wolves' habitat had gone beyond its _____.

(A) Carrying capacity

(B) Feeding capacity

(C) Breeding capacity

(D) Supply capability

(48) Matter can exist in any of the four states named below:

(A) solid, liquid, vapor, and plasma

(B) solid, liquid, gas, and plasma

(C) solid, fluid, gas, and plasma

(D) concrete, liquid, gas, and plasma

(49) There is a table relating to elements and the arrangement of the elements is according to each element's atomic _____, meaning the number of _____ found in their respective nucleus.

(A) mass/protons

(B) mass/neutrons

(C) number/neutrons

(D) number/protons

(50) There is a certain feeding relationship among different species within the same ecological community referred to as a _____.

(A) Food web

(B) Food network

(C) Food sequence

(D) Food chain

(51) _____ causes depletion within the ozone layer.

(A) Chlorofluorocarbons

(B) Carbon dioxide

(C) Nitrous oxide

(D) Methane

(52) The 'Green Revolution' has different significant characteristics, but _____ is not one of them.

(A) Mechanized farming

(B) Monoculture

(C) Use of hybrid seeds

(D) None of the above

How Scientific Methods are Applied – For Questions 53 -62

Scientific methods involve sets of steps allowing people to find accurate answers to 'how' and 'why' regarding the world. Answers derived from scientific methods reflect reality as it is. If there were no scientific methods to find answers, people would hardly have any method that would be considered valid for gathering accurate and quantifiable information pertaining to the world.

The four basic steps of a scientific method are:

(a) Carrying out an analysis of a particular feature of reality, and then proceeding to ask 'how' that feature works or 'why' it exists

(b) Formation of a hypothesis to explain the 'how' or the 'why'

(c) Formulating a prediction regarding the kind of happenings that would result if the hypothesis proves true.

(d) Carrying out an experiment for the sake of testing the prediction you made.

Definitely, these basic steps can vary somewhat according to the branch of science you are studying. For example, in the field of astronomy, you will find experiments eschewed toward evidence of an observational nature when trying to confirm the truthfulness of predictions made. Nevertheless, the basic steps given here are the ones scientists generally follow.

Observing and Analyzing

The very first step of a scientific method is to determine what aspect of reality you are interested in exploring. For instance, perhaps you notice that among your friends those who like eating fruit and vegetables are much healthier than those who like eating meat a lot, particularly red meat with fat. You may even notice the former are more athletic than the latter. So far you have made your observation.

Next, you may wish to answer the question 'why'. Why does it look like your observation is true? This is the point at which, as a scientist, you will begin carrying out research with a view to finding out if there is another person who has studied these observations. During this particular stage as you follow the conventional scientific method, you will also wish to analyze any findings of other people. Carrying out this research and making this kind of analysis is crucial as you get a chance to find out what aspects of the observation they have found to be true and which ones they have found to be false, and both facts will be valuable to you.

The Hypothesis

Once you are finished observing and carrying out some valuable research, you will be ready to begin formulating your hypothesis. Remember you formulate the idea that becomes your hypothesis on the basis of evidence found regarding 'how' your own observation links to reality.

Let us use the diet of your different friends as an example. Probably among your research findings is a discussion on the level of vitamins in different fruit and vegetables. You may have found there are particular vitamins that enhance people's health and their athleticism. From these findings, you may then hypothesize that your friends in the healthy category consume foods containing those particular vitamins, and those vitamins are particularly responsible for their good health.

It is also important to use the research from hypotheses later proven to be wrong because such information helps scientists to refrain from following similar erroneous ways of thinking. You might, for example, find a research paper where a scientist may have hypothesized that the reason fruit and vegetables improve people's athleticism is that the sugars in these foods provide a lot of energy to the consumers. The same paper might have proceeded to give details with crucial information that no such link was found between the sugar in fruit and vegetables and people's enhanced athleticism, on the basis that the energy produced by the proteins as well as carbohydrates in meat and fat far exceeds that from the sugars.

If the link between sugar and athleticism was not found, then you would conclude that the hypothesis was incorrect. As such, you would not waste your valuable time trying to explore that hypothesis.

Making a Prediction

Making a prediction is the third step in the conventional scientific method, and you need to base it on the hypothesis you have formed.

It is important to form predictions as you apply the scientific method simply because if that prediction proves to be correct, it will be confirmation that you were accurate in your hypothesis and hence it can be used to explain some world feature. There is great importance in this since among the scientific method's features is its capacity to objectively demonstrate that the way you understand the world is actually valid.

If, for instance, your car fails to start and you observe that its fuel gage is directed toward the mark of 'empty', you can confidently make a prediction informing the passengers in your car that if the car's gas tank is tested properly it will indicate the car does not have any fuel. This prediction may seem obvious, but the fact is it is such predictions that serve as proof to everyone else that you are really conversant with the workings of a fuel gage and the meaning of its different marks.

Similarly, a prediction formulated from a hypothesis is the singular way to demonstrate properly that the hypothesis represents the real state of affairs or reality. If you follow the hypothesis on vitamins, for example, you could predict that people's health and athleticism can be enhanced just by eating food irrespective of what they consume, so long as they also consume vitamin-based supplements. In the event this particular prediction proves to be true, then you will have demonstrated that it is actually vitamins from fruit and vegetables, and nothing else, which are responsible for making people healthy and athletic. This way you will also have proof of your hypothesis demonstrating the way vitamins actually work.

Carrying Out the Experiment

The scientific method's last step is carrying out an experiment to test the prediction you made.

You could choose to group those friends you consider healthy into three groups – a group to take vitamin supplements and consume no vegetables at all; another group to consume no vegetables but take fake vitamin supplements, and the remaining group to continue with their normal lifestyle and feeding pattern. The last group, the one behaving normally, will serve as the control group.

Having a control group is crucial because you have a person behaving in a 'normal' way and who becomes your reference point when you want to compare the variations of your results. If this particular experiment indicates that members of the group taking real supplements as well as those of the control group have maintained an equal level of health and athleticism, and the members of the group taking fake supplements become weak and even sickly, then you will have proven your hypothesis to be true. However, if you have results that you did not anticipate, it is important that you return to the starting point – step 1 – and begin analyzing all the results you received along the way, making fresh observations and even trying out an entirely new hypothesis.

Any time a hypothesis cannot be proven using an experiment, or in fields like astronomy which depends on observation, such a hypothesis cannot be taken to be true and should be modified or abandoned altogether. This is the point at which the scientists concerned show their human side by deciding to abandon the conventional scientific method and instead follow their beliefs or prejudices when making their deductions. Simply put, whenever scientists get results from their experiments that do not please them, they are sometimes inclined to ignore them completely instead of going back to the drawing board to re-examine their hypothesis.

This happened for a long time in the field of astronomy for almost one thousand years, astronomers attempted to create solar system models that were accurate based on the planet's orbits that were circular in shape, and which had Earth right in the middle. From a philosophical perspective, circles were believed to be 'perfect' so a model with the right elliptical orbits with the sun in the middle of these orbits was rejected. This thinking continued into the sixteenth century even when the rejected models were more accurate in describing everything the astronomers observed.

(53) Any time you are employing the scientific research method, you need to follow the steps of _____.

(A) Defining the question; making observations; offering possible explanations; performing some experiment; analyzing data; and drawing conclusions.

(B) Making observations; offering some plausible explanation; defining your question; performing some experiment; analyzing, and drawing conclusions

(C) Performing some experiment; making observations; defining your question; offering a plausible explanation; analyzing the available data, and drawing conclusions

(D) Making observations; defining your question; offering some plausible explanation; performing some experiment; analyzing data, and drawing conclusions.

(54) There is one principle that advises selecting the hypothesis that is in competition with the one you have, which happens to make the fewest fresh assumptions when you have two hypotheses are similar or equal in every other respect. That principle is referred to as _____.

(A) Hickam's Dictum

(B) Dalton's Law

(C) Boyle's Law

(D) Occam's Razor

(55) There is a prediction stating that a difference observed is actually due to just chance but not as a result of any cause that is systematic. This prediction, which is known as the _____ is tested using statistical analysis and thereafter it is either accepted or it is rejected.

(A) null hypothesis

(B) control

(C) hypothesis

(D) variable

(56) _____ in the field of science is said to be the difference that exists between what you desire of a system or object and the real performance you observe as behavior.

(A) Accuracy

(B) Mistake

(C) Error

(D) Uncertainty

(57) In the fields of science and industry as well as statistics, a measurement system's _____ can be said to be the extent or degree of a quantity's closeness to what its true value is.

(A) error

(B) mistake

(C) accuracy

(D) uncertainty

(58) There is some confidence interval around the value already measured so that the value measured is sure not to fall outside the said interval. This interval of confidence is in reference to that value's _____.

(A) measurement

(B) accuracy

(C) uncertainty

(D) error

(59) Measurement repeatability goes by the term _____, and to know it you do not need to know the true or actual value.

(A) precision

(B) value

(C) accuracy

(D) certainty

(60) Any disagreement in the field of science that occurs between a given measurement and the value accepted or the value that is true is referred to as _____.

(A) error

(B) precision

(C) exactitude

(D) inaccuracy

(61) Sometimes a practical test is designed for the purpose of getting results that are relevant to a given theory, or more than one theory. Such a test is referred to scientifically as _____.

(A) hypothesis

(B) procedure

(C) variable

(D) experiment

(62) A simulation of an actual system, or its approximation, which omits everything except the most basic of system variables is referred to as _____.

(A) a control group

(B) a scientific method

(C) an independent variable

(D) a scientific model

61

(63) The body organs and main parts that comprise the immune system include _____.

(A) thymus; lymphatic system; bone marrow; tonsils; and spleen

(B) veins; heart; capillaries and capillaries

(C) nerve cells; spinal cord; and brain

(D) alveolus; nose; bronchial tubes, trachea, and lungs

(64) One of the organs listed below is a good example of tissue. Which is it?

(A) Chloroplast

(B) Hamstring

(C) Liver

(D) Mammal

(65) A person's adrenal glands are found within the _____ system.

(A) respiratory

(B) endocrine

(C) lymphatic

(D) immune

(66) A person's pineal gland produces a hormone known as _____.

(A) epinephrine

(B) testosterone

(C) melatonin

(D) insulin

(67) The organ systems within the body of a person are _____ in number.

(A) thirteen

(B) four

(C) eleven

(D) seven

(68) A person's brain is found within the _____ system.

(A) endocrine

(B) nervous

(C) respiratory

(D) integumentary

(69) A human being has different types of tissue, and the basic ones are ____ in number.

(A) four

(B) twelve

(C) six

(D) twenty-three

(70) Some blood vessels have less oxygenated blood than others. Which one among the ones listed below has the lowest amount of oxygenated blood?

(A) Capillaries

(B) Vena cava

(C) pulmonary artery

(D) femoral vein

(E) aorta

(71) The place where starch starts to be digested is the _____.

(A) mouth

(B) ileum

(C) stomach

(D) duodenum

(E) pylorus

(72) The primary oocytes are known to produce _____ as the process of oogenesis goes on.

(A) stem cells

(B) eggs

(C) sperm

(D) oogonia

(E) mucus

(73) For any given species, the stages its members follow in their development follows a sequence referred to as _____.

(A) Life cycle

(B) Life sequence

(C) Life journey

(D) Life expectancy

(74) Choose the correct statement from the four options provided below.

(A) Some activities of a chemical and also biological nature must be carried out by every living system within life sequence for the sake of maintaining life.

(B) Every system with the capacity to perceive – those described as being sentient – performs certain activities of a biochemical and also biophysical nature for the sake of maintaining life and combined these activities are referred to as life expectancy.

(C) There are certain activities of both organic and also inorganic nature that every living system must perform for the sake of life maintenance, and together these activities are referred to as life cycle.

(D) The activities of a biochemical and also biophysical nature that every living system must perform for the sake of maintaining life are referred to as life functions.

(75) There are three major processes comprising nutrition that enable living organisms to receive food, and they are made up of different activities. These processes are _____.

(A) Ingesting, digesting and absorbing

(B) Ingesting, diffusing and assimilating

(C) Ingesting, digesting and assimilating

(D) Incorporating, digesting and assimilating

(76) Choose the correct statement from the four options given below.

(A) Assimilation means to take in food, digestion comprises changes of a chemical nature that occur in a person's body, while ingestion means the change particular nutrients go through to become cell protoplasm.

(B) Ingestion means to take in food and digestion is used in reference to the changes of a chemical nature that occur to the food once inside the body, while assimilation means the change particular nutrients go through to become cell protoplasm.

(C) Digestion means to take in food and ingestion is used in reference to the changes of a chemical nature that occur to the food in a person's body, while assimilation means the change particular nutrients go through to become cell protoplasm.

(D) Ingestion means to take in food and digestion is used in reference to the changes of a chemical nature that occur to the food once inside a person's body, while diffusion means the change particular nutrients go through to become cell protoplasm.

(77) Choose the correct statement from the four given below.

(A) When molecules, besides those of water, move from a highly concentrated area to a lower concentrated area, the process is referred to as diffusion.

(B) When molecules, besides those of water, move to a highly concentrated area from a lower concentrated area, the process is referred to as diffusion.

(C) When molecules, other than those of water, move from a highly concentrated area to a lower concentrated area, the process is referred to as osmosis.

(D) When molecules, besides those of water, move from a highly concentrated area to a lower concentrated area, the process is referred to as dispersion.

(78) Choose the correct statement from the four given below.

(A) As diffusion takes place, the solvent passes via a membrane that is semi-permeable from an area where the solvent is less concentrated to one where it is more concentrated.

(B) As osmosis takes place, the solvent passes via a membrane that is impermeable from an area where the solvent is less concentrated to one where it is more concentrated.

(C) As osmosis takes place, the solvent passes via a membrane that is semi-permeable from an area where the solvent is more concentrated to one where it is less concentrated.

(D) As osmosis takes place, the solvent passes via a membrane that is semi-permeable from an area where the solvent is less concentrated to one where it is more concentrated.

(79) Choose the correct statement from the four given below.

(A) Diffusion and osmosis are forms of transport through which materials actively pass across plasma membranes.

(B) Diffusion and osmosis are forms of transport through which materials passively pass across plasma membranes.

(C) Dispersal and osmosis are forms of transport through which materials passively pass across plasma membranes.

(D) Diffusion and synthesis are forms of transport through which materials actively pass across plasma membranes.

(80) The branch of science where the studies appertain to a cell's physiology and life cycle as well cell division is known as _____.

(A) cell science

(B) biochemistry

(C) physiology

(D) biology

(81) One of the statements below regarding mitosis is correct. Which is it?

(A) The process whereby the division of cells culminates in the production of male cells that are identical to the original cells is known as mitosis.

(B) As a result of mitosis, additional cells contain DNA that is less than the parent cells.

(C) The number of chromosomes is doubled through the process of mitosis.

(D) The number of chromosomes is halved through the process of mitosis.

(82) Which one among the statements given below is wrong?

(A) During the process of meiosis, the chromosome number is reduced to half.

(B) The process of meiosis takes place only in cells of eukaryotes.

(C) The process of meiosis takes place during the life cycle stage where sexual reproduction is involved.

(D) None of the choices.

(83) What is the molarity of a given solution if it has two moles of normal salt dissolved in it and the total volume of the solution is one liter?

(A) 2½ M solution

(B) 1 M solution

(C) 2 M solution

(D) 1½ M solution

$$\frac{2 \text{ Moles}}{L} = 2M$$

$$M = \frac{\text{moles}}{L}$$

(84) What is the molarity of a four-liter solution of sugar if it contains eight moles of sugar?

(A) 80 M

(B) 0.5 M

(C) 2 M

(D) 8 M

$$M = \frac{8 \text{ moles}}{4L} = 2M$$

(85) What is the molarity of a 250-milliliter solution with five moles of the solute?

(A) 20 M

(B) 0.104 M

(C) 1.25 M

(D) 15 M

$$M = \frac{5 \text{ moles}}{.25 L} = 20 M$$

(86) What is the number of moles of sodium oxide, or Na2O, which need to be dissolved in water to produce a 2 M solution that is 4 liters in volume?

(A) 2 M

(B) 0.5 mol

(C) 8 Mol

(D) 0.50 M

$$2M = \frac{X \text{ moles}}{4L} \implies x = 2 \times 4 = 8$$

$$x = 8 \text{ moles}$$

(87) What is the number of sodium moles (Na) needed to form a 4½ L solution of 1½ M sodium solution?

(A) 6.75 mol

(B) 0.33 mol

(C) 3 M

(D) 0.33 M

$1.5 = \dfrac{\text{Na moles}}{4.5 \text{ L}}$

(88) The definition of a solution's molarity is _____.

(A) an element's atomic mass

(B) moles of the solution for every liter of the solute

(C) moles of the solute for every liter of the solution

(D) mass of the solvent for every liter of the solution

$M = \dfrac{\text{moles}}{L}$

(89) If the quantity of solute used in a solution is indicated in units of grams while the amount of solution is indicated in units of milliliters, to be able to find the solution's molarity you need to first _____.

(A) Change the grams given to their equivalent in moles but let the amount of solution remain just in milliliters

(B) Change the amount of solution given in milliliters to its equivalent in liters and change grams to become moles

(C) Change the quantity of solute given in grams to its equivalent in moles and also change the amount of solution given in milliliters to its equivalent in liters.

(D) Leave all units as given in the question.

(90) The molarity of a given aqueous solution that has CaCl is defined as:

(A) The number of CaCl moles in every milliliter of the solution

(B) The number of CaCal grams in every liter of the water

(C) The number of CaCl grams in every milliliter of the solution

(D) The number of CaCl moles in every liter of the solution

(91) The rows that are horizontal in the periodic table are called _____.

(A) sets

(B) periods

(C) families

(D) groups

(92) One of the substances listed below enables diffusion to take place the fastest. Which one is it?

(A) Gas

(B) Liquid

(C) Solid

(D) Plasma

(93) The name given to the protons within an atom is the _____.

(A) atomic mass

(B) atomic weight

(C) atomic identity

(D) atomic number

(94) Which of the options below is an empirical formula?

C4H8

C3H6

CH

C2H6

Read the following passage and then answer Questions 95 and 96.

Isotopes

An atom contains a nucleus, and that nucleus has protons as well as neurons. Protons bear one electric charge and it is positive, and neurons also have one electric charge, but this one is neither positive nor negative. It is simply zero.

The nucleus' proton number is known as the 'atomic number', and its abbreviation is 'Z'. The atomic number is responsible for determining the actual identity of any atom in matter. A good example is hydrogen that has just one proton; so Z = 1. In contrast, helium has two protons; so Z = 2.

It is possible for atoms belonging to the same element to vary when it comes to their neutron number within the nucleus of the atom. When added up, an atom's protons and the neutrons produce the atomic mass, which is represented by 'M'. The atomic mass of helium, for example, equals 4, yet there exists another isotope of helium that has its 'M' equaling 3. When writing this isotope's atomic mass you would write: M = 3. The reality in this latter situation is that the helium in this form contains a similar number of protons as the other helium, but this one has just a single neutron.

When there is a reaction of atomic fusion, nuclei are normally in an internal collision, and the force of one nucleus colliding with another continuously breaks the nuclei apart. The new nuclei that are formed as a result could have their atomic mass being lower than their reactants, and the existing difference is discharged in the form of energy. Nevertheless, when all this is happening, there is an electric charge being conserved.

(95) When 2 atoms belonging to helium with an atomic mass equal to 3 collide during some fusion reaction, they produce one helium atom with an atomic mass equal to 4. Incidentally, this is not all this fusion reaction produces. It also produces _____.

(A) one proton & one neutron

(B) two electrons

(C) one neutron

(D) one proton

(E) two protons

(96) The atoms in hydrogen normally have one neutron each. The neutrons in hydrogen's two isotopes, deuterium, and tritium, are 2 and 3 respectively. Assuming you have a hydrogen atom that is electrically neutral, what is the number of electrons that would be orbiting the nucleus of the tritium?

(A) 3

(B) 1

(C) 0

(D) 2

Read the following passage and then answer the questions that follow. Questions 97 – 101.

The Electrochemical Battery

The term 'electrochemical battery' refers to one device that derives its power from oxidation as well as reactions of reduction. These reactions happen to be physically set apart in such a manner as to have electrons traveling via a wire connected to the reducing agent and leading up to the oxidizing agent.

That reducing agent releases electrons or loses them, and it is also oxidized as a reaction occurs within an electrode known as the 'anode'. What follows is the electrons flowing via a wire to reach another electrode known as the 'cathode', and there an oxidizing

73

agent receives electrons and therefore is reduced. For every compartment to remain at a net charge of zero, a limited ion flow goes through a bridge of salt.

For example, in the case of a motor vehicle battery, the reducing agent is being oxidized through the reaction shown below involving an anode of lead, or Pb as well as sulfuric acid, or H_2SO_4. The process produces lead sulfate, or PbSO4, protons, H+, and electrons, denoted by e-.

The formula is Pb + H_2SO_4. = PbSO4 + 2 H+ + 2 e-
                                  s.A.   sulfate

There is then a reaction that takes place affecting the cathode that is made from lead oxide, or PbO2, which is described below, and during which electrons that are produced from the anode are utilized.

The formula is: PbO2 + H2SO4 + 2 e- + 2 H+= PbSO4 + 2 H2O

(97) The reaction of a chemical nature that occurs at the _____ produces electrons.

(A) anode

(B) salt bridge

(C) lead oxide electrode

(D) cathode

(E) oxidizer

(98) Choose the correct statement from the options given below.

(A) During the process of oxidation, there is an oxidizing agent gaining electrons ✓

(B) During the process of oxidation, there is an oxidizing agent losing electrons ✗

(C) During the process of oxidation, there is a reducing agent gaining electrons ✗

(D) During the process of oxidation, there is a reducing agent losing electrons ✓

(E) During the process of oxidation, there is an oxidizing agent reducing an electrode

red agent → releases e-
oxid. agent → receives e-

(99) The term 'aerobic' means _____.

(A) where oxygen is present

(B) heated

(C) anabolic

(D) building of calories

(100) Substances that are impossible to break down to gain a more simplified form of matter are given the name_____.

(A) molecules

(B) nuclei

(C) electrons

(D) elements

(101) Any time atoms belonging to one element are combined with atoms of a different element, what is created is a compound's _____.

(A) electron

(B) enzyme

(C) molecule

(D) ion

(102) The statements given below are about mixtures and compounds. Choose the answer option that is entirely correct.

(A) Mixtures are homogenous and their components' properties are retained, but compounds are heterogeneous and have properties that are distinctly different from those of individual elements that combine to form them.

(B) Mixtures are heterogeneous and their components' properties are retained, but compounds are homogeneous and have properties that are distinctly different from those of individual elements that combine to form them.

(C) Mixtures are heterogeneous and their components' properties are altered, but compounds are homogeneous and have properties that are the same as those of individual elements that combine to form them.

(D) Compounds are heterogeneous and their components' properties are retained, but mixtures are homogeneous and have properties that are distinctly different from those of individual elements that combine to form them.

(103) From the list of answers below, what are the differences between physical and chemical changes?

(A) When a physical change is taking place, there are various aspects of the matter's physical properties that change, but there is no change in the substance identity. Changes of a chemical nature entail a change to the composition of the matter as well as to its structure.

(B) When a chemical change is taking place, there are various aspects of the matter's physical properties that change, but there is no change in the substance identity. Changes of a physical nature entail a change to the composition of the matter as well as to its structure.

(C) When a physical change is taking place, there are hardly any aspects of the matter's physical properties that change, and there is also no change in the substance identity. Changes of a chemical nature entail a change to the composition of the matter as well as to its structure.

(D) There is basically no material variation between changes of a chemical nature and those of a physical nature.

(104) There is one formula written as H – H $_{products}$ – H $_{reactants}$

This formula is best used to _____.

(A) make alterations to the haploid bond ✗

(B) make alterations to the hypothesis ✗

(C) make alterations to the heat content

(D) make alterations to hydration

(105) Choose the correct statement from the list of four options given below.

(A) During a reaction that is exothermic the amount of heat the product has is greater ✓ than that of the reactants, but during a reaction that is endothermic the amount of heat the product has is less than that of the reactants. ✓

discharges heat in rxn to create product — light, or heat

(B) During a reaction that is endothermic the amount of heat the product has is less than that of the reactants, but during a reaction that is exothermic the amount of heat the product has is less than that of the reactants.
✗

(C) During a reaction that is <u>exo</u>thermic the amount of heat the product has is greater than that of the reactants, but during a reaction that is <u>exo</u>thermic the amount of heat the product has is less than that of the reactants.
✗

(D) During a reaction that is <u>endo</u>thermic the amount of heat the product has is greater than that of the reactants, but during a reaction that is exothermic the amount of heat the product has is less than that of the reactants.

endo: absorbs heat from surroundings.
$E_{rxn} < E_{prod}$

exo: $E_{rxn} > E_{prod}$

(106) Choose the correct statement from the list of four options given below.

(A) $E = mc^2$ is a formula whose basis is the second law of thermodynamics, and it states correctly that mass is equal to energy multiplied by the light velocity^2.

(B) $E = mc^2$ is a formula whose basis is the Law of Conservation of Mass and Energy, and it states correctly that energy is equal to mass multiplied by the light velocity^2.

(C) $E = mc^2$ is a formula whose basis is the 1st Law of Thermodynamics, and it states correctly that mass is equal to energy multiplied by the sound velocity^2.

(D) $E = mc^2$ is a formula whose basis is the Law of Conservation of Mass and Energy, and it states correctly that light velocity is equal to energy multiplied by mass^2.

(107) From the list of four options listed below, select the one that is correct.

(A) Any time recording measurements are being done, the major figures comprising digits that are definitely correct and known are recorded, and one additional digit that is not certain is recorded as well.

(B) Any time recording measurements are being done, the significant figures comprising digits that are definitely correct and known are recorded, and one additional digit that is not certain is recorded as well.

(C) Any time recording measurements are being done, the relative figures comprising digits that are definitely correct and known are recorded, and one additional digit that is not certain is recorded as well.

(D) Any time recording measurements are being done, the relevant figures comprising digits that are definitely correct and known are recorded, and one additional digit that is not certain is recorded as well.

(108) Choose the correct statement from the four provided below.

(A) The Kelvin scale is used on the basis of the theoretical temperature that is lowest called absolute zero.

(B) The Celsius scale is used on the basis of the theoretical temperature that is lowest called absolute zero.

(C) The Kelvin scale is used on the basis of the theoretical temperature that is lowest called water's boiling point.

(D) The Centigrade scale is used on the basis of the theoretical temperature that is lowest called water's freezing point.

(109) Choose the correct statement from the four options listed below.

(A) By means of experiments and calculations, it has been confirmed that absolute zero is – 273.15o on the Celsius scale.

(B) By means of experiments and calculations, it has been confirmed that unconditional zero is 0o on the Kelvin scale.

(C) By means of experiments and calculations, it has been confirmed that absolute null is -100o on the Celsius scale.

(D) By means of experiments and calculations, it has been confirmed that absolute zero is – 273.15o on the Kelvin scale.

(110) Choose the correct option from the four statements listed below.

(A) When making use of the system of scientific notation in expressing large numbers, you need to shift the decimal point until you have just 2 digits on the left, and then show the number of decimal point moves as the exponent of 10.

(B) When making use of the system of scientific notation in expressing large numbers, you need to shift the decimal point until you have just one digit on the left, and then show the number of decimal point moves as the exponent of 2.

(C) When making use of the system of scientific notation in expressing large numbers, you need to shift the decimal point until you have just 3 digits on the left, and then show the number of decimal point moves as the exponent of 10.

(D) When making use of the system of scientific notation in expressing large numbers, you need to shift the decimal point until you have only 1 digit on the left, and then show the number of decimal point moves as the of 10.

(111) Choose the correct option from the four statements listed below.

(A) In the field of science, accuracy gives an indication of the reliability or reproducibility of a given measurement, whereas precision gives an indication of the proximity of a measurement to its known or accepted value.

(B) In the field of science, exactitude gives an indication of the reliability or reproducibility of a given measurement, whereas contiguity gives an indication of the remoteness of a measurement to its known or accepted value.

(C) In the field of science, precision gives an indication of the reliability or reproducibility of a given measurement, whereas accuracy gives an indication of the proximity of a measurement to its known or accepted value.

(D) In the field of science, uncertainty gives an indication of the realism or possibility of a given measurement, whereas precision gives an indication of the distance of a measurement to its known or accepted value.

(112) Choose the correct option from the four statements listed below.

(A) The Law of the Preservation of Matter states that, in a chemical change, energy can be neither be created nor destroyed but only changed from one form to another.

(B) The Law of the Conservation of Energy states that, in a chemical change, energy can be neither be created nor destroyed but only changed from atomic number to another.

(C) The Law of the Conservation of Energy states that, in a chemical change, energy can be neither be created nor destroyed but only changed from one form to another.

(D) The Law of the Conservation of Energy states that, in a chemical change, energy can be neither be duplicated or destroyed but only changed from one form to another.

(113) Choose the correct option from the four statements listed below.

(A) A chemical change is a process that transforms one set of chemical substances to another; the substances used are known as products and those formed are reactants.

(B) A biological change is a process that transforms one set of chemical substances to another; the substances used are known as reactants and those formed are products.

(C) A chemical change is a process that transforms one set of chemical substances to another; the substances used are known as reactants and those formed are products.

(D) A chemical variation is a process that transforms one set of chemical substances to another; the substances used are known as reactants and those formed are products.

(114) Choose the correct option from the four statements listed below.

(A) Anabolism is the series of chemical reactions resulting in the synthesis of inorganic compounds, and catabolism is the series of chemical reactions that break down larger molecules.

(B) Anabolism is the series of chemical reactions resulting in the synthesis of organic compounds, and catabolism is the series of chemical reactions that combine larger molecules.

(C) Catabolism is the series of chemical reactions resulting in the synthesis of organic compounds, and anabolism is the series of chemical reactions that break down larger molecules.

(D) Anabolism is the series of chemical reactions resulting in the synthesis of organic compounds, and catabolism is the series of chemical reactions that break down larger molecules.

(115) Choose the correct option from the four statements listed below.

(A) A propellant is a chemical involved in, but not changed by, a chemical reaction by which chemical bonds are weakened and reactions accelerated.

(B) A reagent is a chemical involved in, but not changed by, a chemical reaction by which chemical bonds are strengthened and reactions accelerated.

(C) A catalyst is a chemical involved in, but not changed by, a chemical reaction by which chemical bonds are weakened and reactions slowed.

(D) A catalyst is a chemical involved in, but not changed by, a chemical reaction by which chemical bonds are weakened and reactions accelerated.

(116) Choose the correct option from the four statements listed below.

(A) Nitrogen is the most abundant element in the Earth's crust and appears on the Atomic Table as the letter N.

(B) Oxygen is the most abundant element in the Earth's crust and appears on the Atomic Table as the letter O.

(C) Silicon is the most abundant element in the Earth's crust and appears on the Atomic Table as the letter Si.

(D) Sodium is the most abundant element in the Earth's crust and appears on the Atomic Table as the letter Na.

(117) Choose the correct option from the four statements listed below.

(A) The Law of Multiple Proportions holds that the elements that make up a single chemical compound have weight proportions that are fixed and constant.

(B) The Law of the Preservation of Matter holds that the elements that make up a single chemical compound have weight proportions that are fixed and constant.

(C) The Law of the Conservation of Energy holds that the elements that make up a single chemical compound have weight proportions that are fixed and constant.

(D) The Law of Definite Proportions holds that the elements that make up a single chemical compound have weight proportions that are fixed and constant.

(118) Choose the correct option from the four statements listed below.

(A) The Law of Definite Proportions holds that in any single atom two electrons cannot have the 4 quantum number set.

(B) The Pauli Exclusion Principle states that, in any single atom, no 4 electrons can comprise a similar set of 2 quantum numbers.

(C) The Pauli Exclusion Principle holds that, in any particular molecule, 2 electrons cannot have a different 4 quantum number set.

(D) The Pauli Exclusion Principle states that, in a given atom, two electrons cannot have a similar 4 quantum number set.

(119) From the four choices listed below, choose the most appropriate statement that relates to the principles of Dalton's atomic theory.

(A) Matter of all kinds is composed of small particles that are interconnected, which are referred to as atoms.

(B) An element's atoms are similar in their weight, and the weight depends on the type of atom.

(C) It is possible to sub-divide atoms, and even to create or even destroy them.

(D) When a reaction of a chemical nature is taking place, atoms cannot be combined, rearranged, or separated.

(120) Choose the correct statement from the four choices listed below.

(A) Atoms of varying elements combine in ratios of whole numbers that are simple to form chemical compounds.

(B) Atoms of varying components combine in fractional ratios that are simple to form chemical compounds.

(C) Atoms of the very same elements combine in whole number ratios that are simple, to form chemical compounds.

(D) Atoms of varying elements combine in whole number ratios that are simple to form chemical mixtures.

(121) From the four choices below, choose the statement that is untrue about the atomic theory.

(A) The theory was established during the early years of the nineteenth century through John Dalton's work.

(B) This theory is used in the physics field in describing the characteristics as well as properties associated with the atoms that comprise matter.

(C) This theory is used in describing temperature as the atom momentum.

(D) This theory is used in explaining the phenomenon of a microscopic nature by the behavior involving microscopic atoms.

(122) Choose the correct statement from among the four listed below that indicates something correct about atoms.

(A) Atoms constitute the biggest unit of substance with the capacity to participate in some chemical reaction.

(B) It is possible to chemically break down atoms into forms that are simpler.

(C) Atoms comprise protons and also neutrons within a central or main nucleus that electrons surround.

(D) Atoms vary in terms of their atomic number as well as their atomic mass.

The correct answer is: Ⓒ Atoms comprise protons and also neutrons within a central or main nucleus that electrons surround.

(123) Protons, electrons and also neutrons vary in that:

(A) Protons plus neutrons combine to form the atom nucleus, whereas electrons exist within levels of energy that are fixed around the atom nucleus.

(B) Protons and also neutrons are particles that are charged while electrons happen to be neutral.

(C) Protons plus neutrons create energy levels that are fixed around the atom nucleus as well as electrons situated close to the atom's surface.

(D) Protons, electrons, as well as neutrons, are particles that have been charged.

(124) From the four options listed below, choose the statement that is false regarding quantum theory.

(A) Quantum theory deals with both energy emission and also its absorption by matter, and also with the movement of big particles.

(B) Quantum mechanics, which is a quantum theory-based system, has surpassed Newtonian mechanics as far interpretation of phenomena of a physical nature is concerned regarding the known atomic scale.

(C) Where quantum theory is concerned, energy is taken to be a mere phenomenon that is continuous, whereas it is assumed that matter occupies a region within space that is clearly defined, and also that it is in continual movement.

(D) Quantum theory holds that the reason energy is held is for the purpose of being emitted and also absorbed in amounts that are small and also discrete referred to as quantum.

(125) Among Newton's motion laws are 3 physical laws that serve as the basis for classical mechanics. Which of the four options listed below is one of the three laws?

(A) Any given body stays in a resting position unless some force acts upon it.

(B) Any given body that is moving will change its direction and in due course end up slowing down till it ultimately stops, unless some force acts upon it.

(C) For every given action, there emerges a reaction that is equal but opposite.

(D) Any particular body that a given force acts upon accelerates and follows the direction of that force and its magnitude is proportional to that force.

(126) The term 'electricity' is used generally to encompass a range of phenomena that result from the existence and electric charge flow. From the four choices listed below, choose the correct statement regarding electricity.

(A) When matter is charged electrically, it produces electromagnetic fields that influence that matter.

(B) 'Electric current' means movement or flow of particles that have been electrically charged.

(C) 'Electric potential' means the basic interaction that takes place between a given magnetic field and the existence of an electric charge plus its motion.

(D) When there is influence caused by some electric charge affecting other charges, such influence is essentially an electric field.

(127) One of the following options is not true regarding Ohm's Law.

(A) The existing relationship of power, voltage, current and resistance as symbolized by P, E, I and R respectively is defined under Ohm's Law.

(B) A single ohm can be said to be that value of resistance by which a single volt maintains a current of a single ampere.

(C) It is possible to establish the voltage by using the formula V=IR when I equals the current and R equals resistance, under Ohm's Law.

(D) An ohm can be defined as an electric voltage unit.

(128) Any conductor restricting electron flow internally has the property of _____.

(A) current

(B) friction

(C) power

(D) resistance

(129) In the field of physics, the force opposing 2 bodies' relative motion when those bodies are in contact is referred to as _____.

(A) abrasiveness

(B) antagonism

(C) friction

(D) resistance

(130) If there is any difference at all between potential and kinetic energy, what is it?

(A) Potential energy can be defined as that energy a body has that originates from motion and kinetic energy can be defined as that energy that an object possesses by being in the position it is in or the state it is in, as exemplified by a spring that is compressed.

(B) Kinetic energy can be defined as that energy a body has that is a result of motion, and potential energy can be defined as that energy an object has just by being in the position or state it is in, as exemplified by a spring that is compressed.

(C) Kinetic energy can be defined as that energy a body has that is a result of heat and potential energy is that energy an object has when it is practically chilled.

(D) No difference exists between potential and kinetic energy; both are similar.

(131) The 4 basic forces in nature are _____.

(A) Gravity; nuclear force that is strong; electromagnetic force; and nuclear force that is weak

(B) Nuclear force that is strong; polarity; nuclear force that is weak; and electromagnetic force.

(C) gravity; nuclear force that is strong; nuclear force that is weak; and magnetic force of chemical nature

(D) nuclear force that is positive; electromagnetic force; gravity; and nuclear force that is negative

(132) Organize nature's four fundamental forces in ascending order of their strength.

(A) Gravity; weak nuclear force; electromagnetic force; strong nuclear force

(B) Strong nuclear force; weak nuclear force; electromagnetic force; gravity

(C) Weak nuclear force; gravity, electromagnetic force; strong nuclear force

(D) Gravity; strong nuclear force; weak nuclear force; electromagnetic force

(133) The existing variation between strong nuclear force and weak nuclear force is _____.

(A) The strong nuclear force, which can be termed attractive force, plays the role of binding protons as well as neutrons as it ensures the nuclear structure is maintained, while the weak nuclear force plays the role of radioactive beta decay as well as other different reactions of a sub-atomic nature.

(B) While the strong nuclear force happens to be robust, the weak nuclear force remains feeble.

(C) The strong nuclear force happens to be negative and discharges protons as well as neutrons while threatening the nuclear structure, whereas the weak nuclear force happens to be an attractive force binding protons as well as neutrons while maintaining the nuclear structure.

(D) The strong nuclear force plays the role of radioactive beta decay as well as other different reactions of a sub-atomic nature while the weak nuclear force happens to be an attractive force binding protons as well as neutrons as it continues to maintain the nuclear structure.

(134) Of the four options given below, choose the one that aptly describes what the Law of Conservation states.

(A) Based on all the substances in use, massive gain or loss can be caused by chemical reactions.

(B) As chemical reactions take place, there is no gain or loss that one can detect.

(C) As chemical reactions take place, there is a bit of gain but no loss detected.

(D) Based on the substances in use, a bit of loss can arise during chemical reactions.

(135) From the choices listed below, choose the one that best describes any difference there may be between heat radiation and convection.

(A) Convection can be described as heat emanating from one source and moving to another through fluid, while thermal radiation involves nuclear energy emerging from matter of all kinds owing to the presence of thermal energy.

(B) Convection entails heat transfer from one point to another through fluids, while thermal radiation is light that is not easy to detect that all matter emits owing to the presence of thermal energy.

(C) Convection entails heat transfer from one region to another through fluid movement, whereas thermal radiation entails emission of electromagnetic radiation from all forms of matter because it possesses thermal energy.

(D) Thermal radiation entails heat transfer from one region to another through fluid movement, whereas convection entails emission of electromagnetic radiation from all forms of matter because it possesses thermal energy.

Mathematics Section of the NLN PAX

(136) Write eight as a percentage of forty.

(A) 15%

(B) 25%

(C) 20%

(D) 10%

$\frac{8}{40} = \frac{1}{5} = 20\%$

(137) Write nine as a percentage of 36.

(A) 15%

(B) 20%

(C) 10%

(D) 25%

$\frac{9}{36} = \frac{1}{4} = 25\%$

(138) Three-tenths of ninety is the same as ____.

(A) 45

(B) 36

(C) 27

(D) 18

$\frac{3}{10} \times \frac{x}{90} = 27$

91

(139) Zero point four percent of thirty-six is the same as _____.

(A) 144 ✗

· (B) 0.144

(C) 1.44 ✗

(D) 14.4 ✗

0.4 %

36

3.6 = 1%

(140) What is the ratio of eight to five as a percentage?

(A) 175%

(B) 75%

(C) 150%

· (D) 160%

$\frac{8}{5}$

$\frac{1}{5} = 20\%$
× 3
60% → 160%

(141) What is three-fifths as a percentage of x?

(A) 78%

(B) 75%

(C) 100%

· (D) 60%

$\frac{1}{5} = 20\%$
× 3
60%

(142) What is two-~~thirds~~ fifths expressed in decimal form?

(A) 0.5   1/2

(B) 0.33 1/3

· (C) 0.4 2/5

(D) 0.3 3/10

2/3 = .667

2/5 = 0.4

(143) What is zero point five six (0.56) as a percentage?

(A) 56%

(B) 5.6%

(C) 0.056%

(D) 0.56%

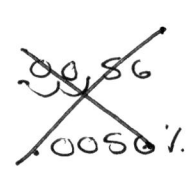

$0.56 = 56\%$

(144) What is eighteen over six written as a percentage?

(A) 300%

(B) 3%

(C) 30%

(D) 150%

$\frac{18}{6} = 3 = 300\%$

(145) What is four over twenty written as a percentage?

(A) 40%

(B) 20%

(C) 15%

(D) 25%

$\frac{4}{20} = \frac{1}{5} = 20\%$

(146) Divide four ninety-one by nine

(A) 54 r. 5

(B) 51 r. 3

(C) 56 r. 6

(D) 57 r. 5

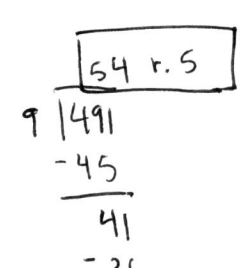

```
   54 r. 5
 9 |491
   -45
   ---
    41
   -36
   ---
     5
```

(147) Seven hundred and three divided by six is:

(A) 118 r. 4

(B) 117 r. 1

(C) 116 r. 5

(D) 116 r. 3

(148) Write 71/1,000 as a decimal.

(A) 7.1

(B) 0.71

(C) 0.071

(D) 0.0071

(149) Four point seven plus zero point nine plus zero point zero one is equal to _____.

(A) 5.7

(B) 5.5

(C) 5.61

(D) 6.51

(150) Zero point three three times zero point five nine is equal to _____.

(A) 0.1947

(B) 0.0197

(C) 0.1817

(D) 1.947

(151) Zero point eight four divided by zero point seven is equal to _____.

(A) 12

(B) 0.012

(C) 0.12

(D) 1.2

(152) Zero point eight seven minus zero point four eight is equal to _____.

(A) 0.39

(B) 0.37

(C) 0.41

(D) 0.49

(153) Rounding 3.864 to the nearest tenth is _____.

(A) 3.9

(B) 4

(C) 3.96

(D) 3.86

95

(154) Which one of the choices listed below is not equal to 10⁴?

(A) 100,000 ✗

(B) 10² x 10² ✓

(C) 10,000 ✓

(D) 0.1 x 10⁵ ✓

(E) 10 x 10 x 10 x 10 ✓

☆ (155) If 10⁴ is multiplied by 10², the answer is _____.

(A) 10²

(B) 10³

·(C) 10⁶ ✓

(D) 10⁸

(E) 10⁻²

$10^4 \cdot 10^2 = $ ~~~~

$10^4 \cdot 10^2 = 10^{(4+2)} = 10^6$

(156) X⁵ ÷ X² = _____

(A) x¹⁰

(B) x²·⁵

(C) x⁷

·(D) x³

(E) x⁴

$X^5 \div X^2 = X^{(5-2)}$
$= X^3$

(157) $8.23 \times 10^9 = $ _____

✗ (A) 823000000000 ✗

(B) 0.00000000823 ✗

(C) 0.000000823 ✗

✓ (D) 8230000000 ✗

(E) 8.23 ✗

(158) 83,000 is equal to _____.

(A) 83.0×10^5

8.3×10^4

✓ (B) 8.3×10^4

(C) 83.0×10^2

✗ (D) 83.0×10^4

✗ (E) 8.3×10^3

(159) Choose the one option that is equal to 0.00875.

(A) 875×10^{-4}

8.75×10^{-3}

· (B) 8.75×10^{-3}

(C) 8.75×10^{-3}

(D) 8.75×10^{-2}

(E) 8.75×10^{-4}

(160) If a particular pool has a volume of 7v liters and there is a tap pouring water in at a rate of y/4 liters per minute, which option below is the correct expression indicating the period of time required for the pool to reach 1/5 full with water?

(A) 35y/4v

(B) 28v/5y

(C) 28y/5v

(D) 7v/20y

(161) There are six employees with equal capacity to work, and they are building a wall. Each day one employee leaves, and that entire job ends up being completed in four days. If no employee left until the work was completed, how many days would it take the employees to complete building the wall?

(A) 2 days

(B) 1 day

(C) 1½ days

(D) 3 days

(162) 10 kg converted to grams is _____.

(A) 10,000 grams

(B) 10.11 grams

(C) 1,000 grams

(D) 100 grams

(163) How many liters are in one gallon?

(A) 4.5 L

(B) 3.785 L

(C) 1 L

(D) 37.85 L

(164) How many milliliters are in 2.5 liters?

(A) 1,500 ml

(B) 2,500 ml

(C) 1,050 ml

(D) 2,050 ml

(165) How many grams are in 210 milligrams?

(A) 2.1 g

(B) 2.12 g

(C) 0.21 g

(D) 0.21 mg

(166) How many kilograms are in ten pounds?

(A) 4.54 kg ✓

(B) 15 kg ✗

(C) 11.25 kg ✗

(D) 10.25 kg ✗

(167) How many milligrams are in 0.539 grams?

(A) 0.53 g ✗

(B) 539 mg

(C) 539 g ✗

(D) 53.9 mg

k H D m D c m

0.539

539 mg

(168) How many gallons are in 16 quarts?

(A) 4.5 gallons

(B) 1 gallon

(C) 4 gallons

(D) 8 gallons

4 gall

4 qt = 1 gall

(169) How many pounds are in 45 kilograms?

(A) 110 pounds

(B) 100 pounds

(C) 10 pounds

(D) 1,000 pounds

1 kg = 2.2 lbs

45 kg × 2.2 lbs / 1 kg = 100 lbs

45 × 2 = 90

4.5 × 2 = 9

90 + 9 = 100

(170) One packet has seven green pencils and twenty-eight red ones. Find the ratio between green and red pencils.

(A) 1 : 4
(B) 1 : 9
(C) 2 : 7
(D) 1 : 8

(171) A certain factory manager says his machines produce 1,450m of woven material within 8 hrs when their efficiency is 100%. Unfortunately, the machines develop problems and they drop efficiency so that 4 of them are running at 95% while the remaining 6 are running at 90%. How many meters of cloth will the factory produce within the normal 8 hrs?

(A) 1,334m
(B) 1,300m
(C) 1,285m
(D) 1,310m

(172) During the presidential elections, 3 local polling stations, A, B, and C, had different rates of turnout. Station A had 1,270 registered voters and 945 of them showed up to vote. Station B had 1,050 registered voters and 860 of them showed up to vote. Station C had 1,440 registered voters and 1,210 of them voted. What percentage of voters turned out locally overall?

(A) 76%
(B) 70%
(C) 74%
(D) 80%

(173) Anne's typing speed is one page per p minutes. How many pages can she type in five minutes?

(A) p + 5

(B) p/5

(C) p − 5

(D) 5/p

(174) Joseph takes four hours to paint a small house, but it takes James six hours to paint the very house. If they did the painting together, how long would it take them to complete painting the house?

(A) 2hr 24min

(B) 3hr 44min

(C) 4hr 10min

(D) 3hr 12min

(175) A store sells dishwashers for $450, and this week it has a 15% sales discount. Normally the employees of the store benefit from an extra 20% discount. If an employee buys a dishwasher this week, how much is he going to pay for it?

(A) $280.90

(B) $292.50

(C) $287.00

(D) $306.00

(176) A car that is on sale has a price tag of $12,590. The discount given to arrive at that price is 20%. Calculate the car's original or initial price.

(A) $15,108.00

(B) $14,310.40

(C) $14,990.90

(D) $15,737.50

(177) Arnold has n employees. He pays each $s every week. Arnold has a total of $x in his bank account. How many days can he afford to employ these employees?

(A) nx/7s

(B) sx/7n

(C) 7x/nx

(D) 7x/ns

(178) Mary purchased 550kg of grain for $165. She sold the grain to her 15 loyal customers at $6.4 per 20kg when grain was still scarce in the town. After one week, she had sold grain to 12 customers at $3.4 per 10kg, and what remained she sold at $1.8 per 5kg. Mary spent a total of $10 to distribute the grain to different customers. What was her profit?

(A) $23.40

(B) $8.60

(C) $10.40

(D) $14.90

(179) What is 15 as a percentage of 200?

(A) 7.5%

(B) 17.5%

(C) 15%

(D) 20%

(180) Little John has 5 blue balls, 3 green balls, and 2 red balls. What percentage of the total balls is red?

(A) 12%

(B) 2%

(C) 20%

(D) 8%

(181) 10% of 300 added to 50% of 20 is_____

(A) 45

(B) 40

(C) 50

(D) 60

(182) What is 75% as a fraction?

(A) 85%

(B) 4/7

(C) ¾

(D) 2%

(183) What is the answer when you multiply three by 25% of forty?

(A) 35

(B) 30

(C) 75

(D) 68

(184) Calculate 10% of 30 times 75% of 200

(A) 450

(B) 45

(C) 20

(D) 750

(185) What is 4/20 expressed as a percentage?

(A) 30%

(B) 20%

(C) 40%

(D) 25%

(186) What is 0.55 expressed as a percentage?

(A) 75%

(B) 45%

(C) 15%

(D) 55%

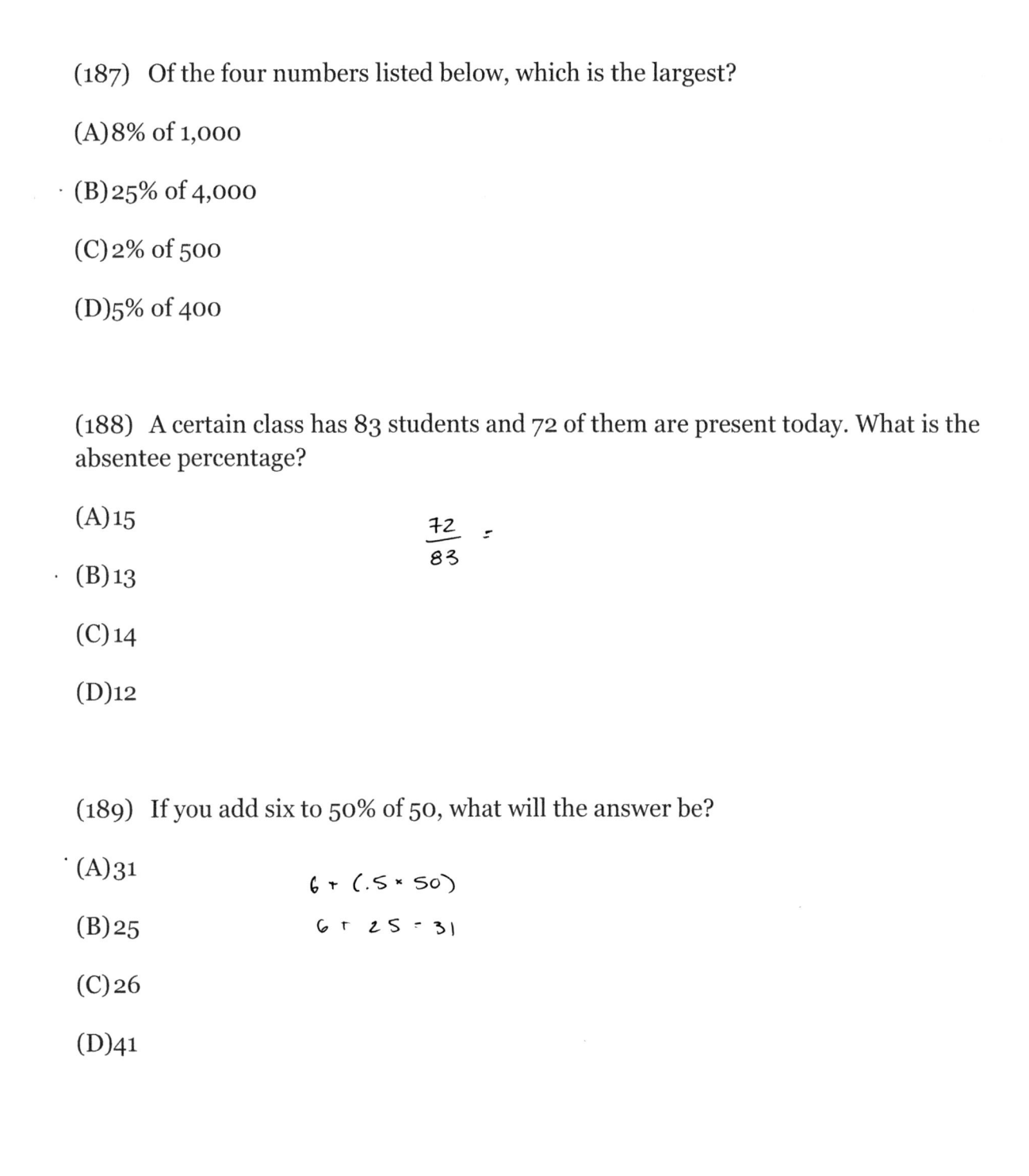

(187) Of the four numbers listed below, which is the largest?

(A) 8% of 1,000

(B) 25% of 4,000

(C) 2% of 500

(D) 5% of 400

(188) A certain class has 83 students and 72 of them are present today. What is the absentee percentage?

(A) 15

(B) 13

(C) 14

(D) 12

$\dfrac{72}{83} =$

(189) If you add six to 50% of 50, what will the answer be?

(A) 31

(B) 25

(C) 26

(D) 41

6 + (.5 × 50)
6 + 25 = 31

(190) A vehicle drives for twenty seconds from a high spot on the road traveling at 10 meters per second. What is the vehicle's acceleration?

(A) 0.5 meters / second²

(B) 1.5 meters / second²

(C) 1 meter / second²

(D) 0.24 meters / second²

(191) A vehicle is traveling at 90 miles per hour and then in five seconds, it accelerates to a speed of 120 miles per hour. What is the vehicle's acceleration?

(A) 6 mph per second

(B) 20 mph per second

(C) 15 mph per second

(D) 10 mph per second

(192) One rocket discharges a satellite that enters an orbit around the earth. This satellite moves at 2,000 m/sec and does this within 25 seconds. Calculate the satellite's acceleration.

(A) 120 m/sec2

✓(B) 80 m/sec2

(C) 100 m/sec2

(D) 60 m/sec2

(193) The velocity of a soccer ball after it has been kicked is 12 m/sec. Within 60 seconds the ball stops. Calculate its acceleration.

(A) -0.2 m/sec² negative

(B) 0.5 m/sec²

(C) 1 m/sec²

(D) 0.2 m/sec²

$a = \frac{m}{s^2}$

$\frac{12m}{s} \cdot \frac{1}{60s} = \frac{12m}{60s^2} = -0.2 \text{ m/s}^2$

(194) If a rocket has traveled three thousand meters within five seconds, how fast was it traveling?

(A) 500 m/sec

(B) 100 m/sec

(C) 200 m/sec

(D) 600 m/sec

$\frac{3000m}{5s} = 600 \text{ m/s}$

(195) If the distance traveled by the space station within five seconds is 1,000 meters, how fast is it traveling?

(A) 500 meters per second

(B) 200 meters per second

(C) 100 meters per second

(D) 50 meters per second

$\frac{1,000m}{5s} = 200 \text{ m/s}$

(196) Rudisha sprints at six meters per second. How far will he have traveled in two minutes?

(A) 800 meters

(B) 720 meters

(C) 600 meters

(D) 760 meters

(197) Find the distance Radcliffe will have walked if she travels 1,000 meters per 20 minutes.

(A) 1000 meters

(B) 50 meters

(C) 25 meters

(D) 100 meters

(198) Tom buys a hundred shares at a hundred dollars per share. Soon the price rises by ten percent and John sells 50 of the shares. After some time the price changes again and this time the price drops by ten percent, and John decides to dispose of all the remaining shares. How much money did he realize from the sale of the last 50 shares?

(A) $5,000

(B) $4,900

(C) $5,050

(D) $5,500

(E) $4,950

(199) Mrs. Smith has three hours to grade scripts from his 35 students. She grades five papers in half an hour. In order to complete grading the remaining scripts in the set three hours, how much faster does Mrs. Smith have to work?

(A) 10%

(B) 25%

(C) 20%

(D) 30%

(E) 15%

(200) What is the prime number that is next in greatness after 67

(A) 76

(B) 68

(C) 71

(D) 73

(E) 69

Practice Test 1 – Answers

English Proficiency Section of the NLN-PAX

(1) The adjective 'corrupted' means:

The correct answer is: (A) adulterated

Something is said to be adulterated when it is impure. For example, when unscrupulous business people add paraffin to petrol and sell it as petrol, one can say the petrol has been adulterated. To be infuriated means the person has been angered. Something harbored is something concealed or held and probably for too long, such as ill feelings against another who offended them in the past. Something inculcated is something instilled into someone, such as the habit of keeping time.

(2) The noun 'eagerness' means:

The correct answer is: (A) Alacrity

Alacrity to do something denotes liveliness or enthusiasm. If there are projects to be done by teams and one of them begins to work on theirs immediately the details are provided, it can be said that particular team has shown alacrity and their eagerness to carry out the work is evident.

Marital has to do with marriage, such as 'marital' status. Happiness means joy and a detonator is a device used to detonate or to blow something up.

(3) The verb that means 'making less harsh' is:

The correct answer is: (B) Alleviate

The verb 'alleviate' means to reduce the harshness or to make something less painful, serious, or severe. A problem or difficulty can be alleviated, meaning it is made less of a difficulty. To suspend means to stop an action for a while and it will resume at a later time. The word 'action' is a noun meaning 'something done'; a deed. The word 'ingrate' refers to someone who does not show gratitude after receiving a favor or after being treated well.

(4) A verb that means to sanctify is:

The correct answer is: (C) Bless

The verb 'sanctify' means to bless or to consecrate, the way a person who lived a holy life is 'sanctified' or 'canonized' after death. To train is to teach or to tutor a person or an animal to do something or learn something. To brand is to assign a name to something or someone. For example, a manufacturer can brand his item so that buyers can consider it unique in character and quality as compared to other items used for a similar purpose. To negate is to contradict or to oppose. People normally negate what others have said when they consider it incorrect, inappropriate, or not worthwhile.

(5) A noun used to refer to someone who donates money or a gift to a charitable organization is:

The correct answer is: (B) Benefactor

The person giving a donation is called the benefactor while the organization or person receiving the donation is referred to as the beneficiary. A teacher is a person who teaches or imparts knowledge or an instructor. What a teacher gives is intangible whereas what a benefactor gives is often tangible. A captain is a leader or a commander, such as a team captain, a ship captain, etc. The word 'source' refers to the origin. For example, if the person donating money used his personal savings, it is correct to say the source of the benefactor's money was his personal savings.

(6) The meaning of the adjective, 'hidden' is:

The correct answer is: (B) Covert

Something covert is an action that is hidden or kept in secret. The word 'surreptitious' could be used particularly when the thing being kept out of the limelight is clandestine. 'Carriage' is a noun that refers to something designed to carry people from one place to another. Accustomed means to have got used to, the word 'hide' is used to mean keeping something out of sight so that other people cannot find it.

(7) 'Straightforward' means the same as:

The correct answer is: (B) Candid

When people are candid, it means they are straightforward and sincere, and they are also open about the issue. It means they are talking about the issue without giving half truths. The word 'illegal' is an adjective used in reference to something that is unlawful; something that can lead to legal proceedings being initiated against the perpetrator. True means factual, accurate, or exact. The adjective 'lawful' means being legal or within the law.

(8) The verb 'fearless' means:

The correct answer is: (C) Dauntless

A person who is described as fearless can also be said to be dauntless, which means the person is not vulnerable with regards to fear and is not easily intimidated. Someone can be said to be extraordinary he or she is special in one way or another; in behavior, in looks, or in any other way. Someone can be said to be feeble if he or she is weak or delicate either physically or emotionally. The opposite of 'feeble' is 'strong' because the latter means being powerful or tough.

(9) An appropriate verb to describe the act of removing a leader from a high position is:

The correct answer is: (C) Depose

The verb 'depose' is generally used in reference to a person already holding a high office, and it means getting that person ousted in a way that does not involve assassination. Some heads of state, for example, have been deposed through a coup. For example, in April 2019, President Omar al-Bashir of Sudan was deposed in a coup led by the military.

To drop is to leave someone out of contention, but it is just general and does not give an indication the position could be a powerful one. To sack is to remove someone from a job, and it could even involve a very junior position. For example, a manager can be sacked the same way a messenger is sacked. The verb, 'suspend' is used to denote temporarily prohibiting a person from acting in their former capacity, and there is a chance that suspension could be lifted and the person allowed to resume normal duties.

(10) To make someone strong in morals or matters of religion can be described using the verb _____.

The correct answer is: (C) Edify

The actual meaning of edify is teaching or providing someone with valuable information so that they become not just knowledgeable but also better off for it. You can edify a person morally or even intellectually by the teachings or instructions you provide. To deceive is to lie. To sanctify is to make holy or to bless, such as when a person dies who has done a lot of good deeds is declared a saint. To pacify is to make peace. For example, if you realize something you did has upset someone, you could go to that person and apologize and by doing so, you are trying to pacify the person.

(11) People are said to be headstrong when _____.

The correct answer is: (B) They are stubborn

People who are headstrong are stubborn and are determined to pursue what they want irrespective of what other people think. (A) is not correct because you may choose not to listen for very good reason and not just because you are obstinate. It is also probable that those people do not listen because they are overwhelmed with work. (C) is also not correct because people who are headstrong are normally not willing to concur with anyone else. Being willing does not have the same meaning as being headstrong. Even (D) is incorrect as being headstrong is not the same as not believing.

(12) Being oblique means _____.

The correct answer is: (B) Being indirect

The meaning of oblique is indirect or not straightforward. For example, politicians sometimes attack each other in an oblique manner as they address voters. Other words that can describe the word 'oblique' include 'obscure', 'sinister', 'underhand' or even 'disingenuous'. Option (A) cannot be correct as being direct is the exact opposite of being oblique. Even a speech can be sharp without being oblique, and being straight is contrary to being oblique.

(13) The word 'temper' can be best described as to _____.

The correct answer is: (C) improve

To temper something is to neutralize it or to make it less harsh. If, for instance, there is a quarrel going on, mentioning something to show that none of the parties is at fault is likely to temper the tense and toxic situation. The other three options are incorrect as they all have the meaning of making something worse. To exacerbate a situation is to make it worse, and that is the same meaning aggravate portrays. To intensify is to make whatever is happening rise a notch higher; so if it is anger, it becomes more intense and more serious instead of being moderated or controlled.

(14) The meaning of 'cryptic' is _____.

The correct answer is: (B) Hard to understand

The meaning of 'cryptic' is 'hard to understand', and this is not necessarily because the writing is in a foreign language, but because the manner of communication is obscure. When a message is said to be cryptic, for example, it means only a few people can understand it because they have a certain advantage other people do not have, like some background information. There is actually some mystery surrounding something that is cryptic.

Option (A) is incorrect since the act of building a house in the graveyard is not given the term 'cryptic'. It may be weird or odd, but not cryptic as everyone can see what is happening. (C) is also incorrect because something cryptic can be represented in coded print or deliver a cryptic message without printing it and without coding it.

(15) To curtail something is to _____.

The correct answer is: (A) reduce its extent or cut it short

If you curtail something it does not continue to increase or to advance, but instead, it stops at that particular point. If something was happening, nothing more happens from the time you curtail it. The meaning of 'curtail' has nothing to do with serving cocktails, and so options (B) is incorrect. Option (C) has the exact opposite of 'curtailing', so it is incorrect. To curtail is not to return something as suggested in (D).

(16)   The verb 'heed' means _____.

The correct answer is: (B) pay attention

To heed is to pay attention. For example, you can heed someone's advice, meaning you will pay attention to it with a view to following it. To heed does not mean to ignore since to ignore means not paying attention. To heed is not to advise. To advise is to offer counsel. For example, you can say, 'He heeded his mother's advice'. To listen is to take note of what is said, but you do not have to take it seriously, which is encompassed in the verb to 'heed'.

(17)   To be oblivious of something is to be _____.

The correct answer is: (D) unaware of something

When you are oblivious it means you are not aware. It is possible to be oblivious of something even when you are near it, and so option (A) is incorrect. In fact 'oblivious' does not bear the notion of distance or being far off, of happiness or unhappiness, or of being close. If you are oblivious, your mind is dwelling elsewhere.

(18)   A podium is a _____.

The correct answer is: (B) platform that is raised

A podium is a platform that is raised that is used by speakers to address an audience. During political campaigns, for example, politicians speak from the podium while giving a speech. Orchestra conductors sometimes stand at a podium as they direct the orchestra.

(19)   To be boorish is to be _____.

The correct answer is: (B) ill-mannered

A boor is a person who is ill-mannered, rude, and uncultured. Being boorish does not necessarily mean being ill-tempered since there are some hot-tempered people who are not necessarily ill-mannered. (C) is incorrect as well considering a person's behavior has nothing to do with how he or she looks. Someone can have good looks and yet be badly behaved. Option (D) is incorrect as being boorish has nothing to do with smelling either nicely or badly.

(20) 'Heresy' is best defined as _____.

The correct answer is: (A) opinion that is at variance with the orthodox

Heresy is an opinion by a group member that radically differs from the beliefs held by the rest of the group. Such a group with a common belief could be in politics, science, philosophy, or any other field. Heresy normally raises controversy as other members of the group are normally not used to opposing opinions.

Heresy is not similar to the orthodox, and so options (B) is incorrect. Option (C) cannot be correct as it does not mean any surprising opinion is heresy. At the same time, when someone expresses some heresy, it means the person has taken a stance different from the usual, and so such a person cannot be said to be open to just any opinion.

(21) The word, 'respite' can be best defined as _____.

The correct answer is: (B) intermission

The meaning of respite is intermission or a short interval. For instance, judging a competition can be exhausting, and so not having to do the judging for a brief time is tantamount to taking a temporary rest. 'Respite' actually means a short period of relief or rest.

The word 'respite' has nothing to do with respect and does not mean short sleep. It does not mean remaining idle or a gadget of technology or any other kind.

(22) What is the meaning of 'passionate' as used in the passage?

The correct answer is: (B) ardent

When a person is passionate about reading, it means he or she likes reading a lot. Being passionate about something means you are a great fan of it and your interest in it is very high. You can, therefore, be termed an ardent reader, an ardent soccer fan and so on.

Doing something fast does not make you passionate about it, and the same case applies to being slow or being lazy. Passionate could have the opposite connotation.

(23) By equating the goodness of Dr. Seuss' books with that of medicine, the inference is that _____.

The correct answer is: (A) People feel better after reading the books

Saying the goodness of the books was like the goodness of medicine infers that people felt better after reading the books the same way they feel better after taking medication. The comparison is a simile that is a compliment to Dr. Seuss for his writing, recommending people to read his books if they want to generally feel good.

Option (B) is incorrect as the passage does not contain any information involving doctors' clinics, and (C) is also incorrect because the kind of goodness the books provided has nothing to do with real diseases. As such, the meaning in the passage is not that people should read the books as a substitute for prescription medicine. Option (D) is not only incorrect but also outrageous as licking books or any other piece of paper cannot serve as a treatment for diseases. In any case, there is no indication in the passage that anyone had the urge to lick any of Dr. Seuss' books.

(24) One publisher who sent Dr. Seuss a book with words is described as being intelligent because _____.

The correct answer is: (D) He knew Mr. Geisel had the talent to create a book which would interest young kids.

The publisher who sent Dr. Seuss the book of words understood that children were not particularly interested in reading and hence needed a nicely written book to gain their interest. He also knew Mr. Geisel was capable of producing such a book and that was the reason he chose to send the book of words to him. He understood that the children would expand their vocabulary without thinking much about it.

Option (A) cannot be correct considering every publisher is literate. This means being literate does not make this one publisher unique. Option (B) is incorrect because it has been mentioned in the passage that the issue of children not being interested in reading was a concern in the early 1950s. In short, it was not just this one publisher who had this information. Whether Dr. Seuss' book would be a bestseller or not has not been mentioned in the passage, so option (C) is not the best choice for an answer.

(25) The passage contains the theme of _____.

The correct answer is: (B) Dr. Seuss influencing generations of young children

The theme running throughout the passage is how Mr. Geisel, who was later nicknamed Dr. Seuss, influenced children from a very young age through reading his books. A number of the books Dr. Seuss wrote are mentioned in the passage, and it is said the books got children interested in reading and many became passionate readers owing to his writing style.

Option (A) is incorrect as the fact that Dr. Seuss was not a medical doctor has been mentioned but it cannot be termed the theme of the passage. This is the same case with the fact that his books rhymed, and so option (C) is incorrect. Although it is suggested it is a good idea to read a book on the birthday of Dr. Seuss, the idea is not discussed at length and cannot be termed the theme of the passage.

(26) To secede means to _____.

The correct answer is: (A) split

The verb 'secede' is used to denote splitting or breaking away from a union or an alliance. In the case of America, there were eleven states that wanted to split and form a separate government and to exist as an independent country. Options (B), (C) and (D) are wrong because 'secede' does not mean to succeed and it also does not mean to join or to expand. In fact, after secession, both sides were smaller as opposed to expanding. The eleven states were not seeking to be welcomed in order to join as they were already part of the USA. They were seeking to leave and cease being a part of the USA.

(27) The following statement summarizes a fact contained in the passage.

The correct answer is: (B) War was declared by Congress after the firing of shots at Fort Sumter.

According to the dates provided in the passage, the firing of shots occurred on the 12th of April, yet the date war was declared by Congress was the 14th of April. This means the declaration of war came after the provocation by shots fired in Fort Sumter. This means option (A) has its timelines wrong, so it is an incorrect answer choice.

Option (C) is wrong as it was stated clearly in the passage that the goal of President Lincoln was to end slavery completely. The reason option (D) is incorrect is that the passage does not disclose where the president was at any one time, or if Congress held a sitting at Fort Sumter.

(28) The Confederacy finally surrendered when _____.

The correct answer is: (C) Richmond, the capital of the Confederacy, was invaded

It is clearly stated in the passage that the leader of the Confederates, Robert Lee, surrendered to the Union leader, Grant, following the capture of Richmond, which was the Confederate capital. For this reason, option (C) is the correct answer choice.

Option (A) is incorrect because even after the battle began at Gettysburg, the Civil War went on for two years. Option (B) is incorrect because there is no mention in the passage about a battle at Bull Run. Option (D) is incorrect because war went on after the march and only after the capital was captured did the war come to an end.

(29) In the context of the passage, 'abolish' means to _____.

The correct answer is: (A) formerly bring to an end

The states in the north had abolished slavery, meaning that no one in those northern states was permitted to keep slaves. It, therefore, means that if someone kept a slave it would have been against the law in those states and slavery had been formerly brought to an end in those particular states, and that makes option (A) the most appropriate choice for an answer.

Option (B) is incorrect as there was no plan to renew slavery after it had been ended, and the term 'abolish' does not have such connotation. Option (C) is also incorrect in that something that has been terminated cannot be improved upon, and in this case, the northern states had terminated slavery. Option (D) is also incorrect since to abolish is not to just to condemn something but to terminate it completely.

(30) What is the meaning of 'Annex' in the context of the passage?

The correct answer is: (A) attic

It is possible to tell that 'annex' in the passage refers to 'attic' considering the 'annex' is said to be somewhere above the building of Otto Frank. Option (B) cannot be correct considering the basement cannot have been above the office block. Office buildings normally do not include bedrooms, and so option (C) is incorrect. Option (D) is also incorrect as an office building is expected to contain offices and not a kitchen, and if there is need to have some space for making simple things like tea or coffee, it is unlikely to be above the office.

(31)   What is the reason the diary that belonged to Anne is now translated into 55 languages?

The correct answer is: (B) So that many people across the globe can learn about the horrors that took place during the infamous Holocaust.

Anne's diary is now published in 55 languages and continues to be printed in an effort to inform as many people as possible about the reality of the Holocaust. The diary is invaluable because it provides an account of a person who lived through those horrors and wrote about them from firsthand experience.

Option (A) is incorrect because the passage does not give any information pertaining to the languages Anne's father, Otto Frank, was able to speak. Option (C), though it gives some idea of the reality, is too vague to be the best choice for an answer. For example, what is it about the diary that people would understand?

Fifty-five languages may not be sufficient to inform everyone about the contents of the diary, considering there are many more languages spoken all over the world. Nevertheless, 55 languages can reach very many people. Option (D), which mentions the three places in which Anne had the opportunity to reside, is wrong considering her diary was not published until after her death.

(32)   What would you conclude is the meaning of 'typhus' from the way the deaths of Anne and Margot have been described in the passage?

The correct answer is: (C) An illness Anne got while she was at the concentration camp

This is the kind of question you can answer by eliminating the most unlikely answers. For one, dying of starvation is an unlikely possibility because it would have been easier to state that outright in the passage if that had been the case. In any case, it is clearly stated that Margot died of hunger. As such, option (A) is incorrect. Option (B) and option (D) are also incorrect for the simple reason that if Anne had been assassinated by the Germans, it would have been a key aspect of Anne's story and would have been stated clearly in the passage. The elimination method thus leaves you with option (C) as the most plausible answer.

(33) What is the meaning of 'outlet' as used in the passage?

The correct answer is: (D) A place where Anne went to express her inner thoughts

From the context, Anne used her diary to release the thoughts going through her mind that she was not able to share with other people. Since the term 'outlet' is used in relation to her diary, it can only have been a vent for her tormenting thoughts and a place for her to pour out what she felt.

Option (A) is not correct as it refers to a wall whereas the outlet in the passage is used in reference to the diary. This means 'outlet' is figuratively used in the passage and should not be taken literally the way option (A) seems to have done. Option (B) is also incorrect as it refers to a store or a shop whereas the passage refers to the place to vent as the diary; the place where she let out her inner thoughts. Option (C) is also incorrect as it is not mentioned in the passage that Anne's outlet was like the annex. In any case, the diary served as the outlet for her thoughts while the family hid in the annex.

(34) The tone of the article is generally _____.

The correct answer is: (B) informal

The passage is not written in official or academic language and does not carry such a tone, but it is written in a rather casual manner. It is clear the passage is not meant as a formal presentation to a class or a group of professionals, or for an official journal. For that reason, option (B) indicates the tone is informal and is the best choice of answer whereas option (D) indicates the tone of the passage is formal and is incorrect.

The language used is not technical at all. The passage is written in such a manner that anyone reading it, even those who are not trained in fish farming, can easily understand the information provided. As such, option (A) is incorrect. Option (C) is not correct because the writer of the passage has presented facts to back up the information provided. A person's opinion does not need to be supported with facts, which is what has been done in the passage.

(35)   Among the answer options provided, one of them cannot be deduced from the passage. Which is it?

The correct answer is: (B) Fewer people maintain aquariums at their place of work than in their homes.

The reason option (B) is the correct answer is that there is no way of verifying or even deducing that of all the people who keep aquariums there are fewer who have them in their offices or other places of work than those who have them in their homes. On the other hand, the assertions in the other three options can be easily deduced.

It is clearly stated in the passage that filters come in varying sizes, and you should use your aquarium size to guide you in selecting the best filter to use. This is the way to deduce that option (A) is correct. As for options (C) and (D), it is easy to tell the information they have is correct because, in the last paragraph of the passage, it is stated that gravel is great for your aquarium especially if you intend to put real plants in the aquarium as opposed to plastic ones. In the same paragraph, it is said that gravel enhances the beauty of the aquarium.

(36)   There is evidence provided in the passage that it is necessary to have aquarium lights. The evidence is _____.

The correct answer is: (B) Both plants and the fish in the aquarium need light.

There is evidence that light is necessary for an aquarium. For one, it is explained that plants need light for photosynthesis, which is the process by which plants make their food. It is also said in the same paragraph that fish also need light. In short, although the point made in option (A) about plant needing light is true, it is not as conclusive as to the facts given in option (B), which states that both plants and the fish need light.

There is also information in the passage indicating that lights make the tank you are using more appealing. However, the beauty of the aquarium is all option (C) addresses, so it cannot be the best answer considering the importance of light to the fish and plants. In any case, making the aquarium more appealing may not always make lighting a necessity. Option (D) is incorrect as it is not stated in the passage how well fish swim depends on the lighting of the aquarium.

(37)   Which of the choices given below is just an opinion?

The correct answer is: (B) An aquarium's aesthetics is enhanced by gravel.

An opinion, unless clearly stated as 'expert opinion', does not need to be supported by facts or even knowledge. It is just a person's perspective. In this case, it is the writer's opinion that aquariums look nice when they have gravel in them. Someone else could have a different opinion. The other options are factual.

Option (A) for example, is instruction on the turnover rate required for a good filter – 3 to 5 times. It is important to adhere to this instruction or expert advice if your tropical fish are to survive in the aquarium. Option (C) states the role of the hood and is factual. The hood keeps unwanted material from the aquarium. That is why (C) does not constitute an opinion. Different species of tropical fish do well at different temperatures, and this is the fact stated in option (D). So, just like options (A), and (C), option (D) does not constitute an opinion but they are stating facts.

(38)   Considering Helen Keller was both blind and deaf, her greatest childhood challenge was _____.

The correct answer is: (A) Difficulty in communication

Communication was such a problem for Helen Keller that her parents engaged the services of a teacher whose name was Anne Sullivan. This confirms that the real challenge Helen faced in childhood was difficulty in communication as indicated in option (A), which her parents sought help to have her overcome.

As for option (B), it is incorrect because it is said that Helen found it difficult to move around, meaning she could move but not easily. Compared to her movement challenge, communication was worse because even learning to talk is described as an 'impossible' task. Option (C) is incorrect as playing comes naturally to a child, whether they can hear, see, or talk. This means if there was a challenge she had that would require a teacher and it could not have been playing. Option (D) is, obviously, incorrect considering without eating Helen could not have survived.

(39)   Soon Helen could tell what someone was saying by the feel of the person's vibrations as they spoke. Helen felt these vibrations through the person's _____.

The correct answer is: (B) Throat

It is expressly stated in the passage that Anne taught Helen how to listen to what is being said by putting her own hand on the throat of the person speaking so that she could feel the sound that was being produced. It is further noted that soon Helen began to have a feel of the words being spoken. This is the information that makes option (A) the best choice for an answer.

All the other options are not correct. Nowhere in the passage is it said that the lips, nose, or the mouth helped Helen to detect what someone was saying.

(40)   It is possible to deduce from the passage that Helen's teacher, Anne Sullivan, had a lot of patience because _____.

The correct answer is: (A) At first Helen would hit her and even bite her, yet she stayed to teach her.

It is possible to deduce that Anne Sullivan had a lot of patience because she did not give up trying teaching Helen Keller to communicate. It is said in the passage that Helen would sometimes bite and hit her teacher, but Anne still continued to work with her until the results were clear for everyone to witness.

Option (B) is incorrect as Anne did not only teach Helen to read but also to communicate. Option (C) is incorrect because not only did Helen have a hearing problem but also a visual problem, and so her teacher's patience cannot be linked solely to her capacity to handle a child with hearing impairment. While it is possible Anne Sullivan could have dedicated her life to teaching, it is not a reason to make someone deduce she was patient. As such, option (D) is incorrect.

(41)   Although Helen Keller could finally speak, Anne Sullivan still found it necessary to translate what she said in public because _____.

The correct answer is: (B) The words Helen spoke were difficult for other people to comprehend.

It is stated in the passage that only Anne Sullivan could understand what Helen said. As such, it was necessary for Anne to listen to Helen and then to convey Helen's message to other people. It has not been stated in the passage that Helen used some foreign language or any other language besides English, and so option (B) is the best choice for an answer while option (A) and the other options are incorrect.

In fact, the insinuation in option (C) that Helen's voice was inaudible is wrong as there is no information in the passage to that effect. The reason given for there being a need for Anne to do the translation for other people has nothing to do with the volume or strength of Helen's voice. In fact, the issue of how loudly or softly Helen spoke was not raised in the passage. Option (D) is also not correct as there is no information in the passage indicating Helen used sign language as opposed to verbal language. On the contrary, it is stated clearly that Helen did manage to learn how to speak.

(42) The major idea in the passage is _____.

The correct answer is: (D) The presidents' wives are important in American culture.

The passage relates significant things some US presidents' wives have done including one who governed for the period her husband was incapacitated by a stroke. There are different First Ladies mentioned in the passage who did memorable things in their days as First Ladies that Americans always remember. Although they support their husbands when they are in office as president, this is not the major point of discussion in the passage, and so option (E) is incorrect.

The issue of humanitarian work among First Ladies was not discussed in the passage. What was highlighted is the humanitarian role played by an individual First Lady, Eleanor Roosevelt. In short, there is no expectation that First Ladies perform humanitarian work. This means option (A) is incorrect. The passage does not point out any First Lady was better at being influential, so option (B) is incorrect. Option (C) is incorrect as the passage does not single out any First Lady as having changed the image of a First Lady.

(43) The major idea in the passage is _____.

The correct answer is: (D) Potatoes are considered a very important vegetable in the US.

The major idea conveyed in the passage is the importance of the potato in America. In fact, there is no mention of either Ireland or a potato revolution in the passage, and this means option (A) is incorrect. Option (B) is also incorrect as it does not constitute the major idea of the passage, and it also gives a wrong statistic of 50 pounds. The information in the passage indicates the per capita consumption of potatoes in America is 100 pounds and not 50.

The passage was not written mainly to inform readers that French fries are produced from potatoes, and so option (C) is incorrect. It was also not the major idea to highlight how historically potatoes have been given different terms although different names used in reference to potatoes was mentioned. In fact, the history of individual terms for potatoes was not discussed in the passage.

(44)   The major idea in the passage is _____.

The correct answer is: (E) The protection patenting of inventions provides to inventors free enterprise as well as creative processes.

This passage gives similar importance to the protection of inventors, free enterprise, and processes of a creative nature, which inventors receive through the law of patents. Option (A) indicates that regulation on patenting helped to enhance free enterprise, which is true, but there is more important in the passage than that one idea. So, this option cannot be said to be the best answer.

Certainly, the point made in option (B) is true, because the US patent laws have protection in the constitution, but that point is not the only idea of importance in the passage. More importantly, this option does not state the major ideas the passage elaborates upon. What is stated in option (C) about patenting in the US having been influenced by the system England used is true, but the option leaves out other major ideas that the passage dwells on. This is the same shortcoming with option (D) – not including the three major ideas of the passage. The fact that patents are important to investors does not on its own make this option correct.

(45)   The major idea of the passage is _____.

The correct answer is: (A) Although it may be correct to say beavers are hard workers, the mechanisms these animals choose are not always the best in efficiency.

There are examples to their efficiency, like cutting trees and leaving them trapped, or beginning to construct a dam at the widest part of a stream as opposed to a narrower part and then giving up midway.

Option (B) is not correct because although dam building has been mentioned as something beavers are good at, this was not the major idea discussed in the passage. Option (C) is incorrect for the same reason as (B), meaning it only gives one point of the passage, which is the biggest dam built by beavers being in New Hampshire while ignoring the major idea. Option (D) has the point that beavers are accomplished in cutting trees, which is true, but that is not the major idea in the passage. As for ((E), it also carries a single point from the passage, which, though true, happens not to encompass the major idea; only that beavers are sometimes not great at surveying aquatic areas.

Science Section of the NLN PAX

(46) When animals and plants are found existing naturally in the same environment, the assemblage is referred to as _____.

The correct answer is: (C) community

The reason option (C) is the correct answer is that the term 'community' is used to refer to a mix of plants and animals thriving together in the same area. Sometimes this community is qualified as a biological community.

Option (A) is incorrect because the term 'population' is generally used in reference to the total number of people or animals living in a given area.

Option (B), which is 'society', is incorrect because when people live together in a community that is somewhat organized and they make common decisions, this is what is referred to as a society. Option (D) biosphere, is incorrect as the term refers to the earth's layer that enables the existence of life, which is the composition of the entire ecosystem.

(47) A ban on wolf hunting was imposed some years ago, and thus their population soared, increasing exponentially. In just a couple of generations, the wolves' habitat had gone beyond its _____.

The correct answer is: (A) carrying capacity

In ecology, the expression 'carrying capacity' is used to refer to how many animals or crops, or even people, a particular area can support, and beyond that number, the environment would be negatively affected. When the population of a certain species exceeds the area's carrying capacity, the environment begins to suffer degradation, and the members of the species living there begin to feel its negative effect.

Often the place cannot produce as much food as required to sustain the species, and there are other spiraling effects. As for people, when the environment is degraded diseases increase, including those of a respiratory nature such as pneumonia and asthma. This is because there are toxins that eventually saturate the environment and pollute the air the people breathe and the water they drink.

(48) Matter can exist in any of the four states named below:

The correct answer is: (B) solid, liquid, gas, & plasma

The correct answer is (B) because the states of solid, liquid, gas and even plasma are the four states that matter can exist in. The state the matter in question is going to be in depends on how strong the bond is that exists among the matter's atoms.

When matter exists in solid form, one can deduce its size and even shape, and it is possible to see it cannot flow the way a liquid like water does or even disappear the way air or gas does. Examples of items in solid form include bones, skin, and even hair.

When matter is in liquid form, it is almost impossible to compress it, and it does not take shape independently. Rather, it takes up the shape of the container it has been poured into. It is important to note that even when the liquid changes containers, its volume remains almost the same, and that is notwithstanding any change in pressure. Liquids, unlike solids, flow.

Matter that takes the form of gas is actually a fluid, and a good example is air. It has no shape and no volume. Nevertheless, it can expand without limit. In fact, air in a given container expands to occupy the entire container. Matter in gas form is also easily compressible. Whenever something in solid form is altered to become gaseous, the matter in the form of gas occupies much more space than the matter in solid form. The same case applies when matter in liquid form is altered to become gaseous. The former will have occupied less space than when it is in the form of gas.

In a hospital environment, for example, there is a substance called ether that is in liquid form when at room temperature, but it has such a low boiling point that it easily turns into vapor, or gaseous form when it comes into contact with something warm – including the human body. This is because its boiling point is 34.6°C, yet a person's body is normally 37°C.

(49) There is a table relating to elements, and the arrangement of the elements is according to each element's atomic _____, meaning the number of _____ in their respective nucleus.

The correct answer is: (D) number/protons

The elements in the elements table are arranged according to each element's atomic number, which means the number of protons in the elements' respective nucleus. The 'atomic number' is the number of protons there are within an atom's nucleus and this is in reference to a chemical element. This atomic number is what determines the position of the particular chemical element in the conventional periodic table.

A 'proton' is a sub-atomic particle that occurs in every atomic nucleus and it has an electric charge that is positive and equal in its magnitude to an electron.

(50)   There is a certain feeding relationship among different species within the same ecological community referred to as _____.

The correct answer is: (A) Food web

The term 'food web' is used in reference to a feeding relationship common to different species within the same ecological community. The term is used to give a description of the feeding relationship in a graphic manner. When you visualize a food web, it should appear different from a food chain. A food chain is simple and linear in nature, and it can even be part of a food web. For example, you can have a food chain that involves a predator preying on an herbivore that feeds on plants. The start of that food chain is the plant that is eaten by the herbivore that then becomes food for the predator – a straightforward line of feeding links.

Food webs constitute a set of feeding relationships that is more comprehensive and involves several food chains that are interconnected and which occur in the same community.

(51)   _____ causes depletion within the ozone layer.

The correct answer is: (A) Chlorofluorocarbons

It is generally feared that deterioration of the ozone layer is caused by the discharge of chemical pollutants that have chlorine as well as bromine in them. Chlorofluorocarbons, also referred in short form as CFCs, are chemicals with chlorine, fluorine, and carbon atoms, and they are mostly put to use when manufacturing packing material, solvents, aerosol sprays, refrigerants, and such other products.

As the ozone layer deteriorates, it leads to a situation where massive quantities of ultraviolet B rays strike the earth and can begin to cause cancer of the skin and cataracts in people. These rays are also harmful to animals.

(52) The 'Green Revolution' has different significant characteristics, but _____ is not one of them.

The correct answer is: (D) None of the answer choices above.

The reason option (D) is the best answer option is that all the other choices are part of the 'Green Revolution'. The 'Green Revolution' involves a concerted effort to increase crop yield, mainly in the countries described as 'developing' by introducing or increasing the use of artificial fertilizers and pesticides, and introduction of crop species known to be high yielding.

Note that when agriculture is mechanized, machinery is used more than hand labor, and productivity generally increases. For example, areas that traditionally used oxen to farm begin using tractors and harvesters to plow the land and harvest the crops. As for monoculture, it involves rearing of a single kind of animal or farming one type of crop at any one time, as opposed to the traditional way of rearing several kinds of animals and farming different kinds of crops at the same time within the same parcel of land. The latter is known as polyculture.

Hybrid seeds are those seeds produced by cross-pollination. Usually, such seeds are produced to replace the more traditional varieties in order to overcome some problems traditional varieties have like being susceptible to certain diseases and weather.

(53) Any time you are employing the scientific research method, you need to follow the steps of _____.

The correct answer is: (A) Defining the question; making observations; offering possible explanations; performing some experiment; analyzing data, and drawing conclusions.

As you follow the scientific research method, you need to follow the steps as mentioned in option (A). You need to define your question so as to be sure what you are looking for at the onset. It is after creating your question that you begin observing to see what is happening, and you are looking to find facts that you are going to rely on for possible explanations. You will then be required to conduct an experiment to establish if your explanation holds true or not, and the only way to properly check the validity of your explanation is by doing a proper analysis of the results of your observation. After that, you can draw an informed conclusion.

(54) There is one principle that advises you to select the hypothesis that in competition with the one you have, which happens to make the fewest fresh

assumptions when you have two hypotheses are similar or equal in every other respect. That principle is referred to as _____.

The correct answer is: (D) Occam's Razor

The principle of 'Occam's Razor' generally gives the advice that where you have two competing hypotheses, it is preferable to choose the one with fewest fresh assumptions, or new ones, as long as these hypotheses are in all other ways equal. In other words, if you are faced with two varying explanations regarding a particular happening or occurrence, you need to choose the one that poses minimal speculation.

This advice is derived from a philosophical perspective, where it is assumed that the more assumptions you have to make the less likely the explanation. In summary, the principle of Occam's Razor assumes that the explanation that is most likely when you have different options is the simplest one.

The principle of 'Hickam's Dictum' welcomes the possibility of as many explanations as possible. That is why in the field of medicine this principle holds that when a patient shows up with varying symptoms they might be reflective of several illnesses. When following the principle of Occam's Razor in a medical situation, it is assumed that the different symptoms showing at the same time have a singular cause. This is the difference between the correct answer (D) and option (A).

Options (B) and (C) are incorrect as they have nothing to do with steps followed in doing scientific research. Rather, they are scientific laws pertaining to gas pressure.

(55) There is a prediction stating that a difference observed is actually due to just chance and not as a result of any cause that is systematic. This prediction, which is known as the _____ is tested using statistical analysis and thereafter it is either accepted or it is rejected.

The correct answer is: (A) null hypothesis

Option (A) is the correct answer because the null hypothesis holds that in any test of a statistical nature when you have specified your population; there is actually no material difference between the populations. If you find any variation it will be because of the manner in which sampling was carried out or due to an error of experimental nature. The word 'null' actually denotes 'nil' value.

(56) _____ in the field of science is said to be the difference that exists between what you desire of a system or object and the real performance or behavior.

The correct answer is: (C) Error

The reason option (C) is correct is that when there is a difference between the true value of a system's performance capacity and the value you get, for example, during an experiment, there is said to be an error. This does not mean that a mistake has necessarily been made in doing the experiment. The variability could be the result of factors you could not control, such as the environmental conditions.

It would be wrong to choose option (A) since accuracy denotes exactness, yet in this case, what is being discussed is variation between two results. Option (B) is incorrect because the variation does not exist because you were wrong in your measurements or the manner in which you carried out your experiment. Often variation is inevitable, although there is usually an acceptable extent. Option (D) is incorrect because the term 'uncertainty' introduces the notion of unreliability, yet this is not applicable in this situation. Results can still be acceptable even with some error as long as it is within the acceptable margin.

(57) In the fields of science, industry, and statistics, a measurement system's _____ can be said to be the extent or degree of a quantity's closeness to what its true value is.

The correct answer is: (C) accuracy

Option (C) is the best answer option because accuracy as used in the fields of science, statistics, and engineering with respect to the system of measurement and is denoted by how close the result is after measuring how close the quantity is to the actual value of that quantity. In the case of medicine, for example, you could take your measurement and think you have calculated the correct quantity, but if the medication has an aspect of evaporation, the actual quantity will vary. In some cases, the container the material is held in might contribute to some slight variation in the results of your measurement.

Another way of explaining 'accuracy' is there is a value held as the standard, which means there is the value that would generally be expected under the circumstances. However, when you do your measuring you may find there is a slight variation from the standard. How close those two values are is what is termed 'accuracy'. Accuracy can determine if your quantity is acceptable for use or not because if the results of your measurement vary greatly from the standard, this can be proof there was inaccuracy in measuring or in the actual quantity and this needs to be rectified for the process to continue with efficacy.

Suppose, for instance, you receive medicine in bulk from the pharmacy in the expected container and the paperwork shows it is 500g as you had ordered, but when you measure it you find the quantity weighs 350g. You can report to the pharmacy that their measurement is inaccurate. Certainly, a difference of 150g is significant for medication, and it might be an indication of a larger problem. If it is the kind of medication prepared in the pharmacy as a mix of different medicines, it could be that the proportions used were wrong, a medication with a lighter density would be more than the required amount. In this case, the composition of the medication sent to you would be wrong and hence the medication inappropriate to use.

(58) There is some confidence interval around the value already measured so that the value measured is sure not to fall outside the said interval. This interval of confidence is in reference to that value's _____.

The correct answer is: (C) uncertainty

The term 'uncertainty' when used in science denotes the range within which probable values fall, and among them are the true or actual measurement values. It should not be confused with a lack of knowledge as to the values or anything else. If the uncertainty range is very wide, you may need to do more research on the relevant topic or the theory concerned with a view to reducing that range and by extension of the number of values that could possibly be correct.

(59) Measurement repeatability goes by the term _____, and to get it you do not need to know the true or actual value.

The correct answer is: (A) precision

If you take the measurements of a given substance three times and in all those times you get the same value – for example, 1st time 2kg, 2nd time 2kg and 3rd time 2kg – it can be said to have precision. The fact that there is repeatability in your measurement does not necessarily mean you have been accurate. The actual weight of the substance might be 2.25kg. In this case, it can be said to have precision but not accuracy. In short, precision is used in reference to the degree of closeness between given measurements. As a nurse, you need to have both accuracy and precision, especially because the difference in recommended dosage could cause fatalities or ineffectiveness - either over-dosing or under-dosing.

(60) Any disagreement in the field of science that occurs between a given measurement and the value accepted or the value that is true is referred to as _____.

The correct answer is: (D) inaccuracy

Accuracy refers to the closeness of a measured value to a given standard, and so when you are looking at how much your measured value disagrees with the true value, the appropriate term to use is 'inaccuracy'.

(61) Sometimes a practical test is designed for the purpose of getting results that are relevant to a given theory, or even more than one theory. Such a test is referred to scientifically as _____.

The correct answer is: (D) experiment

An experiment is normally carried out with the anticipation that confirmation is going to be made that a given theory is true. Before a theory has been established, the relevant hypothesis is tested through an experiment or experiments, and the anticipation is that the results will be as stated in the hypothesis.

Nevertheless, it should be noted that when it comes to a hypothesis, the outcome is just a supposition, and so there is a possibility of the experiment disagreeing with it. In such an eventuality, more research and investigation would need to be done before the hypothesis can be developed into a theory.

(62) A simulation of an actual system, or its approximation, which omits everything except the most basic of system variables is referred to as _____.

The correct answer is: (D) a scientific model

A scientific model is great at representing an idea or a process, or a system, which explains a certain real phenomenon that would be difficult to test or experience directly. That is why it is described as a simulation or approximation. The actual phenomenon has very many features, but during the simulation, only the fundamental ones are incorporated.

Scientific models are used for research and for communicating the basis and validity of various scientific theories. Many times scientific models come in handy when explaining things that are abstract and would otherwise be difficult to show as is done in ordinary experiments. There are times also when scientists use scientific models to make plausible predictions.

(63)   The body organs and main parts that comprise the immune system include _____.

The correct answer is: (A) thymus; lymphatic system; bone marrow; tonsils; and spleen

The role of the immune system is to help the body naturally defend itself against infections. Besides the thymus; lymphatic system; bone marrow; tonsils; and spleen, which is the system's main parts, the immune system also has other parts such as the antibodies and white blood cells, as well as some proteins and chemicals. All the main and minor parts help to enhance the body's defense by attacking bacteria and viruses that are detected to be foreign to the body.

Each of these organs or parts of your body that comprise the immune system also has individual functions. For example, the tonsils and the thymus are responsible for making antibodies, while the lymphatic system made up of the vessels plus the lymph nodes and found all over the body carries the lymph fluid and nutrients as well as waste matter from the tissues of the body to the bloodstream and vice-versa as needed.

As for the bone marrow, which is soft tissue within the long bones of the arms and legs, the pelvic bone and the vertebrae, it is responsible for the production of red as well as white blood cells, and also the platelets. This soft tissue consists of red marrow and yellow marrow that has fat as well as connective tissue responsible for producing some quantity of white blood cells.

The spleen is responsible for filtering blood to remove aged blood cells or the cells already damaged, as well as platelets.

(64)   Which of the organs listed below is a good example of tissue?

The correct answer is: (A) Chloroplast

Chloroplast which is some plastid found within the cells of green plants is an example of tissue. It is the part of the plant that holds chlorophyll and where food for the plant is made through the process of photosynthesis.

The hamstring is an actual muscle in a person's body, normally found at the back of the knee. Since the function of the hamstring has an impact on both a person's knee and the hip, they are often referred to as 'biarticular' muscles. A person's liver is that fleshy organ responsible for detoxification of chemicals and metabolism of drugs, and also preparation of proteins that help in the clotting of blood among other important tasks. A mammal, the one suggested in option (D), is an animal category, just as there are reptiles and insects. A good example of a mammal is a human being, a cow, a goat, and the like – animals known to breastfeed their young ones.

(65)   A person's adrenal glands are found within the _____ system.

The correct answer is: (B) endocrine

Adrenal glands, found within the endocrine system, are responsible for producing hormones for regulating the balance of salt and water in the kidneys. The hormones these glands produce also have an impact on a person's blood pressure and heart rate.

Clearly, the adrenal glands are not part of the respiratory system, the lymphatic system, or the immune system, and so options (A), (C), and (D) are incorrect.

(66)   A person's pineal gland produces a hormone known as _____.

The correct answer is: (C) melatonin

The pineal gland is responsible for producing melatonin, which is a hormone credited with regulating the circadian cycle. This cycle refers to a person's sleep and wakefulness pattern or rhythm. The production of melatonin is highest at night, and it is beneficial in inducing the changes of a physiological nature that enhance sleep including the temperature of the body and the rate of respiration.

The epinephrine is another hormone in the human body, and it is usually produced whenever the body senses danger. This hormone, which is produced by a person's adrenal glands, has several functions, among them hastening of the heartbeat and making it strong, as well as raising the level of blood sugar. Another name for epinephrine is adrenaline.

The set of organs responsible for producing testosterone are the testes. Testosterone is the hormone-charged with the proper development of the sex characteristics of the adult male. Insulin is a hormone produced by the pancreas, and its main role in the body is the regulation of blood glucose. If a person is short of insulin, the person's capacity to convert sugar in the blood to energy declines.

(67) The organ systems within the body of a person are _____ in number.

The correct answer is: (C) eleven

There are eleven organ systems in a person's body and one of them is the integumentary system, which is the entire skin with the appendages inclusive of the hair and nails. The integumentary system is charged with the protection of your body so that it does not suffer damage like losing too much water; it also gives the body protection from ailments. Another task the system accomplishes is the elimination of waste and regulation of body temperature.

There is also the muscular system, which comprises the skeletal muscles, the smooth muscles, and the cardiac muscles. This system enables the body to move properly, maintains body posture, and enhances the circulation of blood throughout the body. Another system is the skeletal system, which is a network comprising tendons and ligaments as well as the cartilage responsible for connecting these two. A person's skeletal system has two hundred and six bones and its major functions include the production of blood cells and regulation of the endocrine, among others.

Another system is the nervous system, which comprises the CNS and PNS, central nervous system and peripheral nervous system respectively. Within the CNS is the brain and the spinal cord, and in the PNS there are the nerves consisting of long fibers in bundles, which are responsible for connecting the CNS to all other areas of the body.

The circulatory system is another system of a human body, which comprises the vessels of the blood and the blood itself, and also the heart. The major roles played by the circulatory system include distribution of oxygen, other nutrients, and hormones to the areas of the body, and the removal of unwanted material in the form of waste from the tissues.

There is the lymphatic system, which comprises a tissue network and other organs that enhance the excretion of toxins and other waste from the body. The basic role played by the lymphatic system is the transportation of lymph, which is a fluid with white blood cells to fight infection.

The respiratory system comprises the lungs and the red blood cells. While the former ensures proper gas exchange during breathing, the latter is in charge of collecting the oxygen already in the lungs and taking it to all other areas of the body.

Another system is the endocrine system, which comprises several important hormone-producing glands. As a whole, this system accomplishes the functions of regulating metabolism, growth, and development, the functions of tissues and sex organs, reproduction, mood, and sleep. The main glands that make up the endocrine system include the hypothalamus and the pituitary, the thyroid and the parathyroids, the adrenals and the pineal body, as well as the ovaries and the testes.

There is also the urinary system, which is also referred to as the renal system. This system comprises the bladder and the kidneys, the ureter as well as the urethra. The urinary system's major role is the elimination of body waste, regulation of a person's blood volume, regulation of the blood pressure, control of electrolyte and metabolite levels, and regulation of the blood pH.

Another body system is the reproductive system, either the female or the male. For the female, the reproductive system is made up of the uterus; the ovaries; the vagina, which is an organ with muscular walls and with the capacity to expand and contract; and the fallopian tubes. For the male, the reproductive system comprises the penis; the urethra that is also part of the urinary system; the testes and the scrotum; the vans deferens; the seminal vesicles and the prostate.

The eleventh system is the digestive system, which comprises the gastrointestinal tract as well as the digestion organs considered accessories, such as the salivary gland, the gallbladder, the tongue, the pancreas, and the liver. The digestive system accomplishes the function of breaking down food so the body can absorb it and assimilate it for use. It is worth noting that although each of the eleven body systems has its distinct function, the efficiency, or lack of it, of one system has a way of affecting the other systems.

(68) A person's brain is found within the _____ system.

The correct answer is: (B) nervous

The brain is a major part of a person's nervous system, and it plays the role of sending messages through the spinal cord to reach the peripheral nerves throughout the body. These are the messages that help in controlling a person's internal organs as well as the muscles.

(69)   A human being has different types of tissue, and the basic ones are ____ in number.

The correct answer is: (A) four

The four major types of tissue a human being has are four, and they include the epithelial, the connective tissue, the nervous tissues, and the muscular tissues.

(70)   Some blood vessels have less oxygenated blood than others. Which one among the ones listed below has the lowest amount of oxygenated blood?

The correct answer is: (C) pulmonary artery

It is the work of the body's pulmonary artery to carry oxygen-depleted blood from the heart to the lungs. In the lungs, the carbon dioxide in that blood is cleared and the blood is replenished with oxygen, and that oxygenated blood is now ready to return to the heart. It passes via the pulmonary vein on its return to the heart, and there it is pumped out for distribution to the rest of the body as oxygenated blood.

The blood with the carbon dioxide gathered from all over the body passes through the pulmonary artery just before it is cleared of the carbon dioxide within the lungs. This means then that the vessel with the least oxygenated blood in the body is the pulmonary artery.

(71)   The place where starch starts to be digested is the _____.

The correct answer is: (A) mouth

When you eat food with starch, the first place that starch begins to be digested is in the mouth as starch digestion is initiated when starch is exposed to amylase, a type of enzyme found in saliva. This enzyme works on the starch, and particularly its glycosidic bonds, and it cleaves them so that they release sugars. It is because of this process that some foods with starch taste a bit sugary when you chew them for a long time. Incidentally, there is more amylase that works on the starch within the small intestines, and this comes from the pancreas. However, this stage of digestion comes after the starch digestion has already begun in the mouth and not before.

(72)   The primary oocytes are known to produce _____ as the process of oogenesis goes on.

The correct answer is: (B) eggs

Oogenesis is the process that goes on within the outer layer of woman's ovary. Here, one of the ovary cells, known as an oocyte, initiates the very first division of a meiotic nature and then halts to continue the process later. The immature eggs within a woman's ovary are known as oocytes. The meiotic division takes place with a view to creating an ovum, which is basically an egg, or in technical language, the gamete. The normal trend is for a single oocyte to mature in every menstrual cycle, first becoming an ootid before becoming an ovum. The 'ootid' is just a middle stage from oocyte to the ovum. These biological words in reproduction beginning with 'oo' are derived from the Greek meaning for 'egg'.

(73)   For any given species, the stages its members follow in their development follows a sequence referred to as _____.

The correct answer is: (A) Life cycle

The sequence living things follow in their development from start to the end of their life is referred to as life cycle and it is inclusive of the stage during which they reproduce. For a person, these stages include childhood and adulthood and then aging. However, different experts opt to split the stages a little differently depending on what they are studying or reporting, so sometimes the stages can be divided into infancy and childhood as the first two stages, followed by adolescence and then adulthood.

(74)   Choose the correct statement from the four options provided below.

The correct answer is: (D) The activities of a biochemical and also biophysical nature that every living system must perform to maintain life are referred to as life functions.

For a person, there are those basic functions that the body must perform in order for life to continue normally. They include movement and responsiveness; metabolism and growth; digestion and excretion; and reproduction. Certainly, these functions must be facilitated, and in the case of human beings, they require oxygen and nutrients, water, and a conducive environment.

(75) There are 3 major processes comprising nutrition that enable living organisms to receive food, and they are made up of different activities. These processes, in the sequence of their occurrence, are _____.

The correct answer is: (A) Ingesting, digesting and absorbing

Every living thing requires food in order to survive, and the entire process of nutrition involves ingesting food and then digesting it in preparation for absorption. For human beings, ingestion involves getting the food including liquids, from where it has been served and putting it in the mouth and then swallowing it.

Digesting food means breaking it down. The body needs energy for movement and other activities, but the food ingested must be broken down to the level of nutrients so that the body is able to take it in from the digestive system for use. The process of absorption is assimilating nutrients into the tissues and all organs of the body, and this happens through osmosis, where the nutrients simply diffuse into the places where they are needed. Even medication, once ingested, is diffused into the blood, tissues, and other organs just like food.

(76) Choose the correct statement from the four options given below.

The correct answer is: (B) Ingestion means to take in food and digestion is used in reference to the chemical changes that occur to the food once inside the body, while assimilation means the change particular nutrients go through to become cell protoplasm.

The reason option (B) is correct is because the food has to be ingested first before anything beneficial to the body can happen. Once inside the mouth, the relevant enzymes will prepare the food for proper digestion further in the digestive system including in the intestines, and the final stage is where the body prepares to benefit from the ingested food by assimilating it into the tissues and all other organs. The nutrients referred to include minerals and vitamins. The process of assimilation takes place in the body's gastrointestinal tract.

(77) Choose the correct statement from the four given below.

The correct answer is: (A) When molecules, besides those of water, move from a highly concentrated area to a lesser concentrated area, the process is referred to as diffusion.

A good example of diffusion in everyday life is what happens with perfume. The reason you are able to smell a scent is that once you open the perfume bottle, the perfume molecules diffuse straight into the air because the space in the bottle is more highly concentrated than the air space. Once the perfume finds its way into the air around you are able to smell it.

Another example is the movement of oxygen from the cells of plant leaves to the atmosphere. The oxygen molecules diffuse into the air and you are able to utilize the oxygen as you breathe in because inside the plant there is a higher concentration of oxygen that is released in the process of making plant food.

(78) Choose the correct statement from the four given below.

The correct answer is: (D) As osmosis takes place, the solvent passes via a membrane that is semi-permeable from an area where the solvent is less concentrated to one where it is more concentrated.

It is correct to say that the solvent's molecules move through a membrane that is partially permeable from an area where the concentration is low to where the concentration is higher. This movement is spontaneous and no other activity needs to be initiated for it to take place. A good example is a process through which plants absorb water from the soil. The roots in direct contact with the soil have sap that is more highly concentrated than the moisture in the soil, and so the moisture or water moves from the soil and into the roots.

(79) Choose the correct statement from the four given below.

The correct answer is: (B) Diffusion and osmosis are forms of transport through which materials passively pass across plasma membranes.

A process is said to be osmosis when there is a variation on either side of a membrane regarding molecular concentration, and the membrane gives way for water, which is the solvent, to pass through while restricting any particles the water may have, even if dissolved. A process is said to be diffusion when there is a variation on either side of a membrane regarding molecular concentration, and the membrane gives way for water, which is the solvent, together with its dissolved particles to pass through. The particles in the solvent are referred to as 'solute particles'.

(80) The branch of science where the studies pertain to a cell's physiology and life cycle, as well as cell division, is known as _____.

The correct answer is: (D) biology

Biology can be explained as the study involving living things, and of course living things are made up of cells. This discipline covers other smaller field, such as the organism's origin, distribution, behavior, and its physiology and morphology as well as anatomy. If someone is asked to study the biology of a lake, for example, it means they are going to study all these areas mentioned regarding not only the aquatic animals dwelling in the lake but also the plants.

Biochemistry is different because of the involvement of chemistry. In the discipline of biochemistry, chemistry is applied in the study of processes of a biological nature. This means the study also covers the molecular composition and processes. Actually, in biochemistry, the aspects of living things or their systems that are studied include their physiology and chemistry in addition to biology.

(81) One of the statements below regarding mitosis is correct. Which is it?

The correct answer is: (C) The number of chromosomes is doubled through the process of mitosis.

The process of mitosis is where cells divide and produce what is termed 'daughter cells', every one of them having a similar number of chromosomes as the nucleus of the parent cells. The chromosomes are also of the same kind as the parent cells. This is the kind of process that takes place to facilitate the normal growth of tissues.

(82) Which one among the statements given below is wrong?

The correct answer is: (D) None of the choices

None of the choices given from (A) to (C) is wrong, and so all of them are correct. During the process of meiosis where the division of cells takes place, daughter cells are produced and there are four. The chromosome number in each of those new cells is exactly half of the ones the original cell had. A good example of how meiosis works is gamete production or the production of a plant's spores. The term 'eukaryote' is used in reference to an organism that has cells with a nucleus that is enclosed inside membranes, a state different from that of bacteria and such organisms.

(83) What is the molarity of a given solution if it has two moles of normal salt dissolved in it and the total volume of the solution is one liter?

The correct answer is: (C) 2 M solution

To calculate the molarity of a solution when you know the number of moles that constitute the solute as well as the number of liters making up the solution you need to apply the formula:

Molarity is: Number of Moles ÷ Liters comprising the solution

Moles of salt = 2 M

Liters comprising the solution = 1 L

Therefore, molarity of the salt solution = 2 M ÷ 1 = 2 M.

This essentially means that in every liter of the salt solution there are two moles of salt.

(84) What is the molarity of a four-liter solution of sugar if it contains eight moles of sugar?

The correct answer is: (C) 2 M

To calculate the molarity of the solution when the number of moles that constitute the solute is 8 and the number of liters making up the solution is 4, the formula to use is:

Molarity is: Number of Moles ÷ Liters comprising the solution

Moles of sugar = 8 M

Liters comprising the solution = 4 L

Therefore, molarity of the sugar solution = 8 M ÷ 4 = 2 M.

This means that in every liter of the sugar solution there are two moles of sugar.

(85) What is the molarity of a 250-milliliter solution with five moles of the solute?

The correct answer is: (A) 20 M

To calculate the molarity of the solution when the number of moles that constitute the solute is 5 and the number of liters making up the solution is 250 milliliters, the formula to use is:

Molarity is: Number of Moles ÷ Liters comprising the solution

Moles of the solute = 5 M

Liters comprising the solution = 0.25 L

If the volume of solution is given in units different from the liter, you need to convert those units to the equivalent in liters. In this case, 250 milliliters are equivalent to 0.25 liters.

Therefore, molarity of the solution = 5 M ÷ 0.25 L = 5 M ÷ ¼ L

5 M ÷ ¼ L= 5 M x 4/1 L = 20 M per liter.

This means that in every liter of the solution there are 20 moles of the solute.

(86)   What is the number of moles of sodium oxide, or Na_2O, that needs to be dissolved in water to produce a 2 M solution that is 4 liters in volume?

The correct answer is: (C) 8 Mol

To calculate the molarity of a solution given the number of moles that constitute the solute and the number of liters making up the solution, the formula to use is:

Molarity is: Number of Moles ÷ Liters comprising the solution

However, in this case, what needs to be calculated is the number of moles. The calculations will look like this:

Molarity = Number of Moles ÷ Liters of the solution

Molarity x Liters of the solution = Number of Moles ÷ Liters of the solution x Liters of the solution

2 M x 4 = Number of Moles

The liters of the solution on the right-hand side will have canceled out.

Number of Moles = 2 M x 4 = 8 Mol

Note that the units of molarity are given per liter, and so when 'Liters of the solution' is introduced on the left side for multiplication the 'L' unit cancels out with the other 'L' unit.

(87) What is the number of sodium moles (Na) you need to form a 4½ L solution of 1½ M sodium solution?

The correct answer is: (A) 6.75 mol

To calculate the molarity of a solution given the number of moles that constitute the solute and the number of liters making up the solution, the formula to use is:

Molarity = Number of Moles ÷ Liters comprising the solution

However, in this case, what needs to be calculated is the number of moles. The calculation will look like this:

Molarity = Number of moles ÷ Liters of the solution

Molarity = 1½ M per liter

A number of moles =?

Liters of the solution = 4½ L

Therefore:

1½ M per liter =? moles ÷ 4½ L

To find the unknown, multiply either side with 4½ L and you will get:

1½ M/1 L x 4½ L =? moles÷ 4½ L x 4½ L

1½ M x 4½ =? moles

In short, you will find out the number of moles by calculating:

? moles = (1½ M x 4½) = 3/2 M x 9/2 = 27/4 mol = 6.75 mol

(88) The definition of a solution's molarity is_____.

The correct answer is: (C) moles of the solute for every liter of the solution

Molarity is used as the unit of concentration of a given solution in the field of chemistry. To get the actual number of units of concentration, you need to divide the figure given as solute moles by the units given in liters as the volume of solution.

(89) If the quantity of solute used in a solution is indicated in units of grams while the amount of solution is indicated in units of milliliters, to be able to find out the solution's molarity you need to first of all _____.

The correct answer is: (C) Change the quantity of solute given in grams to its equivalent in moles and also change the amount of solution given in milliliters to its equivalent in liters.

Since molarity is normally given as a number of moles in the solution whose amount is given in liters, it is important that any other units used to state the concentration of the solution be converted to the conventional units. Hence grams become moles and milliliters become liters.

(90) The molarity of a given aqueous solution that has CaCl is defined as:

The correct answer is: (D) number of CaCl moles in every liter of the solution

Molarity simply refers to the concentration of a given solution by a given solute. In the case of a solution with sodium chloride, or CaCl, it means the concentration of the sodium chloride in the solution, which would be given in units of molarity or 'M'.

(91) The rows that are horizontal in the periodic table are called _____.

The correct answer is: (B) periods

Those rows that are horizontal in the conventional periodic table are referred to as 'periods', whereas the columns that run vertically in the same table are referred to as 'groups' and sometimes 'families'. The periodic table was introduced into chemistry by a person called Dmitri Mendeleev, and the idea he had was to have the elements already known organized as per their similarities. That is the reason the elements contained in any group within a conventional period table have properties that are similar.

Something else worth noting is that the relationships existing among the elements within each period, beginning on the left side to the right are also similar. As such, it is possible to add fresh elements in the periodic table and not disrupt the existing design or necessitate a change.

(92) Which one of the substances listed below enables diffusion to take place the fastest?

The correct answer is: (A) Gas

The reason option (A) is correct is that the process of diffusion happens the fastest through gas and not through liquid, solid, or plasma. In terms of speed with which diffusion is enabled, the sequence after gas is liquid followed by plasma, and then solids follow last. The definition of this process of diffusion in the field of chemistry is the manner in which matter moves following motions of its molecules, which is random in nature. When diffusion is taking place through gas or liquid, their molecules keep perpetually moving. A good example is air. You may observe a mass of air and think it is not moving, but the nitrogen and oxygen molecules that comprise that mass of air are in constant movement, bouncing against one another constantly. As for solids, diffusion takes place minimally, and it rises proportionately as per the solid substance' temperature.

(93) The name given to the protons within an atom is the _____.

The correct answer is: (D) atomic number

The term 'atomic number' is used in reference to the actual number of protons within any one atom. Protons can be explained as the basic units of the atom, which are positive and exist inside the nucleus. When an atom is neutral, meaning the atom is not positive and it is also not negative, the proton number within the nucleus happens to be equal to that of the electrons that continue to orbit the nucleus.

When you want to show the number of atoms forming a molecule, you write that number in subscript – the tiny number at the foot of a letter. For example, when you want to show a water molecule, the symbol is H_2O, which means a water molecule is made up of two atoms of hydrogen and one atom of oxygen.

As for atomic mass, it refers to the units that represent a chemical element's atom, which is roughly equal to the total protons added to the neutrons within the atom.

(94) Which of the options below is an empirical formula?

The correct answer is: (C) CH

CH is a good representation of empirical formula, being the tiniest expression possible for a chemical formula. For any formula to be said to be empirical, it has to be one that cannot be further reduced. Hence option's (A), (B) and (D) cannot be correct. Every one of them can be reduced or simplified further.

It is important to keep in mind that an 'empirical formula' does not have the same meaning as a 'compound', because however a compound is written there is usually room for it to be reduced or simplified further. That is why it is possible to have different compounds sharing an empirical formula yet their molecular formulas vary; the latter representing the real atom number one molecule in the compound contains.

(95) When 2 atoms belonging to helium with an atomic mass equal to 3 collide during a fusion reaction, they produce one helium atom with an atomic mass equal to 4. Incidentally, this is not all this fusion reaction produces. It also produces _____.

The correct answer is: (E) two protons

It is important to note there must be charge conservation when the reaction takes place, and because the reactants, which comprise the two atoms of helium have 2 protons each, ultimately the electric charge totals +4.

As for the product of the reaction, which is helium -4, it has 2 protons. Hence its charge ultimately totals +2. At this juncture, there are 2 charges missing that must be positive in order to have the reaction balanced. Looking at all the answer choices provided in the question, it is only option (E) that has 2 protons and a charge of +2, and this is why it is the best choice for an answer.

(96) The atoms in hydrogen normally have one neutron each. The neutrons in hydrogen's two isotopes, deuterium, and tritium, are 2 and 3 respectively. Assuming you have a hydrogen atom that is electrically neutral, what is the number of electrons that would be orbiting the nucleus of the tritium?

The correct answer is: (B) 1

It must be considered that tritium is actually a hydrogen isotope, and its nucleus has just one proton. This means the charge it produces is +1, and there is no more charge from other neurons. The charge from electrons is -1, and for the sake of neutralizing the one nuclear proton's charge that is positive, it is important that there be one electron continuing to orbit.

(97) The reaction of a chemical nature that occurs at the _____ produces electrons.

The correct answer is: (A) anode

The electrons that are negatively charged are a result of a chemical reaction that reduces the lead anode that is already positively charged. The active reducing agent is oxidized by this same reaction, and the electrons then travel via the wire until they reach the cathode that has a negative charge. On reaching the cathode, these electrons react with the sulfuric acid and the effect is reduction of that acid. As such, what is left is lead sulfate. The anode in an ordinary car battery is shown by a red mark.

(98) Choose the correct statement from the options given below.

When there is a reaction of oxidation taking place, the effect is the oxidizing agent gains electrons, and these come from the reducing agent. Owing to the contribution the reducing agent makes of electrons, it reduces the oxidizer's charge, which means it increases its negative state.

In cases of a motor vehicle battery reducing the anode that has a positive charge has the effect of providing electrons that flow into the cathode where the process of oxidation happens. During oxidation, there is an increase of the reducer's charge by the oxidizing agent, which means the agent increases its positive status of the reducer. The effect is neutralization of the additional electrons within the cathode whose charge is negative, and it is the oxidizing agent that is responsible.

(99) The term 'aerobic' means _____.

The correct answer is: (A) where oxygen is present

The literal meaning of 'aerobic' is 'with oxygen' and the word is used in reference to the utilization of oxygen during the processes of energy generation in tissues or muscles.

When aerobic is taking place, there is breaking down of glycogen which results in the production of glucose. Nevertheless, if there is no glycogen to be broken down, then fat is metabolized instead.

(100) Substances that are impossible to break down to gain a more simplified form of matter are given the name_____.

The correct answer is: (D) elements

The term 'element' indicates a substance impossible to break down to make into some form of matter that is simpler. The periodic table is one place where the characteristics of different elements are summarized. The element's symbol, its atomic number, and its atomic mass are noted on the table.

(101) When atoms belonging to one element combine with atoms of a different element, what is created is a compound's _____.

The correct answer is: (C) molecule

When atoms from two different elements are joined, the combination forms molecules of a compound. It is important to note that all atoms in a given element are similar, and so no matter how many there are, they cannot form something new. However, when atoms from different elements come together what they form is different from the individual elements including its chemical properties. For example, when atoms of hydrogen and oxygen combine in a given ratio, they form water, and when atoms of sodium combine with those of chlorine they form sodium chloride.

(102) The statements given below are about mixtures and compounds. Choose the answer option that is entirely correct.

The correct answer is: (B) Mixtures are heterogeneous and their components' properties get retained, but compounds are homogeneous and have properties that are distinctly different from those of individual elements that combine to form them.

The way to make a compound is to combine elements through a chemical process, and these elements have to be combined to bond in preset proportions. As for a mixture, the way to form it is to combine different substances physically, and these substances also have to be combined to bond together in preset proportions. After the chemical process that combines the different elements, a substance that is pure is produced and is a compound. After the physical combination of substances, a substance that is impure is formed, which is a mixture.

(103) Which of the options below reflects the differences between physical and chemical changes?

The correct answer is: (A) When a physical change is taking place, there are various aspects of the matter's physical properties that change, but there is no change in the substance identity. Changes of a chemical nature are changes to the composition of the matter and its structure.

To understand chemical changes better, think of a process where the changes are not easily reversible. They cause a chemical reaction with the substances involved so that their atoms are fundamentally rearranged. A chemical reaction can form a new substance by also combining more than two substances. As well, one chemical reaction can produce one or more distinct substances.

Changes of a physical nature can be described as processes that affect substances physically without altering their chemical form or composition. A process of physical change to separate different substances from a mixture can be used, but it is not possible to separate substances using a physical process if they have been combined through a chemical process.

Changes of a physical nature can be exemplified by breaking a piece of stick, breaking of a glass plate, or melting a cube of ice. As for changes of a chemical nature, these can be exemplified by frying of an egg, infusion of herbal leaves, or rusting of a piece of metal.

(104) There is one formula written as: $H - H_{products} - H_{reactants}$

This formula is best used to _____.

The correct answer is: (C) make alterations to the heat content

When pressure remains constant and a given reaction releases heat into the environment in which it is happening, there is a decline in the system's enthalpy. Enthalpy means some thermodynamic quantity that is the equivalent of all the system's amount of heat.

(105) Choose the correct statement from the list of four options given below.

The correct answer is: (D) During a reaction that is endothermic the amount of heat the product has is greater than that of the reactants but during a reaction that is exothermic the amount of heat the product has is less than that of the reactants.

Option (D) is correct as measuring the energy molecules have in totality is quite impossible. For this reason, for the sake of credible data in experiments involving reactions, what is used is the heat change that occurs and it is referred to as 'enthalpy'.

A reaction is termed exothermic if it is of a chemical nature and discharges energy through either light or even heat. Exothermic reactions are actually the opposite of endothermic reactions. Exothermic reactions can be exemplified by evaporation of water or even melting of salts that are originally in solid form.

As for an endothermic process, it utilizes energy from its surroundings by absorbing it, and the process can be of a chemical nature or not.

(106) Choose the correct statement from the list of four options given here below.

The correct answer is: (B) $E = mc_2$ is a formula whose basis is the Law of Conservation of Mass and Energy, and it states correctly that energy is equal to mass multiplied by the light velocity^2.

This Law of Conservation of Energy is a basic physics concept, and it holds that the energy amount in its totality maintains its constancy whenever in some isolated system. This means the energy cannot be created and it cannot be destroyed. However, it can take a different form from what it was before.

(107) From the list of four options listed below, select the one that is correct.

The correct answer is: (B) Any time recording of measurements is being done, the significant figures comprising digits that are definitely correct and known are recorded, and one additional digit that is not certain is recorded as well.

By 'significant figures' is meant those digits included when expressing a measurement recording to the necessary extent of accuracy. The significant figures are considered beginning the very first digit that is not of zero value.

'Relative figures' could mean 'relative numbers', meaning that their value is dependent on the values of other numbers normally said to be absolute.

(108) Choose the correct statement from the four provided below.

The correct answer is: (A) The Kelvin scale is used on the basis of the theoretical temperature that is lowest, called absolute zero

Option (A) is the most suitable answer as the 'Kelvin scale' is actually based on the temperature known theoretically to be the lowest, which is referred to as 'absolute zero'. As for the Celsius scale, it is used as a tool for measurement of temperature and it works on the basis that water's freezing point is zero degrees while its boiling point is 100°. Centigrade actually means the same as Celsius; only the term 'Centigrade' is old fashioned. The word 'Celsius' came into use in 1948 and the name came from an astronomer from Sweden called by that name who invented the scales.

(109) Choose the correct statement from the four options listed below.

The correct answer is: (A) By means of experiments and calculations, it has been confirmed that absolute zero is – 273.150 on the Celsius scale.

It has been established and internationally accepted after scientific experiments and credible calculations that the proper definition of absolute zero is -273.15°C on the Celsius scale. The same is simply 0 K when using the Kelvin scale.

The variation between these two scales, Kelvin and Celsius, is in their point of starting. Whereas in the Kelvin scale zero degrees is absolute zero, zero degrees in Celsius represents the point at which water freezes. If you want to convert the temperature given in Celsius to degrees in Kelvin, you need to add 273.15° to the figure you have in Celsius. For example, water's boiling point in Celsius is 100°C, but that measurement in Kelvin would be 373.15° (100°+273.15°).

(110) Choose the correct option from the four statements listed below.

The correct answer is: (A) When making use of the system of scientific notation in expressing large numbers, you need to shift the decimal point till you remain with just 2 digits on the left, and then show the number of decimal place moves as the exponent of 10.

Scientific notation serves as a way of expressing an enormous number or an extremely tiny one, and it is used in writing numbers when any digit within the range of one to ten is multiplied by any power of ten. For example, the way to denote 750,000,000 in scientific notation is 7.5 x 10^8.

(111) Choose the correct option from the four statements listed below.

The correct answer is: (C) In the field of science, precision gives an indication of the reliability or reproducibility of a given measurement, whereas accuracy gives an indication of the proximity of a measurement to its known or accepted value.

The term 'precision', when used in regards to a given system of measurement, refers to reproducibility, or how possible it is to repeat the measurement and get the exact same outcome when all conditions are unchanged; this is termed repeatability. It is important to note there is a possibility of measurement being accurate while not being precise, or precise while not being accurate. Other times, the measurement could be neither accurate nor precise, and yet there are times when the measurement could be both accurate and precise.

No matter how precise or accurate a given measurement is found to be, there is always some extent to which there is uncertainty. Such uncertainty depends on the limitation associated with the instrument being used for measuring as well as the skill the person doing the measuring.

(112) Choose the correct option from the four statements listed below.

The correct answer is: (C) The Law of the Conservation of Energy states that in a chemical change, energy can neither be created nor destroyed but only changed from one form to another.

This 'Law of Conservation of Energy' in chemistry holds that an isolated system's entire energy keeps constant and as time goes on it is conserved. Also going by this law, it is not possible to create energy or to destroy it, but the only thing possible is transforming it to a different form from the original or to transfer it.

(113) Choose the correct option from the four statements listed below.

The correct answer is: (C) A chemical change is a process that transforms one set of chemical substances to another; the substances used are known as reactants and those formed are products.

The term 'chemical change' can be substituted with the term 'chemical reaction', and it refers to that process of one or more substances being altered to become a different substance or two or more substances. This is a process where atoms are rearranged, and hence the substance is transformed.

That substance that is the subject of transformation is called the 'reactant' - the one undergoing change. The newly formed substance is called the product, and it is the product of the chemical change. For example, when water is poured onto sodium, a chemical reaction takes place and results in the production of two products, namely, sodium hydroxide and hydrogen.

(114)   Choose the correct option from the four statements listed below.

The correct answer is: (D) Anabolism is the series of chemical reactions resulting in the synthesis of organic compounds, and catabolism is the series of chemical reactions that break down larger molecules.

The term 'anabolism' in chemistry is used in reference to the synthesizing of molecules that are complex in organisms that are alive. Anabolism basically builds up molecules that are larger from molecules that are smaller. As for catabolism, it is the breaking of molecules. Anabolism and catabolism are different reactions of a metabolic nature that occur within a given cell. Reactions of an anabolic nature are known for using energy, and they happen to be endergonic. During the process of anabolism, large molecules are formed by having smaller ones join together.

(115)   Choose the correct option from the four statements listed below.

The correct answer is: (D) A catalyst is a chemical involved in, but not changed by, a chemical reaction by which chemical bonds are weakened and reactions accelerated.

Enzymes have the function of catalyzing reactions and allowing several reactions of a chemical nature to take place in a living system's environment with constraints of a homeostatic nature. Enzymes have the capacity to act speedily. For example, in the case of the enzyme, carbonic anhydrase, the chemical reaction is a hundred and seven times faster than when there is no enzyme present. This enzyme helps inter-conversion to happen rapidly where carbon dioxide plus water are converted to form carbonic acid, bicarbonate ions, and protons.

Carbonic hydrase is found in red blood cells. In fact, in people the minute these cells enter the lungs carbonic hydrase plays a big role in the conversion of the bicarbonate ions so that they can resume their original state, which is carbon dioxide – and this is how a person's lungs get the carbon dioxide to release during exhalation.

(116) Choose the correct option from the four statements listed below.

The correct answer is: (B) Oxygen is the most abundant element in the Earth's crust and appears on the Atomic Table as the letter O.

In terms of volume, the atmospheric air that is dry comprises 78.09% of nitrogen and 20.95% oxygen, while argon makes up 0.93% and carbon dioxide is 0.04%. There are also other gases whose volume is insignificant. This air contains some water vapor, but the amount varies from one location to another or according to different atmospheric conditions. At sea level, this vapor content is usually 1% but generally, it is 0.4%.

(117) Choose the correct option from the four statements listed below.

The correct answer is: (D) The Law of Definite Proportions holds that the elements that make up a single chemical compound have weight proportions that are fixed and constant.

According to this law, a given chemical compound has mass proportions of its individual elements that are not only fixed by constant. A good example of the Law of Proportions applies to water, which is itself a compound. Water composition is made up of 2 hydrogen atoms and one oxygen atom, and this is why water is written as H_2O.

(118) Choose the correct option from the four statements listed below.

The correct answer is: (C) The Pauli Exclusion Principle holds that, in any particular molecule, 2 electrons cannot have a different 4 quantum number set.

According to the 'Pauli Exclusion Principle', one atom – or even molecule – cannot contain any electrons that are two in number and they have 4 electronic quantum numbers that are exactly the same. For example, an orbital can have 2 electrons as the maximum, and their spins must be opposing.

(119) From the four options listed below, choose the most appropriate statement that relates to the principles of Dalton's atomic theory.

The correct answer is: (B) An element's atoms are similar in their weight, and the weight depends on the type of atom.

As per the principles of Dalton's atomic theory, all the atoms present in a given element happen to have similar weight, with this weight being specific to the type of the atom. This theory states that matter comprises particles referred to as atoms, which are indivisible, and when they are part of an element, they are all similar or identical, and that the atoms cannot be created and nor can they be destroyed. Atoms are also used in combinations of tiny ratios to form compound atoms, and the name given to such compound atoms is 'molecules'.

(120) Choose the correct option from the four statements listed below.

The correct answer is: (A) Atoms of varying elements combine in ratios of whole numbers that are simple to form chemical compounds.

Elements happen to be the simplest form a chemical substance can exist, and every element matches only one entry among the ones in the periodic table. All the atoms that make up an element are of the same type, and every single atom type has protons that are equal in number. In short, the number of protons in one atom of an element is the same number of protons in any other atom in that same element.

Elements are linked together by bonds of a chemical nature, and once they are bound together they create molecules that are complex, and which essentially form a compound. It is important to note that a compound cannot comprise a single element – the elements must be of two types at the minimum, bound together through an ionic bond.

To be able to divide an element into units that are smaller, energy must be used in great amounts. This is different from the case of compounds as it is possible to break the bonds in them with normal quantities of energy. For example, heat generated from ordinary fire has the capacity to break down compounds.

(121)   From the four options listed below, choose the statement that is untrue about the atomic theory.

The correct answer is: (C) This theory is used in describing temperature as the atom momentum.

Option (C) is not correct as the atomic theory describes temperature to be the atom motion and not its momentum. That atom momentum provides an explanation for the outward moving pressure normally exerted.

The atomic theory states that the matter comprises small particles that are indivisible and as per modern interpretations pertaining to this theory these atoms are identical although varying between different elements.

(122)   From the four choices listed below, choose the correct statement that indicates something correct about atoms.

The correct answer is: (C) Atoms are made up of protons and neutrons within a central or main nucleus that electrons surround.

Atoms are known to comprise protons, which are particles of extremely small size, as well as neutrons and electrons that are equally tiny. The protons and the neurons are found in the central part of an atom, and they comprise the atom's nucleus. The charge level is the same for the proton as it is for the electron, with the difference being that both are oppositely charged. Considering there is a tendency for charges that are opposite to attract, it follows that normally the protons and the electrons are drawn to one another.

(123)   Protons, electrons and also neutrons vary in that:

The correct answer is: (A) Protons plus neutrons combine to form the atom nucleus, whereas electrons exist within levels of energy that are fixed around the atom nucleus.

An atom's nucleus is formed by the combination of protons and neutrons, whereas electrons exist in energy levels that are fixed around the atom's nucleus. It is important to remember that apart from many hydrogen atoms, atoms of other elements contain neutrons within their own nucleus. Neutrons are not associated with any charge at all, and this makes them different from protons and electrons that are always charged.

(124) From the four options listed below, choose the statement that is false regarding the quantum theory.

The correct answer is: (C) Where quantum theory is concerned, energy is taken to be a mere phenomenon that is continuous, whereas it is assumed that matter occupies a region within space that is clearly defined, and that it is in continual movement.

Quantum theory is about matter as well as energy, and it is defined on the basis of the quanta concept particularly quantum mechanics. 'Quanta' is quantum in plural form, and it refers to a discrete amount of energy whose magnitude is proportional to the actual frequency of radiation that it happens to represent.

(125) Among Newton's motion laws are 3 physical laws and they serve as the basis for classical mechanics. From the four options listed below, choose is one that is one of the three laws.

The correct answer is: (B) Any given body that is moving will change its direction and in due course end up slowing down till it ultimately stops unless some force acts upon it.

The answer given is associated with the first law of motion created by Newton that indicates that unless there is some force acting upon a given body, the body remains in a position of rest while a body that is already in motion continues its movement using the same speed and in a straight manner.

(126) The term 'electricity' is used generally to encompass a range of phenomena that result from the existence and electric charge flow. From the four choices listed below, choose the correct statement regarding electricity.

The correct answer is: (C) 'electric potential' means the basic interaction that takes place between a given magnetic field and the existence of electric charge plus its motion.

Essentially the term 'electric potential' is used in reference to the capacity an electric field has to work upon a given electric charge that is mostly measured in units of volts. Electromagnetism is the magnetic field, the electric charge that is present and the motion of the electric charge.

(127) One of the following options is not true regarding Ohm's Law.

The correct answer is: (D) An ohm can be defined as an electric voltage unit.

An ohm is known in the field of physics to be a unit used in the measurement of electric resistance and is considered the international standard. It transmits current of a single ampere whenever it is a subject of one-volt potential difference. Ohm's law relates the difference in voltage between different points – actually 2 points – the amount of electric current effectively flowing in between the points, and the electric current path's resistance. The mathematical representation of Ohm's Law looks like this:

V = IR; and in this case 'V' represents voltage difference, 'I' represents current in terms of amperes, while 'R' represents resistance in terms of ohms.

(128) Any conductor restricting electron flow internally has the property of _____.

The correct answer is: (D) resistance

The word 'resistance' used in the field of physical science refers to friction, which goes against a body motion's direction while tending to deter the body from moving; or to slow it down. It can also be described as that measurement of the degree or level, or extent, to which a given substance inhibits the electric current flow as prompted by some voltage. The unit in which resistance is measured is called an 'ohm'.

(129) In the field of physics, the force opposing 2 bodies' relative motion when those bodies are in contact is referred to as _____.

The correct answer is: (C) friction

Friction is the force which resists the movement of surfaces that are solid, layers of fluid, and elements of material that slide against one another. Friction is of several types. For example, there is dry friction that can be explained as some force opposing the relative motion of a lateral nature involving two surfaces that are solid and in contact with each other.

(130) What is the difference between potential and kinetic energy?

The correct answer is: (B) Kinetic energy can be defined as that energy a body has that is a result of motion, and potential energy can be defined as that energy an object has just by being in the position or state it is in, as exemplified by a spring that is compressed.

For a better understanding of kinetic energy as used in the field of physics, it can be explained as that energy a given object possesses by virtue of being in motion. It is taken to be the work required in order to accelerate the body of a particular mass so that it leaves its rest position and be in some given velocity. Once a body has gained kinetic energy as it accelerates, it retains its magnitude unless there is a speed change in the motion of the body.

(131)   The 4 basic forces in nature are _____.

The correct answer is: (A) Gravity; nuclear force that is strong; electromagnetic force; and nuclear force that is weak

What is referred to as 'electromagnetic force' is electricity. When the term 'gravity' is used in the field of physics, it refers to gravitational force or that force that makes all masses within the universe attract, and especially that attraction that the mass of the earth has toward the bodies close to its own surface.

As for 'weak nuclear force', it is that mechanism through which particles that are sub-atomic interact. This force also referred to as 'weak interaction' or 'weak force', is the one that causes radioactive atom decay. This force is normally studied in the area of particle physics just like a strong nuclear force that is also referred to as strong interaction.

Of the four fundamental forces, the strong nuclear force is considered the strongest. Despite its strength, its range is the shortest, which means particles have to be very close for its effect to be felt. Its major responsibility involves holding together those nuclear particles that are sub-atomic, meaning the protons that are positively charged, as well as the neutrons that do not have any charge; the particles collectively referred to as nucleons.

(132)   Organize nature's four fundamental forces in ascending order of their strength.

The correct answer is: (A) Gravity; weak nuclear force; electromagnetic force; strong nuclear force

Option (A) has the best series of nature's fundamental forces as arranged in how strong each of them is with the least strong starting off the series. It is important to note that even though gravity or gravitational force happens to have the least strength, its force is felt over big distances. In comparison, nature's electromagnetic force compared to the gravitational force is 1,039 times stronger.

(133) The existing variation between strong nuclear force and weak nuclear force is _____.

The correct answer is: (A) The strong nuclear force, which can be termed attractive force, plays the role of binding of protons as well as neutrons as it ensures the nuclear structure is maintained, while the weak nuclear force plays the role of radioactive beta decay as well as other different reactions of a sub-atomic nature.

The strong nuclear force is sometimes referred to as simply the 'strong force'. Among nature's four fundamental forces it is the one that has the greatest strength and this can be detected from the name it has been given. Within this force, the protons detect a force that repels them from different protons in the neighborhood. Energy is needed in order to have protons already charged coming together so that they stand against electric repulsion directed at them. This force is also instrumental in the storage of energy used in the manufacture of nuclear power.

The weak nuclear force is effective only within a limited distance, hence the name it has been given. However, it plays a big role in enabling the sun to provide energy to the earth by permitting the change of a single element to become a different element. This force is actually known for initiating some fusion reaction of a nuclear nature that ends up fueling the sun.

(134) Of the four options listed below, choose the one that aptly describes what the Law of Conservation states.

The correct answer is: (B) As chemical reactions take place, there is no gain or loss that one can detect.

It is worth noting that no gain whatsoever that is detectable within the mass, and no loss as well, which occur as reactions of a chemical nature take place. Nevertheless, in such chemical reactions, the given substance could have its state altered. A good example is when substances that are initially solid have their state altered as chemical reactions take place and they become gaseous. Effectively, although the form of substance will have changed, the mass itself will not have changed.

(135) From the choices listed below, choose the one that best describes any difference there may be between heat radiation and convection.

The correct answer is: (C) Convection is heat transferred from one region to another through fluid movement, whereas thermal radiation is the emission of electromagnetic radiation from all forms of matter because it possesses thermal energy.

In the field of physics, the word 'fluid' means any matter or substance with the capacity to deform under stress. Such substances include liquids, gases, plasmas, and certain solids made of plastic. An example of electromagnetic radiation is sunlight, which is solar and is a generation of the sun's hot plasma, which is the thermal radiation that heats the earth.

Mathematics Section of the NLN PAX

(136) Write eight as a percentage of forty.

The correct answer is: (C) 20%

The calculation is as follows:

8/40 x 100% = 20%

(137) Write nine as a percentage of thirty-six.

The correct answer is: (D) 25%

The calculation is as follows:

9/36 x 100% = 25%

(138) Three-tenths of ninety is the same as _____.

The correct answer is: (C) 27

The calculation is as follows:

3/10 x 90 = 27.

(139) Zero point four percent of thirty-six is the same as _____.

The correct answer is: (B) 0.144

When a number is given as a percent, it simply means that number over 100. Therefore the calculations are as follows.

0.4% x 36 = 0.4/100 x 36

0.4/100 x 36 = 0.004 x 36

0.004 x 36 = 0.144.

(140) What is the ratio of eight to five as a percentage?

The correct answer is: (D) 160%

Eight over five and then multiply by 100%.

8/5 x 100% =?

Cross multiply: ((8 x 100)/5)%

((8 x 100)/5)% = (800/5)% = 160%.

(141) What is three-fifths as a percentage of X?

The correct answer is: (D) 60%

The calculation is as follows:

8/40 x 100%, which gave you 0.2 x 100% and finally 20

Now that you have 3/5 as a percentage of X, the working should be like:

3/5 ÷ X x 100%

In order to leave the unknown, X, on its own side, you need to multiply either side of the equation with X as follows:

3/5 ÷ X x 100% x X = 1 x X

X = 3/5 x 100%

X = 0.6 x 100%

X = 60%.

(142) What is two-fifths expressed in decimal form?

The correct answer is: (C) 0.4

To express a fraction in the form of a decimal, all you need to do is divide the numerator by the denominator as follows:

2/3 means 2 ÷ 5 = 0.4

(143) What is zero point five six (0.56) as a percentage?

The correct answer is: (A) 56%

In the case of 0.56, it would need to be written as 56/100 = 56%.

(144) What is eighteen over six written as a percentage?

The correct answer is: (A) 300%

The calculation is as follows:

18/6 x 100%

Cross multiply so that you have ((18 x 100) ÷ 6) %

((18 x 100) ÷ 6)% = (1800÷ 6)%

(1800÷ 6)% = 300%

(145) What is four over twenty as a percentage?

The correct answer is: (B) 20%

The calculation is:

4/20 x 100% = %?

You can cross multiply and you will get:

((4 x 100)/20)% = (400/20)% = 20%

(146) Divide four ninety-one by nine

The correct answer is: (A) 54 r. 5

169

The expression is as follows:

491 ÷ 9 = 54 because 54 x 9 = 486, but then there will be 5 remaining.

For that reason, the answer is given as 54 remainder 5; and this is abbreviated as 54 r. 5

(147) Seven hundred and three divided by six is:

The correct answer is: (B) 117 r. 1

The calculation is:

703 ÷ 6 = 117 and a remainder of 1; abbreviated as 117 r 1

(148) Write 71/1,000 in the form of a decimal.

The correct answer is: (C) 0.071

The calculation is:

71/1,000 = 71 ÷ 1,000

If you take the assumption that every whole number has a decimal point on its extreme right end, then the decimal point for 71 will be immediately after the number one (1). To divide a number by a thousand, move the decimal point of that number 3 places to the left.

In the case of 71 ÷ 1,000, move the inferred decimal point (71.0) 3 places to the left. Because there is no digit to the left of 7, a zero (0) is placed there. The number is now .071 or 0.071.

(149) Four point seven plus zero point nine plus zero point zero one is _____.

The correct answer is: (C) 5.61

The calculation is follows:

Four point seven plus zero point nine plus zero point zero one is the numerically:

4.7 + 0.9 + 0.01

4.7 + 0.9 + 0.01 = 5.61

(150) Zero point three three multiplied by zero point five nine is equal to _____.

The correct answer is: (A) 0.1947

The calculation is as follows:

0.33 x 0.59

0.33 x 0.59 = 0.1947

When you multiply decimal numbers, the answer must have as many decimal places as those in all the numbers. In this case, 0.33 has two decimal places and 0.59 has two decimal places as well. Both numbers have a total of four decimal places and thus the answer.

(151) Zero point eight four divided by zero point seven is equal to _____.

The correct answer is: (D) 1.2

Zero point eight four divided by zero point seven is written numerically as:

0.84 ÷ 0.7

0.84 ÷ 0.7 =?

The easiest way to work out such a problem is to multiply both numbers with as many tens as will turn them into whole numbers before doing the division. Also, whatever number of tens the dividend requires to become a whole number should be used with the divisor and vice-versa.

To calculate 0.84 ÷ 0.7, multiply both sides with 100 first

0.84 x 100 = 84

0.7 x 100 = 70

84 ÷ 70 = 1.2.

Since both numbers are increased by the same amount, nothing needs to be done about the decimal place. The answer remains 1.2.

(152) Zero point eight seven minus zero point four eight is equal to _____.

The correct answer is: (A) 0.39

The calculation is as follows:

0.87 − 0.48

0.87 − 0.48 = 0.39

When subtracting decimals, the same method is followed when subtracting whole numbers. However, as you put one number is placed above the other, ensure they have the same number of digits (even if the digits are zero) and that the decimal points are under each other. Those zeros effectively have no value but they help avoid confusion.

0.87

0.48-

0.39

(153) Rounding of 3.864 to the closest tenth produces _____.

The correct answer is: (A) 3.9

The number immediately to the right of the decimal is the tenth position. If the number next to it to the right is five or larger, you round up and if it is less than 5, you round down. In this case, the number in the tenth position is eight (8), and the number next to it on the right is six (6) so you round up by adding another tenth to the eight tenths already there so 8 changes to 9. After you have done that you need to ignore all the other numbers that come after the rounded up number. That is why the correct answer, in this case, is 3.9.

(154) Among the choices listed below, one of them is not the same or equal to 10^4. Which one is it?

The correct answer is: (A) 100,000

100,000 is the correct answer because it is the same as 10^5 or equal to 10 x 10 x 10 x 10 x 10. It is also equal to 10^2 x 10^2 x 10.

(155) When 10^4 is multiplied by 10^2, the answer is _____.

The correct answer is: (C) 10^6

If you are multiplying similar numbers with powers, meaning the base is the same but the exponents are different, add the exponents. In this case, the numbers to be multiplied are 10^4 and 10^2, and so the answer base will be a ten.

10^4 x 10^2 = 10^6.

(156) $X^5 \div X^2$ = _____

The correct answer is: (D) X^3

When the problem requires dividing numbers whose bases are similar, subtract the exponent of the divisor from the exponent of the dividend. In this case, the problem is $X^5 \div X^2$. The base remains X and the exponent is calculated by 5 − 2 = 3.

(157) 8.23 x 10^9 = _____

The correct answer is: (D) 8,230,000,000

To multiply 8.23 x 10^9, take note of the number of decimal places the main number has, and in this case 8.23 has two decimal places represented by '2' in the position of the tenth and '3' in the position of the hundredth.

Begin by getting rid of these decimals, and to do this, take two zeros from the given exponents. It will be the same as multiplying 8.23 by 100. You will now have 823 x 10^7.

173

Any number multiplied by 10 with an exponent means that number added the number of zeros equal to the exponent. In this case, 823 x 10^7 is the same as 823 with seven zeros at the end; 8,230,000,000.

(158) 83,000 is the same or equal to _____.

The correct answer is: (B) 8.3 x 10^4

Option (B) requires that the decimal in 8.3 to be moved once to the right to match one of the exponents so that you now have 83 x 10^3.

83 x 10^3 means you are required to add 3 zeros at the end of 83, and so you will have 83,000. As for options (A), (C), and (D), the number of zeros you add after the whole number given should be equal to the exponents of 10, and this is because the zero after the decimal point has no effect, and cannot be considered a decimal number. However, option (E) would have to forfeit one zero to change 8.3 to 83, and because ten will have been left with 2 exponents only two zeros can be added to 83. Hence 8.3 x 10^3 = 8,300

(159) Choose the one option that is equal to 0.00875.

The correct answer is: (B) 8.75 x 10^{-3}

To multiply 8.75 x 10^{-3}, you need to shift the decimal three places to the left, and the first shift will give 0.875 x 10^{-2}. To multiply 0.875 x 10^{-2} you need to shift the decimal two places to the left, so you will have 0.00875. In fact, you do not need to go through 2 steps. You could simply shift the decimal from its original position to the left three places.

The important thing to note is that when the exponent is positive you shift the decimal to the right, meaning the number becomes larger, but when the exponent is negative you shift the decimal to the left; meaning the number becomes smaller in value.

(160) If a particular pool has 7v liters as its volume and there is a tap pouring in water at a rate of y/4 liters per minute, which option here below gives the appropriate expression indicating the period of time required to for the pool to reach 1/5 full with water?

The correct answer is: (B) 28v/5y

Take total pool volume to be 7v.
This means 1/5 of the pool volume = 7v/5
The rate at which the tap pours in water is y/4 liters per minute
Therefore, to pour in 7v/5 liters, how many minutes are required?
Let the unknown, which is time taken to fill in 7v/5 liters, be X.

The calculation is as follows:

y/4 L = 1 min
7V/5 L = X min
Cross multiply so you will get:
X * y/4 = 7V/5
X = (7V/5) ÷ y/4
This is the same as:
X = (7V/5) * 4/y
X = 28V/5y

(161)   There are six workers with equal capacity to work, and they are building a wall. Each day there must be one worker leaving, and that entire job ends up being completed in four days. Supposed no worker left till the work was completed. How long in terms of days would it take the workers to complete building the wall?

The correct answer is: (D) 3 days
Total number of workers =6

Assume that every worker did x amount of work every single day.
Work done in Day 1 = 6 * X = 6X
Work done in Day 2 = 5 * X = 5X
Work done in Day 3 = 4 * X = 4X
Work done in Day 4 = 3 * X = 3X

By the 4th day the work is completed, hence the total amount of work done is:
6X + 5X + 4X + 3X, which totals 18X

It has already been established that all the 6 workers manage to complete 6X work in a day. Therefore, if the entire work to be done totals 18X, how many days will it take the 6 workers together? The expression is as follows:

Total work available ÷ A day's work = 18X ÷ 6X

18X ÷ 6X = 3 days.

175

(162) 10 kg converted to grams becomes _____.

The correct answer is: (A) 10,000 grams

If one kilogram is equal to 1,000 grams, to find how many grams make 10 kilograms you need to multiply:

10kg x 1,000 = 10,000 grams

(163) How many liters are in one gallon?

The correct answer is: (B) 3.785 L

One US gallon is the equivalent of 3.78541178 liters. Option (B) is the same volume but rounded up to 3 decimal places.

(164) How many milliliters are in 2.5 liters?

The correct answer is: (B) 2,500 ml

One liter is the equivalent to 1,000 milliliters
Therefore, 2.5 liters = (2.5 x 1,000) ml = 2,500 ml

(165) How many grams are in 210 milligrams?

The correct answer is: (C) 0.21 g

The calculation is as follows:

1,000 mg = 1 g
210 mg = (1/1,000 x 210) g
(1/1,000 x 210) g = (0.001 x 210) g
(0.001 x 210) g = 0.21 g

(166) How many kilograms are in ten pounds?

The correct answer is: (A) 4.54 kg

The calculation is as follows:

One pound is equivalent to 0.454 kg
10 pounds are equivalent to:
0.454 kg x 10 = 4.54 pounds

(167) How many milligrams are in 0.539 grams?

The correct answer is: (B) 539 mg

The calculation is as follows:

One gram is equivalent to 1,000 milligrams
Therefore 0.539 g = 0.539 g x 1,000
0.539 g x 1,000 = 539 mg
When multiplying a decimal number by 1,000, move the decimal point 3 places to the right. It is important to avoid mixing up the units. In this case, what you have just calculated is the number of milligrams in 0.539 grams, and so the answer needs to be in milligrams (mg).

(168) How many gallons are in 16 quarts?

The correct answer is: (C) 4 gallons

The calculation is as follows:

Four quarts equal one gallon
Therefore to find out the number of gallons in 16 quarts the expression is:
6 quarts ÷ 4 = 4 gallons

(169) How many pounds are in 45 kilograms?

The correct answer is: (B) 100 pounds

The calculation is as follows:

1 kg is equal to 2.202 pounds

Therefore, in 45 kg, the number of pounds should be:
45 kg x 2.202 = 99.09 pounds
It is apparent the answer has been rounded up to become 100 pounds. In any case, there is no closer option than that in the answer choices list.

(170) One packet has seven green pencils and twenty-eight red ones. Find the ratio between green and red pencils.

The correct answer is: (A) 1 : 4

The calculation is as follows:

The ratio between the green and red pencils is 7 : 28 and then simplify that ratio. Seven is used to simplify the ratio: 7 divided by 7 equals 1, and 28 divided by 7 equals 4. The ratio in its simplest form is 1 : 4.

(171) A certain factory manager says his machines produce 1,450m of woven material within 8hrs when their efficiency is 100%. Unfortunately, the machines develop problems and they drop their efficiency, 4 of them running at 95% while the remaining 6 runs at 90%. How many meters worth of cloth will the factory produce within the normal 8hrs?

The correct answer is: (A) 1,334m

The calculation is as follows:

When working @100%, 1 machine yields 1,450/10 (Total cloth ÷ total no. of machines)

When working @95%, 4 machines yield ((1,450/10) * 95%) * 4

What this formula means is that once you determine what one machine produces at 100% efficiency (1,450/10), determine what that amount could have been if produced under circumstances of 95% efficiency. This is (1,450/10) * 95%. The output of one machine at 95%, multiplied by the number of machines working at 95%, and there are 4. The formula is:

((1,450/10) * 95%) * 4 = (145 *95%) * 4

(145 *95%) * 4 = 137.75 * 4 = 551m

The same method is used to determine the length of cloth the 6 machines should produce in 8hrs while working at 90% efficiency.

((1,450/10) * 90%) * 6 = (145 *90%) * 6

(145 *90%) * 6 = 130.5 * 6; and 130.5 * 6 = 783m

All 10 machines will, therefore, produce at their respective efficiencies:

551m + 783m = 1,334m

Note that there has not been any need to carry out time calculations because the information on machine output has been based on 8hrs.

(172)   During the presidential elections, 3 local polling stations, A, B, and C, had different rates of turnout. Station A had 1,270 registered voters and 945 of them showed up. Station B had 1,050 registered voters and 860 of them showed up to vote. Station C had 1,440 registered voters and 1,210 of them voted. What percentage of voters turned out locally on the overall?

The correct answer is: (D) 80%

In order to establish what the entire turnout was, it is important to know the proportion of voter number to registered voter number.

The calculation is as follows:

Actual voters (A + B + C) 945 + 860 + 1,210: Registered (A + B + C) 1270 + 1050 + 1440

The proportion of voters who turned out to registered voters is 3,015 : 3,760

Therefore the required percentage is: (3,015/3,760) x 100%

(3,015/3,760) x 100% = 0.80186 x 100%

0.80186 x 100% = 80.186%, which can be rounded to 80%.

(173)   Anne's typing speed is one page per p minutes. How much, in terms of pages, can she type in five minutes?

The correct answer is: (D) 5/p

This is another problem that is easily solved using proportions. If Anne is able to type one page in p minutes, let the number of pages she can type within five minutes be x.

The calculation is as follows:
1 : p and x : 5

Next, cross multiply: xp = 5

The value of x is calculated by dividing both sides by p as follows:

xp/p = 5/p

The left side can be simplified by canceling out the p in the numerator and denominator, so the equation is:

x = 5/p

(174) Joseph takes four hours to paint a small house but it takes James six hours to paint this very house. If they did the painting together, how long would it take them to complete painting the house?

The correct answer is (A) 2hr 24min

This kind of problem is referred to as a problem of inverse ratio. Use the formula:

1/x = 1/a + 1/b, and in this case, 'a' stands for the time Joseph takes to do the painting alone, while 'b' stands for the time it takes James to do the painting on his own. As for 'x', it represents the time taken by both Joseph and James painting together.

Substitute the known values, meaning the time it takes either of them to do the painting, and you will have: 1/x = ¼ + 1/6

Using the LCM or lowest common multiple the fractions are:

1/x = 6/24 + 4/24; which will become 1/x = 10/24

1/x = 10/24 can be worked out through cross multiplication and you will have:

10x = 24, and in order to find the value of x alone you need to divide either side by 10

10x/10 = 24/10; which means x = 24/10 or 2.4

Remember the question asks how long it would take to do the painting when both Joseph and John paint together, and that is the time represented by x and 2.4 represents the number of hours they spend. Two hours is clear, but how many minutes is 0.4 of an hour? Since an hour has 60 minutes, 0.4hr is the same as 40% of 60 minutes, which is 24 minutes. That is why the answer is 2h 24min.

(175)   A store sells dishwashers at $450, and this week it has a 15% sales discount. Normally the employees of the store benefit with an extra 20% discount. If an employee buys a dishwasher this week, how much is he going to pay for it?

The correct answer is: (D) $306.00

The dishwasher ordinarily costs $450

Customers' discount is 15% of $450, which amounts to $67.50

Customers' price after 15% off = $450 - $67.50 = $382.50

The price of $382.50 is the price from which the store employee will get 20% discount.

20% of $382.50 = $76.50 and the employee's discounted price = $382.50 – $76.50, which is $306. That is how option (D) as the correct answer is arrived at.

(176)   A car that is on sale has a price tag of $12,590. The discount given to arrive at that price is 20%. Calculate the car's original or initial price.

The correct answer is: (D) $15,737.50

The initial price is unknown, so call it X.

The current price is 20% less than X, and you can express that as 100%X – 20%X

100%X – 20%X = 80%X. The discounted price is the current price that has been given as $12,590, therefore: 80% X = $12,590

When you find the value of X you will have found the car's original price. In order to leave X alone on one side, divide either side by 80% and you will have:

X = $12,590 ÷ 80%, which is the same as $12,590 ÷ 80/100 or $12,590 x 100/80

$12,590 \times 100/80 = \$1,259,000/80 = \$15,737.50$. That is how option (D) is the correct answer.

(177) Arnold has n employees. He pays each $s every week. Arnold has a total of $x in his bank account. How long, in terms of days, can he afford to employ these employees?

The correct answer is: (D) 7x/ns

One employee is paid $s per week and therefore n employees are paid $s x n per week

$s x n = $sn; the amount Arnold spends every week and the amount Arnold spends on the employees each day = $sn/7

Considering all Arnold has available to pay the employees is $x, to find out for how long he can afford to employ them, divide what he has with the amount he spends each day. The formula will be:

$x ÷ $sn/7, which is the same as $x * 7/$sn

$x * 7/$sn = $7x/sn or $7x/ns

Whether you write 'ns' or 'sn' it does not matter as they both mean s times n.

(178) Mary purchased 550kg of grain for $165. She sold to her 15 loyal customers at $6.4 per 20kg when grain was still scarce in the town. In a week's time, she sold to 12 customers at $3.4 per 10kg, and what remained she sold at $1.8 per 5kg. Mary spent a total of $10 in distributing grains to different customers. How much profit did she make from the business?

The correct answer is: (B) $8.60

Mary has done her grain distribution at 3 varying rates and also 3 varying amounts.

15 customers had a rate of $6.4 per 20kg. This means at $6.4 she sold 15 x 20kg = 300kg; at $3.4 she sold 12 x 10kg = 120kg. From 550kg she managed to sell at the 2 prices 300kg+120kg, which is 420kg.

What remained was 550kg − 420kg = 130kg, which Mary sold at $1.8 per 5kg. To sell all the remaining grain, Mary must have sold to:

130kg / 5kg = 26 customers

It is now time to calculate the actual amount Mary earned in each category of distribution.

300kg sold at the rate of $6.4 per 20kg means: $6.4/20 x 300kg = $96

120kg sold at the rate of $3.4 per 10kg means: $3.4/10 x 120 = $40.8

130kg sold at the rate of $1.8 per 5kg means: $1.8/5 x 130 = $46.8

The total amount Mary earned from selling all her grain was: $(96+40.8+46.8) = $183.6

To calculate Mary's profit, subtract the cost of distribution and the cost of buying the grain from the total amount received. So the profit will be calculated as:

$183.6 – ($10+165) = $183.6 - $175 = $8.6. That is how option (B) is the correct answer.

(179) What is 15 as a percentage of 200?

The correct answer is: (A) 7.5%

The calculation is as follows:

15/200 = x/100%

Cross multiply: 1500 = 200x%

x = (1500/200) % = 7.5%

The question requires you to determine what 15 is as a percentage of 200, and not what 15% of 200 is.

(180) Little John has 5 blue balls, 3 green balls, and 2 red balls. What percentage of the total balls are the red ones?

The correct answer is: (C) 20%

The total balls = 5 + 3 + 2 = 10 and the red balls are 2.

The calculation is as follows:

2/10 x 100% = 20%.

(181) What is the answer after adding 10% of 300 and 50% of 20?

The correct answer is: (B) 40

The calculation is as follows:

10% of 300 = 10/100 x 300 = 30

50% of 20 = 50/100 x 20 = 10

30 + 10 = 40. That is how (B) was arrived at as the correct answer.

(182) What is 75% converted to a fraction?

The correct answer is: (C) ¾

In this question divide 75 by 100, simplified it equals ¾.

(183) What is three multiplied by 25% of forty?

The correct answer is: (B) 30

The calculation is as follows:

25% of 40 is the same as 25/100 x 40

Multiply that by 3 which is:

(25/100 x 40) x 3, and this is the same as (1/4 x 40) x 3

(1/4 x 40) x 3 = 10 x 3 = 30

(184) Calculate 10% of 30 multiplied by 75% of 200

The correct answer is: (A) 450

The calculation is as follows:

Solve 10% of 30, which is 10/100 x 30 = 3

Solve 75% of 200 which is 75/100 x 200 = 150

Next multiply the two amounts: 3 x 150 = 450.

(185) What is 4/20 expressed as a percentage?

The correct answer is: (B) 20%

When expressing a number as a percentage, divide it by 100. In this case, it is 4/20.

The expression is:

4/20 ÷100%, which is the same as (4/20 x 100/1)%, which is (400/20)%

(400/20)% = 20%

(186) What is the answer after converting 0.55 to a percentage?

The correct answer is: (D) 55%

The calculation is as follows:

0.55 ÷ 100 which is the same as 0.55 x 100/1 = 55%

(187) Of the four numbers listed below, which is the largest?

The correct answer is: (B) 25% of 4,000

The best way to determine the option with the largest amount is to calculate every option in absolute figures. 5% of 400 = 20; 25% of 4,000 = 1,000; 2% of 500 = 10; and 8% of 1,000 = 80

Among all the four numbers, the largest is 1,000 that is a product of 25% of 4,000.

(188) A certain class has 83 students and 72 of them are present today. What is the absentee percentage?

The correct answer is: (B) 13

The first step is to find out the number of students who are absent by subtracting the number of those present from the total number of students: 83 – 72 = 11

To find the percentage, put the number of absentees over the total number of students and then multiply by 100%:

The calculation is as follows:

11/83 x 100% = 13.25%

The answers are provided in whole numbers, and since the decimal part of 13.25 is .25 and is less than 0.5, the number can be rounded down to 13.

(189) What is six added to 50% of 50?

The correct answer is: (A) 31

The calculation is as follows:

6 + (50% of 50) = 6 + 25 = 31

(190) A vehicle drives for twenty seconds from a high spot on the road traveling at 10 meters per second. What is the vehicle's acceleration?

The correct answer is: (A) 0.5 meters / second²

The formula to calculate acceleration is:
A = (Vf – Vo) / t
Take the final velocity and divide it by the time taken.

The calculation is as follows:

10m/sec ÷ 20sec, which works out to 10/1sec X 1/20sec
10m/1sec X 1/20sec = 1/2m/sec² or 0.5m/sec²

(191) A vehicle is traveling at 90 miles per hour and then for five seconds, it accelerates, moving at a speed of 120 miles per hour. What is the vehicle's acceleration?

The correct answer is: (A) 6 mph per second

Use the acceleration formula A = (Vf – Vo)/t

The calculation is as follows:

Acceleration = (Final velocity – Initial velocity) / time taken; the final velocity = 120 miles per hour; Initial velocity = 90 miles per hour; Time taken = 5 seconds
Acceleration = (120m/hr – 90hr/sec) / 5 sec
Acceleration = 30m/hr per 5sec = 6m/hr per sec

(192) One rocket discharges a satellite that enters the orbit that is around the earth. This satellite moves at 2,000 m/sec and does this within 25 seconds. Calculate the satellite's acceleration.

The correct answer is: (B) 80m/sec^2

Use the acceleration formula of A = (Vf – Vo) / t

The calculation is as follows:

A = (2,000 m/sec – 0) / 25 sec, which works out to 2,000 m/sec per 25 sec, which when simplified becomes 80 m/sec per sec or 80 m/sec^2.

(193) The velocity of a soccer ball is 12 m/sec and this is how it travels after it has been kicked. Within 60 seconds the ball stops. Calculate its acceleration.

The correct answer is: (A) -0.2 m/sec^2

Acceleration = Final velocity – Initial velocity0 / t

Since the ball soon came to a stop, the final velocity is zero.

As such, the calculation is as follows:

187

A = (0 − 12m/sec) / 60 sec, which becomes -12 m/sec per 60 sec
-12 m/sec per 60 sec simplified is -1 m/sec per 5 sec.
Since a fifth is the same as 0.2, the correct answer is -0.2 m/sec²

(194) If a rocket has traveled three thousand meters within five seconds, how fast was it traveling?

The correct answer is: (D) 600 m/sec

Speed is that rate at which a given object changes its position.

The calculation is as follows:

Speed = Distance traveled / Time taken

In this case, the distance traveled is 3,000 meters and the time taken is 5 seconds. Using the formula given:
Speed = 3,000m / 5 sec, which is 600m/sec

(195) If the distance traveled by the space station within five seconds is 1,000 meters, how fast was it traveling?

The correct answer is: (B) 200 meters per second

Using the normal formula of Speed = Distance over time taken:

The calculation is as follows:

Speed of the space station = 1,000m ÷ 5 sec, which is 200 m/sec

(196) Rudisha sprints at six meters per second. How far will he have traveled in two minutes?

The correct answer is: (B) 720 meters

Speed = Distance ÷ Time taken

We know the speed and the time to be taken, which are 6 m/sec and 2 min respectively.

The calculation is as follows:

6 m/sec = Distance / 2 min

You can convert the minutes to seconds to work with like terms and the calculation is:

6 m/sec = Distance / 120 sec. To isolate Distance on one side, multiply both sides by 120 sec. Distance = 120 sec x (6m/sec)
The second units will cancel out leaving 120 x 6m, which equals 720 meters.

(197)   Find the distance Radcliffe will have walked if she travels 1,000 meters per 20 minutes.

The correct answer is: (B) 50 meters

Speed = Distance / Time taken.

The speed is known to be 1,000 m/min/20 min. The minute units cancel out and the calculations equal 50 meters.

(198)   Tom buys a hundred shares at a hundred dollars per share. Soon the price rises by ten percent and John sells 50 of the shares. After some time, the price changes again and this time it is a price decrease of ten percent, and John decides to dispose of all the remaining shares. How much money did he make from the sale of the last 50 shares?

The correct answer is: (E) $4,950

The calculation is:

100 shares bought @ $100 each = $10,000 spent

50 shares sold @ ($100 x 1.10%) = ($10,000 ÷ 2) x 1.10% = $5,500

Remaining 50 shares sold @ ($110 x 90%) = $5,500 x 90% = $4,950

(199)   Mr. Smith has three hours to grade scripts from his 35 students. She grades five papers within half an hour. In order to complete grading the remaining scripts within the set three hours, how much faster does Mr. Smith have to work?

The correct answer is: (C) 20%

Mr. Smith's working speed has been ten scripts per hour, and you can deduce that by considering he had marked 5 scripts in 30 minutes. With 30 papers remaining and 2½hrs at his disposal, how many scripts does Mr. Smith have to grade per hour? You can check the ratio of remaining papers to remaining time first.

The calculation is as follows:

2.5 hrs : 30 scripts; therefore, in one hour he grades 30 scripts/2.5hrs = 12 scripts/hr

Initially, the rate was 10 scripts / hr, which means there is an increase of 2 scripts this time around. 2 scripts /10 scripts = 1/5, which is the same as 20%. This is the extra speed Mr. Smith has to put in order to have graded of all the scripts completed within the scheduled time.

(200) Find out the prime number that is next in greatness after 67

The correct answer is: (C) 71

It is important to remember that prime numbers are the numbers that are divisible by themselves and one, but by no other number without causing a remainder. In this case, the number has to be greater than 67 and all the numbers given as options fit that criterion, but the one that cannot be divisible by a third number without having a remainder is only 71. Option (A) cannot be correct as 76 is divisible by 4. Option (B) is divisible by 4 also. Although 73 can be a prime number, it is not the next greatest to 67, so option (D) is incorrect. Option (E) is divisible by 3 in addition to itself and one.

Practice Test 2 – Questions

English Proficiency Section of the NLN-PAX

(1) She chose the red dress as she found it _____ than the purple dress.

(A) pretty

(B) prettier

(C) prettiness

(D) more prettier

(2) He felt unwell and chose to _____ down.

(A) lain

(B) lay

(C) lie

(D) laid

(3) Choose the correct sentence from the four listed below, taking note that they are all punctuated differently.

(A) Owing to her laziness she was left behind.

(B) Owing to her laziness; she was left behind.

(C) Owing to her laziness: she was left behind.

(D) Owing to her laziness, she was left behind.

(4) Choose the correct sentence from the four listed below, taking note that they are all punctuated differently.

(A) The pupil, who is leading the class; was appointed prefect last semester.

(B) The pupil who is leading the class was appointed prefect last semester.

(C) The pupil who is leading the class was appointed prefect last semester.

(D) The pupil, who is leading the class, was appointed prefect last semester.

(5) Learning grammar will make you speak _____.

(A) goodly

(B) well

(C) clear

(D) good

(6) Of the four listed below, choose the sentence that is most clear.

(A) She had 20 years of cooking experience when she burned food for the first time.

(B) She had been cooking for 20 years when she finally burned food.

(C) She was cooking for 20 years when she burned food.

(D) She cooked for 20 years and then she burned food for the first time.

(7) From the four listed below, choose the sentence that is grammatically correct.

(A) I'm not going to repeat it again. Just reconsider it again.

(B) I'm not going to repeat it. Just reconsider.

(C) I'm not going to repeat it again. Just think again and reconsider.

(D) I'm not going to repeat just think again before reconsidering.

(8) From the four listed below, choose the sentence that is most clear.

(A) The chef in the kitchen has photos of his mother in different dresses.

(B) The chef has photos in different dresses of his mother in the kitchen.

(C) The chef has photos in the kitchen of his mother in different dresses.

(D) In the kitchen in different dresses, the chef has photos of his mother.

(9) From the four listed below, choose the sentence that is grammatically correct.

(A) The last panelist, which was my former teacher, entered.

(B) The last panelist, whom was my former teacher, entered.

(C) The last panelist, what was my former teacher, entered.

(D) The last panelist, who was my former teacher, entered.

(10) This issue is between _____.

(A) him and me

(B) he and me

(C) he and I

(D) him and I

In the next 10 questions, if there is no error, simply indicate 'No error' as the answer.

(11) The last opportunity to draw in the charity lottery will go to whomever is the last in line. The underlined word(s) incorrectly used is/are _____.

(A) to draw in

(B) whomever

(C) is

(D) the last in

(12) There were several people who think that she has often got a lot more than her reasonable share. The underlined word(s) incorrectly used is/are _____.

(A) who

(B) often

(C) got

(D) than

(13) Susan felt so good yesterday that she volunteered to do the cooking herself instead of being waited on. The underlined word(s) incorrectly used is/are _____.

(A) good

(B) yesterday

(C) volunteered

(D) herself

(14) <u>Whom</u> did Jane find <u>yesterday</u> at the rear verandah <u>in</u> the resort's <u>restaurant</u>? The underlined word(s) incorrectly used is/are _____.

(A) Whom

(B) yesterday

(C) in

(D) restaurant

none

(15) <u>Since</u> they <u>felt demoralized</u>, the three <u>top</u> trainees discussed the matter <u>between</u> themselves. The underlined word(s) incorrectly used is/are _____.

(A) Since

(B) felt demoralized

(C) top

✓ (D) between

between = 2 people / things

(16) <u>After</u> the tutor had instructed <u>her</u> to do her research again, the diligent student scribbled a note '<u>redue</u>' for <u>herself</u> on her paper. The underlined word(s) incorrectly used is/are _____.

(A) After

(B) her

(C) redue

(D) herself

195

(17) When someone through a stone, smashing one of his windows, Tom suspected the person was among the rioters. The underlined word(s) incorrectly used is/are _____.

(A) through

(B) smashing

(C) was

(D) rioters

(18) All the presidential candidates agreed that none of them hadn't sworn to incite their followers. The underlined word(s) incorrectly used is/are _____.

(A) that

(B) them

(C) hadn't

(D) followers

(19) The moment I walked in the room I sensed the place had been abandoned with no-one there. The underlined word(s) incorrectly used is/are _____.

(A) walked

(B) in   — into

(C) abandoned

(D) no-one there

(20) "Whose sweater," Mum inquired, "is this? By the way, who's in charge of the sweaters today?" The underlined word(s) incorrectly used is/are _____.

(A) Whose

(B) Mum

(C) inquired,

(D) W=who's

none

(21) The character seen in the leader's administration mirrors his profligate behavior.

Profligate means:

(A) Excessive

(B) Productive

(C) Generous

(D) Immoral

(22) The staff has been charged with expediting the matter by the executive.

Expediting means to:

(A) Relieve of

(B) Speed up

(C) Make easier

(D) Eliminate

(23) The very querulous woman from the ball had dressed beautifully.

Querulous means:

(A) Flirtatious

✓ (B) Full of Complains

(C) Inquisitive

(D) Fashionable

(24) She just acquiesced to that whole process.

Acquiesced means:

(A) Comment on

(B) Object to

(C) Enthused over

(D) Submit to

(25) The new land was fecund according to the settlers.

Fecund means:

(A) Pretty

(B) Fertile

(C) Rotten

(D) Filthy

(26) Throughout the study, the researchers controlled their data due to participant attrition.

Attrition refers to:

(A) Variety

(B) Attitude

✓(C) Loss

(D) Gain

(27) The contestant abhors many kinds of socialism and that is his stand.

Abhors means:

(A) Uses

· (B) Hates

(C) Grasps

(D) Loves

(28) Everyone had a viable reason to consider Rita's behavior frugal.

Frugal means:

(A) Generous

(B) Old-fashioned

· (C) Economical

(D) Flighty

(29) The treatises written by this philosopher are too esoteric for common readers.

Esoteric means:

(A) Lengthy

(B) Enigmatic

(C) Controversial

(D) Accessible x

(30) The bluish color on the patient's lunulae worried the doctor.

Lunulae are found in:

(A) The beds of your fingernails

(B) Bodily extremities

(C) The gums in your mouth

(D) The whites of your eyeballs

Raisins – For Question 31

The raisin venture was accidentally discovered by the San Joaquin Valley farmers of California in 1873. Just before the farmers harvested their grapes that year, a heat wave that was by far the worst ever was experienced in the valley. The heat was so severe that all the grapes began to dry on the vines and that is how California had a raisin crop harvest for the very first time.

To the people's surprise, the raisins were really enjoyable and they all wanted more. This led the farmers of San Joaquin to venture into the newly discovered raisin business. The grapes are now, however, treated with better care and are not left to dry on the vines.

The grapes begin to ripen toward the end of August and the farmers test them to check if the grapes are sweet. They have to wait for the sugar level to be 21% and when this is achieved, the farmers know that their grapes are ready for picking. Skilled workers hand-pick these grapes in bunches. They then place the picked grapes into flat pans which are emptied onto square papers that are usually placed between the long rows of grape vines.

The grapes then sit under the sun for about half a month or sometimes even longer. During this time, both sides of the grapes should be given enough time to dry and until they turn to the desired color. The drying process continues until only 15% of the grape's moisture remains. At this point, the grape is said to be a raisin.

These raisins are then rolled up inside the papers that were used during the drying process and then they are taken from the farms in trucks. After this, the raisins are collected in big boxes known as sweatboxes with a carrying capacity of 160 pounds. Here, the raisins that have less moisture are able to get moisture from the ones with too much and after some time, all the raisins have just the right amount of moisture needed.

The boxes are then trucked near the packaging plants and emptied onto a conveyer belt that gently shakes the raisins to remove the stems. The stems are then whisked away by blasting air. The raisins are then taken through a water bath. After these steps, the big brown raisins are inspected and rechecked for sugar and moisture. They then go through a belt and onto packaging machines where they are put into packages, weighed automatically, and sealed. At this point, the raisins can be considered market-ready.

(31) What is the major idea in the passage?

(A) In the US, raisins were created by accident.

(B) Several steps are required in the process of developing raisins.

(C) Once on the shelves of the grocery stores, the raisins are taken through a process of fermentation.

(D) Cleaning of raisins is done at the plant where packing takes place.

(E) For a long time, California has led to the development of raisins in America.

Sichan Siv – For Question 32

Sichan Siv was a man who was desperately trying to flee Cambodia in 1976 and years later, in 1989, he would end up working in Washington, D.C. inside the White House as the advisor to the United States President. At this point, you are probably wondering how this came to be.

Like many other Cambodians at that time, Siv found himself in the middle of a brutal civil war. The government of Cambodia and a group known as the Khmer Rouge were at war and the situation became worse after the government lost to the opposing group. Countless people were butchered, in some cases, entire families wiped out, and many people were forced into labor.

Siv was from a big family that lived in Cambodia's capital. On completing high school, he worked at an airline company for some time and then he went to teach English. Later, he worked with CARE, an American charity group that was helping war victims.

Siv's hope had been to flee his country before it was taken over by the Khmer Rouge but he was unfortunately delayed. Because of this, he was taken from his home together with his family and forcefully made to work in the rice fields but luckily he was able to escape. On an old bike, he rode for miles aiming to get to Thailand where there would be freedom and safety for him. For the next three weeks, Siv slept on the hard ground and hid from soldiers who were searching for him. When he was finally caught, his fear was that they would kill him but he was brought to a forced labor camp instead where he would work for 18 hours every day with no rest.

Once again, he escaped after a few months, but this time it was a successful escape. The journey was quite terrifying as he staggered through thick bamboo for miles on foot for three days and he finally managed to get to Thailand. The experience he had gained while working for the American charity organization made it easy for him to get a job at a refugee camp and soon he set off for the USA On arriving in June 1976, he got his first job as an apple picker. Later he became a cook in a fast-food eatery. He was, however, not satisfied with what he was doing because his passion was actually to work closely with people like himself who had gone through the difficulties of fleeing from their countries. Siv knew that the ideal way to get ready for that kind of a job was to enroll at a college and so he sent letters to various universities and colleges. His bravery and school records made an impression and in 1980, Siv got an opportunity to study at Columbia University in the city of New York.

After he completed his studies, the UN gave Siv a job. He later married an American woman and became an American citizen. After a few more years, Siv felt like he belonged to his new nationality, and in 1988, he received a job offer from the White House where he worked for the closest advisors of President Ronald Reagan. The job was tough and he often had to put in long hours, but it was all worth it since he got the chance to help refugees.

(32)   What is the major idea in the passage?

(A) Persistence and even courage are ideas of a global nature.

(B) Siv's travels took him to many places in his young and adult life.

(C) Siv had to persevere before escaping Cambodia.

(D) Siv went through a lot of problems in order to reach America and to assist others.

(E) Siv had to persevere in order to gain American citizenship.

The American Flag – For Question 33

If you are hanging the flag of the United States of America over a street, you should hang it in a vertical manner and make sure that the blue area, also known as the union, faces the north and east-west street. If you want to display the American flag together with another flag using crossed staffs, remember that the other flag should be on the left with its staff behind that of the American flag. When hoisting the flag, you should hoist it quickly, but when lowering it, you should do so slowly and all this should be done in a respectful manner. When you want to fly it at half-mast, you should raise it up to the very top for a while before you lower it to half-mast. In a case where you are flying the flag together with other banners from cities or states, you should begin by raising the banner that represents the nation first and it should also be the last to be lowered. Remember that the flag should never touch the ground at any point.

(33)   What is the major idea in the passage?

(A) The flag of America serves as the symbol of US freedom.

(B) The flag of America has 50 stars.

(C) The government would intervene in a case where the flag of America is inappropriately placed.

(D) One should fly the flag of America differently according to different situations.

(E) It is important to lower the flag quickly and also with respect.

The Bamboo – For Question 34

Would you believe it if someone said that there is a type of grass whose height is equivalent to that of very tall trees? What if they told you that this grass can become very strong like steel and that boats, furniture, houses, and many other important products can be derived from it? On top of that, what if you learned that you could also eat this grass? Well, believe it or not, this is true. Bamboo is the grass we are referring to.

You may argue that bamboo resembles wood. Nevertheless, this plant belongs to the plant family that includes oats, barley, and wheat. This type of grass not only provides material to make useful products but also provides food for human beings. In most Asian foods, for example, young bamboo and other vegetables are mixed and cooked together.

Bamboo is found in many different countries in the world. It does well in a warm and wet climate especially in Asian countries and the South Pacific Ocean islands. In the USA, it mostly grows in Virginia, Indiana, Florida, Texas, and Louisiana.

In many Asian countries, bamboo is almost as valuable as rice. Most people in Asia make their houses, furniture, and mats from bamboo. They also use bamboo for fencing and caging their pigs and chickens.

You can glue bamboo in layers to make it as strong as steel and use it to construct large buildings. On some South Pacific islands, bamboo is used to make water pipes. You can also make some musical instruments like recorders and flutes using bamboo. For many years, artists have valued paper that is made out of bamboo.

Bamboo is strong and light and it does not break when bent. It also floats well on water, hardly wears out, is quite cheap to grow, and grows easily. In fact, nothing else in the world grows faster than bamboo. There are even times when you can actually see bamboo grow. According to records of botanists, bamboo can grow more than 3 feet in only 24 hours! It is also a hollow plant with strong roots that continue to grow and spread. Bamboo only dies after flowering, a rare event that happens once in 30 years.

There are over 1,000 types of bamboo with the smallest being only 3 inches tall with a one-tenth inch diameter while the largest type is over 200 feet tall with a seven-inch diameter. It is no surprise that many consider bamboo a sign of good fortune and happiness. Indeed, almost half of the world's population would suffer greatly if there was no more bamboo.

(34) What is the major idea in the passage?

(A) It is possible to use bamboo a minimum of 2,000 ways.

(B) Bamboo is mainly found in Asia and its growth is amazing.

(C) Bamboo is an amazing type of grass with multiple uses.

(D) The different types of bamboo can total at least a thousand.

(E) There are times bamboo can be considered to be a flower.

Marathon in the Moroccan Desert – For Question 35

Since 1986, the Moroccan desert hosts the world's bravest runners every year. Here, they participate in a race that is considered to be among the toughest race competitions in the entire world. 'The Marathon of the Sands', the name given to the race, covers more than a 125-mile stretch of mountain wilderness and desert. The runners are expected to finish the entire course in less than 7 days while carrying their clothing, sleeping bags, and food.

Patrick Bauer founded the marathon in 1986 with the idea of giving the runners that gathered there from all around the world a different type of adventure. Deep friendships are formed among the runners as they spend their nights and days in this desert. The runners also learn a lot about themselves as well as each other as they battle total exhaustion and terrible heat.

Most runners enter because of the challenge that the race provides. On day one, there is a 15-mile distance stretching across the desert full of thorny bushes, rocks, and sand. Most runners have raw and blistered feet by the end of the day. For each day during the entire race, they are only allowed less than 9 quarts of drinking water and this causes dehydration. The runners are also exhausted by the time they get to their campsite to spend the night.

On day two, the runners are up by 6 a.m. and just a couple of hours later, the temperature rises to 100 degrees, but the participants have to keep going. On this day, they are required to complete an 18-mile distance. They then rest throughout the night in preparation for the following day.

On day three, the runners are required to climb gigantic sand dunes which are the first they have seen in the seven-day marathon. Their sweat mixes with sand and dust and soon enough, their faces look muddy. Fifteen miles later, the runners arrive at their next camping site.

For the next four days, the race goes on in the same manner. Out of all the days, day four and five are usually the worst. Despite the level stretch of ground and the beautiful oasis of trees that the runners go through on day four, on day five, they also go through more than 21 miles of sand dunes and rocks. Many runners concede defeat as the temperature rises to 125 degrees and these fallen runners are rushed by helicopter to receive medical help. Those who survive day five know that they have conquered the worst part of the race.

On day six, the rocks and the heat are unbearable. The wind grows stronger in Draa valley and causes the heat to pound against the runners with a lot of force and this makes them more exhausted.

On day seven, the final day, the runners only have 12 miles to cover. The tired, blistered, dusty runners begin the journey at daybreak. By the time the runners get to the finish line, everyone is excited and the children race alongside them. At this point, the runners who have completed the entire marathon are proud of themselves for achieving what many could not. One racer who had participated twice in the marathon said that during the tough moments, he would think and question why he was part of the marathon and then realize that he was in it to test how far he could push himself.

(35)   What is the major idea in the passage?

(A) The race dubbed 'Marathon of the sands' tests people's endurance limit.

(B) The participating runners run at the pace they wish.

(C) This race makes the strong runners stumble while those who are weak fail to finish.

(D) The toughest day of this race is the seventh.

(E) Every participating runner competes in order to establish what they are capable of accomplishing.

Machu Picchu – For Question 36

Machu Picchu is an ancient city in the Andean Mountains of Peru. The reason behind the building of this exceptional city is not known and it will perhaps remain a mystery forever. Nevertheless, the city is a significant site that reveals some details about the Inca people, ancient people who lived in South America.

A significant area of South America was once ruled by the Incan empire. The empire had been in place for over 500 years before the first explorers from Spain made their way onto the continent in search of gold.

The Inca people were very advanced. Their engineering skills enabled them to construct sturdy bridges and pave their roads. They also plowed their land such that when it rained, the valuable soil would not be washed away and they dug trenches that would carry water to the dry areas to facilitate farming. The Incas had no knowledge of the wheel but they could move large stone blocks weighing up to 10 tons to the mountainsides to construct walls. They could fit blocks so tightly without any kind of cement that nothing can slip between them, not even a thin blade. Earthquakes and storms have destroyed countless modern buildings but the walls of the Incan empire still stand firm.

The Inca people were also skilled artists who created beautiful objects from silver and gold as these valuable metals were in high supply during those days. Today, Incan items are treasured greatly for their magnificent designs.

The Incas used knotted strings with different colors and lengths to keep their accounts because they did not have a written language. The size of a knot and the distance between the knots represented numbers.

The empire had about 30 million residents at its peak. The Inca emperor ruled his subjects cruelly. He dictated where they would live, what they would plant, how many hours they would work, and whom they would marry. The emperor owned everything and so he would decide what to give to the people, the quantity to give and when to give it.

In 1533, the Spanish explorers, with Francisco Pizarro as the leader, killed the Inca emperor. The successor to the empire had earlier been killed also and this left the Incas, a people who always fully depended on their leader, without a recognized authority. The Spaniards were able to conquer the empire easily and strip it of all its riches.

The South American people, however, can still trace their heritage to the Incas. In Peru, which was once the core of the empire, 80% of the 20 million people can trace their roots back to the Incas. What is left of the ancient city now stands as a tribute to the once mighty empire.

(36) What is the major idea in the passage?

(A) There was a time the Incas occupied the old city called Machu Picchu.

(B) The Incas lived mainly in Peru.

✓ (C) The Spaniards plundered the Incan empire that can be traced in different cities of ancient times.

(D) Destruction of the Incan empire by the Spaniards took place during the 13th century.

(E) The Incan empire had Machu Picchu as its capital.

Piaget Part 1 – For Questions 37 – 41

Jean Piaget was born in Switzerland in 1896 in an area populated by French speakers. One of his parents was a professor at the university. As a child, Piaget was intellectually gifted with an interest in nature and biology studies. Piaget originally trained to be a botanist but his interest in psychology was influenced by Sigmund Freud whose practice and theory of psychoanalysis began to develop and become popular during the time when Piaget was young. Piaget became a Swiss philosopher and developmental psychologist who developed a theory of cognitive development that was among the most significant in his field.

Upon finishing his studies at the university and graduating, Piaget relocated to Paris to teach in a school. The director of the school, Alfred Binet, developed some standardized tests designed to assess intelligence and these tests are used today. As Piaget assisted in scoring the tests, he noticed that the younger children were making consistent errors that were not made by adults and older children. He then developed a hypothesis suggesting that children's reasoning is different from that of adults. This would mark the start of Piaget's theory of progressive and distinct stages in cognitive development universally experienced by people while growing up.

In 1921, he returned to Switzerland and became a director of the Rousseau Institute in Geneva. Piaget and his wife were blessed with three children and he analyzed their learning and behavior from the time they were born through their early years. To study them, he used a direct observation technique as well as a case study, which is a technique that develops a comprehensive profile on different aspects of each child. He called children 'little scientists' that learn through interacting with, acting upon, and exploring their environments.

Piaget's theory proposed that when learning, human beings adapt to the environment through accommodation and assimilation processes just as is the case with biology. He suggested that young children form constructs in their minds that represent the world they see, a concept he referred to as schemata. To relate to new information, infants fit it into a schema that already exists and when it fails to fit, they form a new schema or modify the existing one. Piaget was called the great founder of constructivism because he emphasized the role that children play in actively creating their own understanding of reality. Constructivism is a theory that suggests that we build knowledge from interactions between our thoughts and encounters.

(37) Going by the information provided in the passage, it is clear _____ was Piaget's initial discipline in the field of science.

(A) botany

(B) philosophy

(C) cognitive development

(D) developmental psychology

(38) Piaget applied the principle of _____ in developing the proposal pertaining to how human beings adapt to their environment.

(A) direct child observation

(B) the biology he had learned

(C) Freudian psychoanalysis

(D) Binet's intelligence test

(39) One of the statements below is true about the experience Piaget had with the tests of Alfred Binet's intelligence.

(A) Piaget realized those tests were unsuitable for children of a younger age.

(B) Piaget took note of patterns of errors that made the results of the tests invalid.

(C) According to Piaget, the way children of a younger age thought varied from the way adults thought.

(D) Piaget became helpful to Alfred Binet by ensuring the development of intelligence tests.

(40) Which of the following statements is in regard to Piaget's theory?

(A) The belief that children of a younger age commit errors yet adults cannot

(B) A continuous and also gradual progression pertaining to cognitive development, the progression that varies in its entirety from one person to another

(C) Universal development stages that are progressive, which every human being undergoes.

(41) There is a theory that holds that people build their knowledge from the interactions they make with their thoughts as well as their experiences. This theory is known as _____.

(A) cognitive development

(B) constructivism

(C) developmental psychology

(D) biology

Piaget Part 2 – For Questions 42 - 46

Piaget observed his children and those of his colleagues at the university as they built their knowledge on their surrounding by trying different things and this helped to form his idea. His theory explains that a baby is in a stage called the sensorimotor stage in cognitive development. In this stage, infants acquire information via their senses when they get involved in motor activity, after which they receive feedback on their motor activity from the given environment.

Piaget named stage two a pre-operational stage. This stage comprises children between two to seven years. At this age, children begin to gain motor skills and their thinking is marked by egocentrism which is an attitude of thinking that everything is all about them and there is no alternative viewpoint. This age is also characterized by animism whereby they attribute human behavior and characteristics to an inanimate object. Magical thinking is also typical at this stage and they believe that their actions or thoughts cause unassociated external events. At this stage, children still cannot think logically or retain properties like numbers, amounts, or volume in their minds despite the changes in appearance, arrangement, or shape.

The next stage is the concrete operational stage that continues until around the age of eleven. At this stage, children start to have logical thinking and can perform mental operations as Piaget called them. They can, however, only do those mental operations with concrete objects that they can touch, see, and manipulate. They can learn simple science and arithmetic. They also cease to think egocentrically. At this stage, they are able to solve some conservation problems that involve concrete materials by first understanding that the quantities of liquids or solids are equal even when the shapes and the containers' shapes change and that even if you arrange objects differently, the number remains constant. They, however, still cannot think abstractly or tackle purely mental operations.

Formal operations stage begins right before puberty. This continues into adolescence and into adulthood. At this stage, youngsters are able to tackle purely mental operations. They can also consider philosophical ideas, logical arguments, and understand abstract ideas, such as democracy, justice, beauty, and truth. They are also able to consider issues of morality. Piaget had, in fact, developed one theory of moral development which later influenced psychologists who came after him, such as Lawrence Kohlberg. Kohlberg used Piaget's theory as the basis for his developmental theory of moral reasoning that expanded on Piaget's foundations. Jean Piaget died in 1980.

(42) Based on the passage and according to Piaget, the stage of cognitive development that_____ are in is the pre-operational stage.

(A) toddlers

(B) teens

(C) infants

(D) adults

(43) A child might hold the belief that it was her disobedience that brought about a thunderstorm, a belief that can exemplify what Piaget referred to as _____.

(A) conservation

✓(B) magical thinking

(C) animism

(D) egocentrism

(44) Based on the passage, which of the four options listed is true regarding the concrete operations stage?

(A) Children are not capable of performing operations of a mental nature.

(B) Children still have the capacity to think in an egocentric manner at this particular stage.

(C) Children have the capacity to think in a logical manner at this particular stage.

(D) Children have the capacity to think in an abstract manner at this particular stage.

(45) During a typical Piagetian experiment, one researcher poured some liquid in a beaker that was narrow and tall and then transferred that liquid into another beaker that was short and wide, and all that was done before a student who was watching. The researcher then asked that student to identify the beaker that held a larger amount of liquid. The student's reply was that the two beakers held an equal amount of liquid. Among those defined by Piaget, which earliest stage is the student experiencing?

(A) Sensorimotor

(B) Formal operations

(C) Concrete operations

(D) Pre-operational

(46) Choose the answer option that provides the truth regarding the theory by Lawrence Kohlberg according to the information in the passage.

(A) The theory focuses mainly on cognitive development.

(B) The theory falls under cognitive theory and opposes the theory by Piaget.

(C) The theory is not at all related to Piaget's.

(D) The theory provides expansion for Piaget's theory on moral development

213

Science Section of the NLN PAX

(47) From the choices below, which one is a component grouped under lipids?

(A) Fatty acids

(B) Nucleic acids

(C) Zinc

(D) Plasma cells

(48) Which chromosome is affected by Down's syndrome?

(A) Chromosome 13

(B) Chromosome 15

(C) Chromosome 23

✓(D) Chromosome 21

(49) Blood enters the lungs through which chamber of the heart?

(A) Left atrium

(B) Right Ventricle

(C) Left Ventricle

(D) Right atrium

(50) When you take alcohol excessively over a lengthy period, you are likely to destroy a certain organ of your body. Which one is it?

(A) Liver

(B) Gallbladder

(C) Kidney

(D) Pancreas

(51) There are various types of radiation rays. Which of the following is not one of them?

(A) Alpha

✓ (B) Infrared

(C) Gamma

(D) Beta

(52) How many oxygen molecules can be held by one hemoglobin molecule in the blood during transportation?

(A) 8

(B) 6

✓ (C) 4

(D) 2

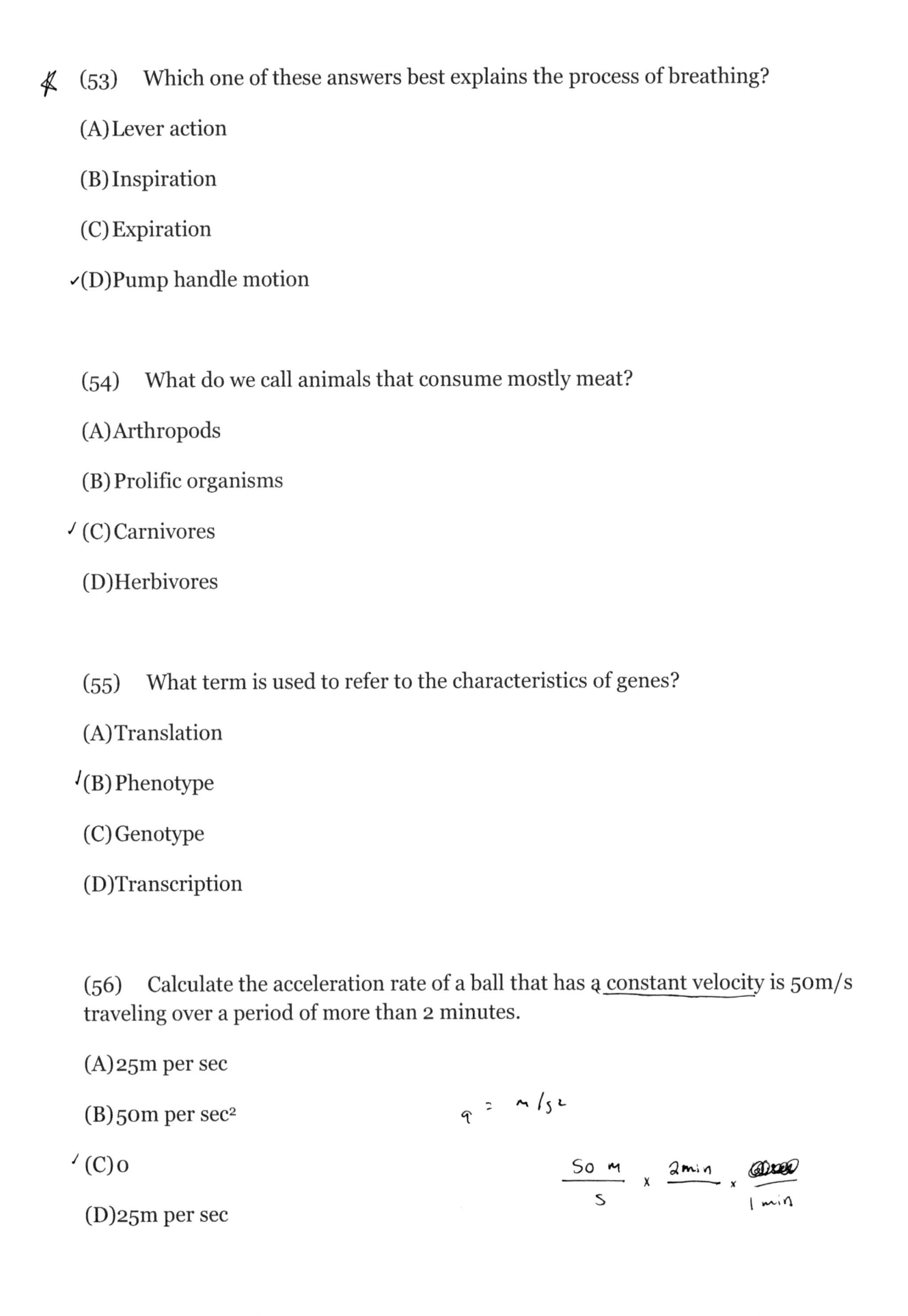

(53) Which one of these answers best explains the process of breathing?

(A) Lever action

(B) Inspiration

(C) Expiration

✓(D) Pump handle motion

(54) What do we call animals that consume mostly meat?

(A) Arthropods

(B) Prolific organisms

✓(C) Carnivores

(D) Herbivores

(55) What term is used to refer to the characteristics of genes?

(A) Translation

✓(B) Phenotype

(C) Genotype

(D) Transcription

(56) Calculate the acceleration rate of a ball that has a constant velocity is 50m/s traveling over a period of more than 2 minutes.

(A) 25m per sec

(B) 50m per sec²

✓(C) 0

(D) 25m per sec

(57) What term refers to the site where neurons connect?

✓ (A) Synapse

(B) Docking station

(C) Synergy

(D) Terminal site

(58) The kneecap can also be referred to as _____.

(A) Meniscus

(B) Pisiform

✓ (C) Patella

(D) Popliteal bursa

(59) Which one of these terms is used to refer to the joint in the shoulder?

(A) Hinge joint

✓ (B) Ball and socket joint

(C) Pivot joint

(D) Saddle joint

(60) Which area of the body is the organ of Corti found?

(A) Ear

(B) Nose

(C) Lungs

(D) Mouth

(61) A person suffering from rickets is likely to be lacking what vitamin in their body?

(A) D

(B) A

(C) Z

(D) C

(62) Under what group does a steroid fall?

(A) Weak acid

(B) Enzyme

(C) Protein

(D) Lipid

(63) Cranial nerve X is also referred to as the _____ nerve.

(A) Vagus

(B) Facial

(C) Hypoglossal

(D) Abducens

(64) From the following PH ranges, which is a strong base?

(A) 7.1 to 9.0 w.B

(B) 1.3 to 2.0 acid

✓ (C) 11.2 to 12.0 SB

(D) 4.5 to 5.2 newt

(65) Which of the chambers in the heart is responsible for pumping blood in systematic circulation?

(A) Right atrium

✓ (B) Left ventricle

(C) Right ventricle

(D) Left atrium

(66) Newton's second law of motion is represented by the formula _____.

(A) P = mv

✓ (B) F = ma

(C) V = d/t

(D) F = mva ✗

(67) In which phase do chromosomes arrange themselves in the mitosis?

(A) Anaphase

(B) Prophase

✓ (C) Metaphase

(D) Telophase

(68) Digestive enzymes are contained in which cellular organs?

(A) Ribosomes

(B) Lysosomes ✓

(C) Golgi Apparatus

(D) Nucleus

(69) The process by which organs <u>replace</u> their worn out tissues is called_____.

(A) Transformation

(B) Mitosis

(C) Meiosis

(D) Cellular differentiation

(70) What is the model regarded as efficient during an enzyme action?

(A) Lock and Key model ✓

(B) Transformation Model.

(C) Transcription Mode.

(D) Enzyme Interaction model.

(71) Select the statement on enzymes that is false.

(A) Almost all enzymes are proteins.

(B) Enzymes operate most efficiently at optimum PH. ✓

(C) Enzymes are catalysts. ✓

(D) Enzymes are destroyed during chemical reactions. ✗

(72) Select the statements on prostaglandins that are false?

(A) Prostaglandins can lead to pain and fever.

✓ (B) Prostaglandins can only constrict blood vessels.

(C) Prostaglandins promote inflammation.

(D) Prostaglandins are made in the renal medulla

(73) LDL Cholesterol stands for_____.

✓ (A) Low-density lipoproteins

(B) Level-density lipoproteins

(C) Level-density lysosomes

(D) Low-density lysosomes

(74) What is the process by which arteries harden?

✓ (A) Atherosclerosis

(B) Microcirculation

(C) Hypertension

(D) Venous narrowing

(75) What does the highest blood pressure level show?

(A) Optimum pressure

(B) Diastolic pressure

(C) Transient pressure

✓ (D) Systolic pressure

(76) When subjected to a strong base, a blue litmus paper will turn or stay_____.

(A) Red

(B) Green

(C) Blue

(D) Orange

(77) Which compound affects alveoli surface tension in the lungs and is necessary during breathing.

(A) Plasma

(B) Sodium Chloride

✓ (C) Surfactant

(D) Potassium

(78) Which function is not regarded as a kidney function?

(A) Filtration

(B) Secretion

✓ (C) Transport

(D) Reabsorption

(79) What is referred to as the kidney's functional unit?

(A) Pyramid

(B) Medulla

(C) Glomerulus

✓ (D) Nephron

(80) Select the ideal gas law.

(A) PV= knT or PV=RnT   PV = nRT

(B) KTV =PR

(C) V=Kt

(D) PV = k

(81) Select a property that is not a characteristic of a type of gas.

(A) Mass

(B) Pressure

(C) Volume

(D) Particles

(82) 'A particular body that is submerged in a liquid has some upward force act on it that is of similar weight with that of the liquid the body displaced'. This statement describes _____.

(A) Archimedes' principle

(B) Boyle's law

(C) Anderson's principle

(D) Charles' law

(83) What name is given to fluids that easily evaporate?

(A) Evaporative fluids

✓(B) Volatile fluids

(C) Transient fluids

(D) Viscous fluids

(84) Which of the following is used to describe high-frequency sound waves?

(A) Consonance waves

✓(B) Overtones

(C) Dissonance waves

(D) Fundamental waves

(85) _____ was the first citizen of America to be awarded the Nobel Prize for being able to measure how fast light can travel.

(A) Grimaldi

✓(B) Albert Michelson

(C) Thomas Young

(D) Albert Einstein

(86) What is the anatomical structure connecting the mouth and the stomach called?

(A) Spinal column

(B) Hepatic duct

(C) Trachea

✓(D) Esophagus

(87) Select the correct statement among the following:

(A) The life of all organism starts as one cell.

(B) All of the above answers are incorrect.

(C) The life of organisms starts as multiple cells.

(D) Other organisms begin their life as one cell while others begin as multiple cells.

(88) According to scientists _____ has taken place through _____

(A) Reproduction/homeostasis

(B) Natural selection/evolution

(C) Differentiation/ evolution

(D) Homeostasis/ natural selection

(89) Name two science measurement types that very important.

(A) Descriptive and qualitative.

(B) Scientific and numerical.

(C) Quantitative and numerical.

(D) Qualitative and quantitative

(90) A common sperm must have:

(A) A, B, and C.

(B) B and C.

(C) 23 chromosomes.

(D) Y chromosome.

(E) X chromosomes.

(91) Living things on earth use:

(A) Sexual reproduction.

(B) Oxygen

(C) Neurotransmitters.

(D) Light.

(E) A triplet genetic code.

(92) The main reason why sexual reproduction is preferred over an asexual form is that:

(A) It needs chromosomes

(B) It leads to diversity.

(C) It is easily done at any time during the year.

(D) It results in multiple offspring.

(E) It needs two people.

(93) In an organism scientific name, what do we call the second section of the name?

(A) Species.

(B) Population.

(C) Kingdom.

(D) Phylum.

1. genus
2. species

(94) When a bacterial cell divides into two new cells, what has the cell has gone through?

(A) Meiosis.

(B) Replication.

(C) Mitosis.

(D) Fission.

reg. chromosomes

(95) The following are found in a bacterial cell. Which one among them is not a component of a bacterial cell?

(A) Mitochondria

(B) Ribosomes.

(C) DNA

(D) Vesicles

(96) Young children are likely to suffer from drastic acute malnutrition described as:

✓ (A) Age Z height score <-3 or age Z weight score<-3 or edema.

(B) Age Z weight score.

(C) Age Z height score < -3 or age Z weight score <-3 edema

(D) Age Z height score <-3 and edema.

(97) Children lacking vitamin A are likely to suffer from:

(A) Poor bone growth

(B) Goiter

(C) Poor cognitive development

✓ (D) High mortality risk

(98) Lack of Iodine in the body is caused by:

(A) Consuming fewer calories.

✓ (B) Consuming only central Africa staple foods.

(C) Not getting enough sunlight.

(D) Consuming fewer vegetables and fruits.

(99) Anemia is caused by a lack of which nutrients among the following;

A) Protein and zinc

✓ B) Iron and copper

C) Zinc and vitamin D

D) Vitamin C and iodine

(100) Among the following statements, which one has not been regarded as a result of kwashiorkor edema?

(A) Abrupt weaning from breastfeeding.

(B) A change in intestinal bacteria

(C) Insufficient consumption of nutritious antioxidant.

✓(D) Lack of iron

(101) According to the UNICEF model, malnutrition causes are categorized in several levels; basic, underlying, and immediate. Select from the following causes the one that is not in the underlying category in accordance with the UNICEF model.

✓(A) Lack of sufficient rainfall needed for agricultural purposes.

(B) Lack of proper mother and child care.

(C) Lack of proper health services and a healthy environment.

(D) Restricted access to food.

(102) Which category of people is highly recommended by the World Health Organization to take zinc supplements?

(A) Children from low-income regions who are at a high risk of reduced growth rate

✓(B) Children suffering from diarrhea or malnutrition

(C) Poor older individuals

(D) Women that are breastfeeding or pregnant

(103) The core reason why a well-nourished individual can suffer from only vitamin D deficiency is?

(A) Vitamin D in a particular type of food is fully dependent on the type of soil where the food was grown and not the age or wealth of a person.

(B) Meals with enough growth nutrients will lead to increased demand for vitamin D thus leading to deficiency.

(C) The vitamin D required by our body is not solely dependent on food; therefore, food is not a necessary vitamin D determinant.

(D) In most cultures, vitamin D foods are consumed by both the rich and the poor.

(104) Which one of the following statements is <u>not a reason</u> why elderly people from highly developed countries suffer from mineral or vitamin deficiency?

(A) Reduced inherent factor in the stomach

(B) High priced nutritional food that can't be met by the low income of the citizen

(C) Less time spent on outdoor activities such as walking to get sufficient sunlight

(D) Renewal of tissues requires high nutritional meals.

(105) Lack of iron can also lead to an infection as many compounds of iron status are most likely affected by the infection. A person suffering from iron deficiency as well as infection is likely to have which combination of iron status markers?

(A) High serum transferrin receptors, high hepcidin, low hemoglobin, high ferritin

(B) Low serum transferrin receptors, High hepcidin, low hemoglobin, low ferritin

(C) High serum transferrin receptors, low hepcidin, low hemoglobin, low ferritin

(D) Normal serum transferrin receptors, high hepcidin, low hemoglobin, low ferritin

(106) Discoloration of brass, when exposed to air, is caused by which gas among the following:

(A) Nitrogen.

✓(B) Hydrogen sulfide. — corrodes metal

(C) Oxygen.

(D) Carbon dioxide.

(107) Select the non-metal that will stay in its fluid state when exposed to room temperature.

(A) Chlorine.

✓(B) Bromine.

(C) Helium.

(D) Phosphorous.

(108) The central metal of chlorophyll as a natural chelate compound is:

(A) Calcium.

✓(B) Magnesium.

(C) Copper

(D) Iron

(109) Name the component used to make pencils.

✓(A) Graphite

(B) Charcoal

(C) Phosphorous

(D) Silicon

(110) Select the metal that when combined with other types of metals will form an amalgam.

(A) Zinc.

amalgam = mercury + metal

✓(B) Mercury

(C) Tin

(D) Lead.

(111) State the chemical formula of water.

(A) CaSiO3

✓(B) H2O

(C) NaAlO2

(D) Al2O3

(112) Which gas is often used to fill electric bulbs?

✓(A) Nitrogen

(B) Oxygen

(C) Hydrogen

(D) Carbon dioxide

(113) Washing soda is a name popularly used to refer to:

✓(A) Sodium carbonate

(B) Sodium bicarbonate - baking soda

(C) Calcium carbonate

(D) Calcium bicarbonate

(114) Quartz clocks are made of quartz crystals which are chemically composed of:

✓(A) Silicon dioxide

(B) A combination of silicon dioxide and germanium

(C) Sodium silicate

(D) Germanium oxide

(115) Select the gas commonly known as a greenhouse gas.

(A) Nitrous oxide.

(B) Carbon dioxide

(C) Methane

(D) Hydrogen

(116) Which of the following statements describe bromine?

(A) Colorless gas.

(B) Red liquid

(C) High inflammable gas

(D) Black solid

233

(117) Which of the following is known as the hardest substance on earth?

(A) Platinum

(B) Gold

✓ (C) Diamond

(D) Iron

(118) Which type of coal has its deposit containing identifiable marks of the parent plant material?

(A) Anthracite

(B) Lignite

(C) Bitumen

(D) Peat

(119) Which of the following is the major use of tetraethyl lead?

(A) Mosquito repellant

(B) Pain killer

(C) Fire extinguisher

(D) Petrol additive

(120) Select the compound from the following that is used as a lubricant.

(A) Graphite

(B) Iron oxide

(C) Diamond

(D) Silica

(121) Which inert gas do deep sea divers use to breathe as a substitute for nitrogen?

(A) Krypton

(B) Argon

(C) Helium

(D) Xenon

(122) Which combination of gas is commonly used in most welding types?

(A) Acetylene, nitrogen, hydrogen, and oxygen.

(B) Argon, oxygen, and acetylene

(C) Hydrogen and oxygen.

(D) Acetylene and oxygen.

(123) Which name is given to the quality of the substance that absorbs moisture when exposed to air?

(A) Desiccation

(B) Deliquescence

(C) Osmosis

(D) Efflorescence

(124) Silicon carbide is commonly used for:

(A) Decontaminate water ponds

(B) Creating statue casts

(C) Breaking strong substances

(D) Manufacturing cement and glass

(125) What is the average saline level of sea water?

(A) 2%

(B) 3.5%

(C) 3%

(D) 2.5%

(126) During the rusting of an iron nail, iron oxide is created_____.

(A) Without a difference of the nail color or weight

(B) Without a difference of the nail weight

(C) With an increased nail weight

(D) With a decreased nail weight

(127) The coat used in galvanizing iron sheets is made up of:

(A) Tin

(B) Lead

(C) Zinc

(D) Chromium

(128) For most allotropes of carbon,_____.

(A) The softest one is coke whereas the hardest one is diamond.

(B) The softest is lampblack while the hardest is the diamond.

(C) The softest one is graphite while the hardest one is diamond.

(D) The softest one is graphite whereas the hardest one is coke.

(129) Fe, Co, and Ni are in a category of metals best known as:

(A) Transition metals

(B) Alkali metals

(C) Rare metals

(D) Main group metals

(130) What is described as heavy water?

(A) Deuterium oxide

(B) Rain water

(C) Tritium oxide

(D) PH7

(131) To impart a detectable smell to a gas, ethyl mercaptan and the odorless LPG cooking gas are added together. The chemical ethyl mercaptan is a compound of:

(A) Chlorine

(B) Bromine

(C) Fluorine

(D) Sulfur

(132) What element is found in all acids?

(A) Hydrogen

(B) Sulfur

(C) Oxygen

(D) Carbon

(133) Which of the following is used in coating nonstick cooking utensils?

(A) Teflon

(B) Black paint

(C) Polystyrene

(D) PVC

(134) Which of the following categorizes monazite as its ore?

(A) Zirconium

(B) Iron

(C) Titanium

(D) Thorium

(135) Graphite, carbon, and diamond are categorized as:

(A) Allotropes

(B) Isomorphs

(C) Isotopes

(D) Isomers.

136) We use potassium nitrate to make:

A. Fertilizer

B. Glass

C. Salt

D. Medicine

137) What can we add to water to remove permanent hardness?

A. Alum

B. Lime

C. Sodium carbonate

D. Potassium permanganate

138) Soda water has:

A. Nitrous acid

B. Carbon dioxide

C. Sulfuric acid

D. Carbonic acid

139) Which is the main ore of the aluminum metal?

A. Calamine

B. Bauxite

C. Calcite

D. Galena

140) From the choices below, which one dissolves best in water?

A. Sulfur

B. Sugar

C. Camphor

D. Common salt

141) Which of these was discovered first on the sun's chromospheres layer?

A. Xenon

B. Krypton

C. Helium

D. Neon

142) When at room temperature, which of the following is in a liquid state?

A. Francium

B. Sodium

C. Cerium

D. Lithium

143) In what liquid should you keep sodium metal?

A. Water

B. Petrol

C. Kerosene

D. Alcohol

144) Which mineral gives us radium?

A. Limestone

B. Rutile

C. Pitchblende

D. Haematite

145) What gas is referred to as laughing gas?

A. Hydrogen peroxide

B. Nitrous oxide

C. Sulfur dioxide

D. Carbon monoxide

146) Which atomic numbers represent elements called actinides?

A. 101 – 115

B. 97 – 104

C. 36 – 43

D. 89 – 103

147) Which two elements are often used to make transistors?

A. Germanium and silicone

B. Aluminum and boron

C. Columbium and niobium

D. Tungsten and iridium

148) Electric bulbs have filaments that are made of:

A. Graphite

B. Tungsten

C. Iron

D. Nichrome

149) What does LPG mainly consist of?

A. Ethane, nonane, hexane

B. Methane, hexane, ethane

C. Propane, butane, methane

D. Hexane, methane, nonane

150) Which of the following best describes air?

A. Mixture

B. Element

C. Compound

D. Electrolyte

(151) In case of a fire outbreak associated with petroleum, from the list below, what category of fire extinguisher would be appropriate to use?

(A) The powder type

(B) The liquid type

(C) The foam type

(D) The soda acid type

(152) Which one of the materials listed below is often referred to as 'polyamide'?

(A) Orlon

(B) Nylon

(C) Terylene

(D) Rayon

(153) You can use epoxy resins as _____.

(A) moth repellants

(B) detergents

(C) adhesives

(D) insecticides

(154) Many detergents that people use for their laundry and also for cleaning utensils have _____.

(A) nitrates

(B) bicarbonates

(C) sulphonates

(D) bismuthates

(155) From the list below, choose the one that is a protein.

(A) Natural rubber

(B) Cellulose

(C) Cobalamin

(D) Starch

(156) When manufacturing _____, wood is the major raw material.

(A) gun powder

(B) paper

(C) paint

(D) ink

(157) In the chemical sense, rayon can be considered _____.

(A) cellulose

(B) amylase

(C) pectin

(D) glucose

(158) Which of the phrases below best describes soap?

(A) Silicate salts

(B) Fatty acid esters

(C) Sodium salts or even potassium salts made of heavy fatty acids

(D) Glycerol & alcohol mixed

(159) From the list below, choose the item that is petroleum wax.

(A) Paraffin wax

(B) Bees wax

(C) Carnauba wax

(D) Jonoba wax

(160) When a barometer reading is dropping, it is a signal of _____.

(A) intense heat

(B) snow

(C) storm

(D) rainfall

Mathematics Section of the NLN PAX

(161) John has a 4½ yard line. How many 3-inch lengths can he get from it?

(A) 84

(B) 15

(C) 54

(D) 45

(E) 64

(162) A dress ordinarily costs $138. If there is a sale and the dress is being sold for a discount of 25%, what will be the sale price of the dress?

(A) $125

(B) $103.5

(C) $113

(D) $67

(E) $34.50

(163) At the harbor, there is a raised crane supporting a beam of steel that weighs 3,300 pounds while the beam's other end is on the ground. The weight of the beam borne by the crane is 30%. How many pounds is the crane supporting?

(A) 2,310 pounds

(B) 990 pounds

(C) 1,100 pounds

(D) 700 pounds

(E) 330 pounds

(164) A taxi charges $5.50 to cover the initial one-fifth of a mile, and after that, the charge changes to $1.50 per every added fifth of a mile. The waiting charges for the taxi are 20 cents for every minute. Mary rode in the cab from her house to a flower store that was a distance of eight miles away. There she bought some flowers and then rode to her mother's house that was an additional 3.6 miles away. The driver waited for Mary for nine minutes as she bought the flowers. What was Mary supposed to pay the driver?

(A) $90

(B) $20

(C) $92.80

(D) $91

(E) $120.20

(165) Calculate two hundred and thirty-six plus three hundred and one.

a. 535

b. 507

c. 505

d. 537

(166) Add four thousand, three hundred and seven to one thousand, eight hundred, and sixty-four.

a. 5,161

b. 6,171

c. 5,271

d. 6,271

(167) Given x = 3 and y = -2, calculate the value of $x^2+3xy-y^2$

a. -13

b. 5

c. -20

d. -4

(168) Subtract one hundred and sixty-seven from three hundred and fifty-six.

a. 211

b. 189

c. 198

d. 298

(169) Subtract three thousand four hundred and eighty-seven from five thousand three hundred and six.

a. 1,819

b. 2,189

c. 2,119

d. 1,181

(170) Write 34 as a percentage of 80.

a. 42.5%

b. 34%

c. 44.5%

d. 40%

(171) Divide nine hundred and seventeen by seven.

a. 145 R 4

b. 131 R 4

c. 145

d. 131

(172) Multiply seven hundred and seven by seventeen.

a. 17019

b. 17049

c. 12049

d. 12019

(173) Convert 48/100 to a decimal number.

a. 0.48

b. 0.038

c. 0.0038

d. 3.8

(174) 6.68 + 4.4 + 17.21 + 4 = _____

(A) 32.49

(B) 31.29

(C) 22.29

(D) 32.29

(E) 31.49

(175) (36.1 + 3.9) * 5.4 * 0 * (13.45 – 9.1) = _____

(A) 0

(B) 280.5

(C) 50.49

(D) 704.7

(176) -5 + (-12) + 10 = _____

(A) 1

(B) -7

(C) 19

(D) -27

(E) -1

(177) 33 − (-28) = _____

(A) 13

(B) -61

(C) 15

(D) -15

(E) 61

(178) (30 ÷ 5) + (12 ÷ 3) = _____

(A) 8

(B) 6

(C) 4

(D) 10

(E) 5

(179) 1,040 ÷ (-26) = _____

(A) -40

(B) -30

(C) 28

(D) 30

(E) 40

(180) (5 + 6) * (8 – 2) = _____

(A) 96

(B) -132

(C) 66

(D) 132

(E) -66

(181) 3 x (-5) x 8 x 2 = _____

(A) -240

(B) 80

(C) -120

(D) 120

(E) -80

(182) 5.791 – 3.81 = _____

(A) 2.171

(B) 1.981

(C) 2.709

(D) 2.181

(E) 1.911

(183) $4^6 \div 2^8 =$ _____

(A) 64

(B) 2

(C) 16

(D) 8

(E) 32

(184) From the list given below, choose the expression that equals X^{mn}.

(A) $(x^m)^n$

(B) nx^m

(C) $x^m x^n$

(D) x^{m+n}

(185) Tim places a penny on a checkerboard's first square; on the second square, he places two pennies; on the third square, he places four pennies; on the fourth square, he places eight pennies and so on until the last square which is the 64th. How many pennies did he place on the last square?

(A) 2^{64}

(B) 2^{64-2}

(C) 2^{63}

(D) 2^{63+1}

(E) 2^{64-1}

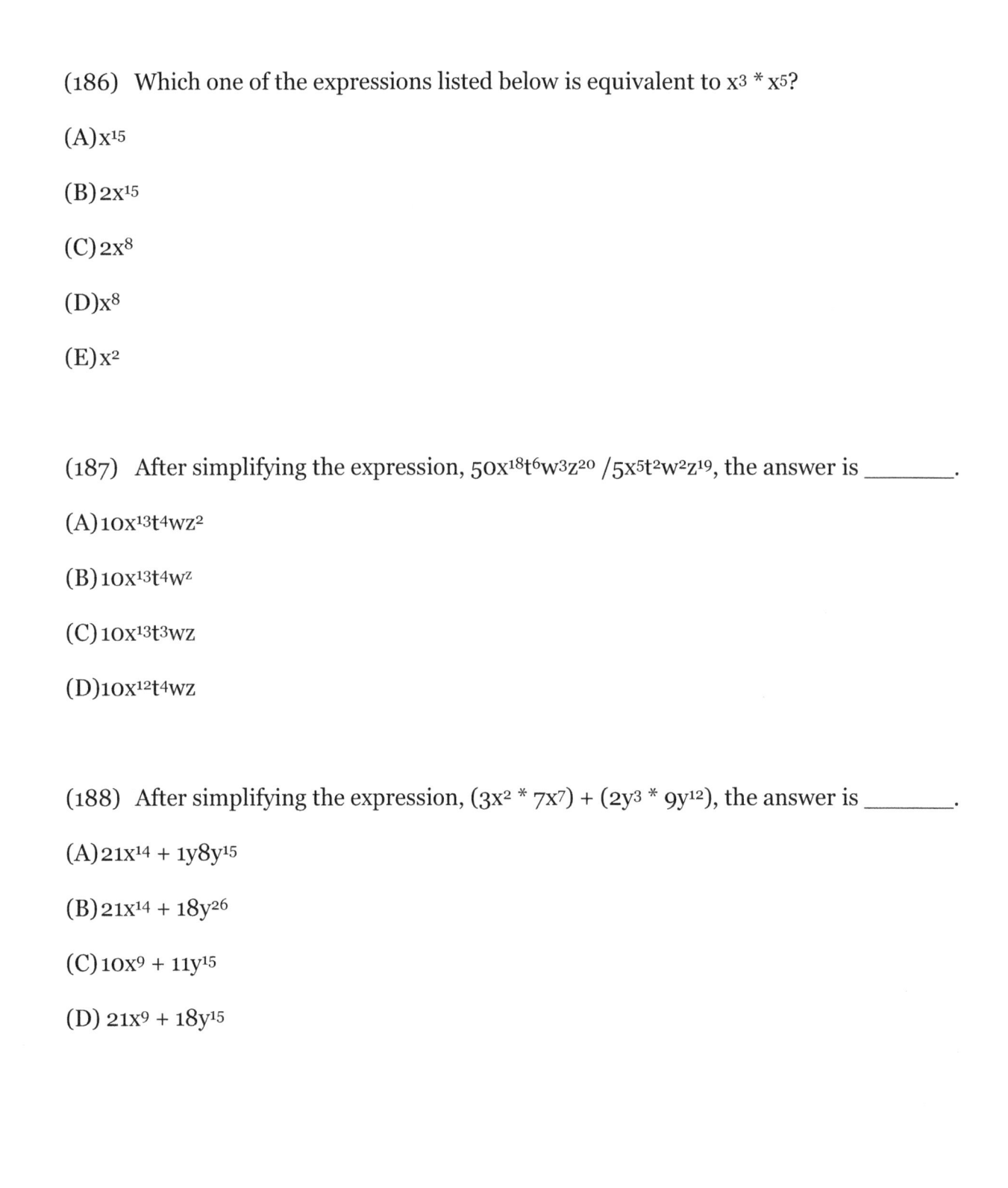

(186) Which one of the expressions listed below is equivalent to $x^3 * x^5$?

(A) x^{15}

(B) $2x^{15}$

(C) $2x^8$

(D) x^8

(E) x^2

(187) After simplifying the expression, $50x^{18}t^6w^3z^{20} / 5x^5t^2w^2z^{19}$, the answer is _____.

(A) $10x^{13}t^4wz^2$

(B) $10x^{13}t^4w^z$

(C) $10x^{13}t^3wz$

(D) $10x^{12}t^4wz$

(188) After simplifying the expression, $(3x^2 * 7x^7) + (2y^3 * 9y^{12})$, the answer is _____.

(A) $21x^{14} + 1y8y^{15}$

(B) $21x^{14} + 18y^{26}$

(C) $10x^9 + 11y^{15}$

(D) $21x^9 + 18y^{15}$

(189) After simplifying the expression, $(2x^4y^7m^2z) * (5x^2y^3m^8)$, the answer is _____.

(A) $10x^5y^{10}m^{10}z$

(B) $10x^6y^6m^{10}z$

(C) $7x^6y^{10}m^{10}z$

(D) $10x^6y^{10}m^{10}z$

(190) Find the value of x if $2^4 = 4^x$.

(A) 2

(B) 6

(C) 4

(D) 8

(191) Find the value of x when $3^4 = 9^x$.

(A) 2

(B) 8

(C) 4

(D) 16

(E) 6

(192) $6^x \div (6^2 + 6^2 + 6^2) = 1/3$. Find x.

(A) 2

(B) 4

(C) 3

(D) 5

(193) Given the diameter of a circle as 16, what is the circle's area?

(A) 8π

(B) 256π

(C) 64π

(D) 128π

(E) 16π

(194) Using the dimensions provided in the shape below, what is the perimeter?

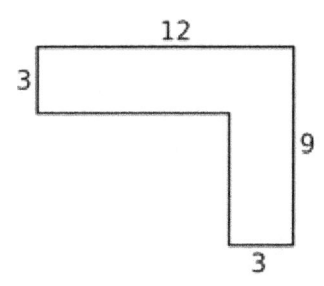

(A) 48

(B) 27

(C) 33

(D) 42

(E) 36

(195) Given the values of two angles of a triangle as 95° and 35°, what is the value of the third angle?

(A) 45°

(B) 55°

(C) 40°

(D) 50°

(E) 35°

(196) Given a circle's circumference is 30π, calculate the area of that same circle.

(A) 900π

(B) 225π

(C) 3000π

(D) 15π

(E) 400π

(197) What do the inner angles of a hexagon add up to?

(A) 1440°

(B) 720

(C) 1080

(D) 540

(E) 810

POLYGON: $\dfrac{(n-2) \times 180°}{n}$

TRIANGLE = 180°
QUADRILATERAL = 360°
PENTAGON = 540°
HEXAGON = 720°

(198) A right-angled triangle has two known sides, one 5 centimeters, and the other 8 centimeters. What is the area of this triangle?

(A) 20

(B) 35

(C) 80

(D) 30

(E) 40

(199) In a given parallelogram, the 2 inner angles on the right are $(4x + 12)°$ and $(3x + 14)°$. The value of x is _____.

(A) 24

(B) 10

(C) 9

(D) 22

(E) 20

(200) Of the options provided below, which one is a set of 3 sides of a right-angled triangle?

(A) 4, 5 & 6

(B) 5, 10 & 15

(C) 3, 13 & 14

(D) 4. 9 & 10

(E) 5, 12 & 13

Practice Test 2 – Answers

English Proficiency Section of the NLN-PAX

(1) She chose the red dress as she found it _____ than the purple dress.

The correct answer is (B) prettier

The word 'prettier' is used as a comparison of two things. Prettiest compares more than two things. Adding 'more' to the word 'prettier' is redundant and it is certainly not grammatical. As for 'pretty', it does not compare and is not used with 'than'. As for the word 'prettiness', it would be wrong to use it in the sentence as it is a noun yet what is required is an adjective to describe the dresses.

(2) He felt unwell and chose to _____ down.

The correct answer is: (C) lie

The word 'lie' is the infinitive of 'to lie', which is a verb, and it can also be used in a sentence like, 'Go lie down', which is normally said to be imperative use. You can also use it in a sentence like 'You will have time to lie down after work', and this is 'lie' used as a verb in the present tense.

The word 'lay' and 'laid' is used when referring to something being placed or a chicken producing an egg. For example, '*Lay* that book on the desk', the teacher said, and the student *laid* the book on the desk. As for 'lain', it is correct to say 'He has lain there long enough; we better take him to hospital'.

(3) From the list below, choose the correct sentence, taking note that they are all punctuated differently.

The correct answer is: (D) Owing to her laziness, she was left behind.

Any time a sentence has a dependent clause or one that is subordinate, and it precedes an independent clause, the correct punctuation is to separate the two by use of a comma. A semi-colon is used to separate two independent clauses, where each clause can stand on its own. For example, 'Jane is the wrong person for the job; she can't even speak audibly'.

A colon is used when you want to introduce a list of things, or another sentence to give a better explanation of the preceding sentence. For example: 'Here are what you should buy: toys, colors, paint, brushes, pencils, and rubbers'. Colons are also acceptable in salutations used in business letters.

(4) From the list below, choose the correct sentence, taking note that they are all punctuated differently.

The correct answer is: (C) The pupil who is leading the class was appointed prefect last semester.

Whenever you have a sentence where someone has been specifically mentioned, the adjectival clause is not really essential, and for that reason, it is enclosed in commas. For example, 'John, who is leading the class, was appointed prefect last semester'. However, in the given sentence, 'pupil' is general and not specific. As such, it would be incorrect to enclose the clause that describes the pupil in commas. Use of a semi-colon and a single comma is also incorrect.

(5) Learning grammar will make you speak _____.

The correct answer is: (B) well

This sentence requires an adverb. It already has a verb, speak, and it is the one that requires describing. Thus, the word 'well' is correct as it describes the way you will speak after learning grammar.

The word 'good' is an adjective; a word used to describe a noun. For example, you could say, 'That was a good speech'. The word 'goodly' is not correct in modern language and is not an adverb. Once upon a time, it was used in place of the word 'good', which is an adjective, but it is now archaic. The word 'clear' is not correct as it is an adjective and cannot describe a verb. It would need to be converted into its adverbial form to fit in the given sentence; meaning becomes 'clearly'.

(6) From the list below, choose the sentence that is most clear.

The correct answer is: (A) She had 20 years of cooking when she burned food for the first time.

The other options sound as if the writer never stopped to do anything else but continued cooking for a whole 20 years before having the incident of burning food.

(7) From the list below, choose the sentence that is grammatically correct.

The correct answer is: (B) I'm not going to repeat it. Just reconsider.

Considering the word 'repeat' has been used in the given sentence, using 'again' is redundant because 'repeat' connotes doing something again. Option (D) has no commas or any other punctuation within, yet there are two clauses in it. That is incorrect as there should be either some form of punctuation or the use of a conjunction to link the two clauses grammatically.

(8) From the list below, choose the sentence that is most clear.

The correct answer is: (C) The chef has photos in the kitchen of his mother in different dresses.

The photos are of the chef's mother and it is the mother who is in different dresses in different photos. It is also the chef who has those photos in the kitchen. The correct sentence must bring out these facts clearly, and this is what option (C) does. The remaining options have their modifiers misplaced and this causes confusion in meaning. Option (A), for example, describes the chef being personally in the kitchen, yet what is required is to show the photos of his mother are in the kitchen. Option (B) is actually given a ridiculous meaning, insinuating photos are in different dresses. Option (D) erroneously portrays the chef as being in different dresses while in the kitchen.

(9) From the list below, choose the sentence that is grammatically correct.

The correct answer is: (D) The last panelist, who was my former teacher, entered.

All the options have an adjective clause, and its role is to modify 'panelist'. Since the noun being modified is a person, the correct pronoun to introduce the modifying clause is 'who'. The option that has 'who' introducing the modifying clause is (D), and that makes it the correct option.

There are many cases of people using the pronoun 'which' to introduce modifying clauses, but this is incorrect as 'which' is preferable when modifying a thing; something inanimate, e.g. a table, conference, interview, etc. 'Whom' is inappropriate in this case and could only be used correctly in reference to an indirect object. Example: 'My former teacher, with whom I had just spoken, entered'. You could also use it in reference to a direct object as in, 'My former teacher, whom I clearly saw, entered'.

(10)   This issue is between _____.

The correct answer is: (A) him and me

'Is' happens to be the verb being modified by the pronouns, and these pronouns are linked by the word 'between', which is a preposition. In a prepositional phrase such as 'between her and me', the pronouns are always used as if they were objects. Option (A) is correct as it has the pronouns 'him' and 'me', which are objective and not subjective.

You can try out different quick tests to see if you have picked out the right pronoun. For example you can say 'Take a picture with the flower vase', 'Take a picture with it', 'Take a picture with John', 'Take a picture with him', 'Take a picture with me', but you cannot say 'Take a picture with he' or 'Take a picture with I'.

(11)   The last opportunity to draw in the charity lottery will go to whomever is the last in line. The underline word(s) wrongly used is/are _____.

The correct answer is: (B) whomever

In such a sentence, the correct word to use is 'whoever' and not 'whomever', the reason is that the word 'whoever' is used as the subject of the clause; meaning 'whoever' happens to be last in line. The word 'whomever' is used as an object and is not a subject. Examples: She wanted to give the last ticket to whomever she wanted. She wanted to give the first ticket to the person whom she saw first.

(12)   There are several people who think that she has often got a lot more than her reasonable share. The underlined word(s) wrongly used is/are _____.

The correct answer is: (C) got

The sentence should read: There are several people who think that she often got a lot more than her reasonable share. The way the verb is currently used is in the simple past

– got. This is incorrect when the tense the auxiliary includes 'has' because it denotes present perfect tense.

(13)   Susan felt so good yesterday that she volunteered to do the cooking herself instead of being waited on. The underlined word(s) wrongly used is/are _____.

The correct answer is: (A) good

To describe how Susan felt, an adjective is required. Yet in this sentence, the word 'good' is used and it is an adverb. 'Good' can be correctly used to describe a book, a play, or anything else, but it cannot be used to describe Susan's feelings. The feeling is just like running or playing in the sense that they are verbs, and to modify them, adverbs are required. However, if it were Susan being described in entirety, it would be fine to say, 'Susan is good' or 'Susan is a good lady'. To describe how Susan felt the adverb 'well' would be the appropriate word. Just as it is correct to say 'She runs well', so is it correct to say 'Susan felt so well yesterday…'.

(14)   Whom did Jane find yesterday at the rear verandah in the resort's restaurant?

The answer is: No error

 'Whom' is used properly as it is the direct object of the verb, and the verb is referred to is 'find'. 'Whom' has not been used as the clause or sentence subject, which would have been the wrong usage.

As for 'yesterday', it has been used as an adverb, just as 'in' has been used properly as a preposition. 'Restaurant' is a noun and it has been correctly used, and the question ends aptly with a question mark.

(15)   Since they felt demoralized, the three top trainees discussed the matter between themselves.

The correct answer is: (D) between

The word 'between' is a preposition used to compare two things or people. It cannot be used when comparing three or more things. While the use of 'between' in reference to three trainees is wrong, it is correct to say: 'Two of the three top trainees discussed the matter between themselves'.

As long as the comparison being made involves three or more things or people, the appropriate word to use is 'among'. All the other underlined words have been correctly used in the sentence.

(16) After the tutor had instructed her to do her research again, the diligent student scribbled a note 'redue' for herself on her paper.

The correct answer is: (C) redue

There is no such word as 'redue', and so it can be reasonably deduced that the student meant 'redo', meaning to do it again. It is easy to tell that the student meant she was to redo the research; in any case, that was the instruction given by her tutor. To do is to perform or execute, and to 'redo' is to perform or execute something again.

(17) When someone through a stone smashing one of his windows, Tom suspected the person was among the rioters.

The correct answer is: (A) through

The word 'through' has been used incorrectly; the appropriate word is 'threw'. The word 'threw' is the past tense of the word 'throw'. If a window was smashed by a stone, then it means someone must have 'thrown' it. 'Thrown' is the past participle of the verb 'throw'.

The writer must have understood the meaning because the rest of the sentence is correct, but mistook the spelling for that of the preposition 'through', which means inside passage.

(18) All the presidential candidates agreed that none of them hadn't sworn to incite their followers.

The correct answer is: (C) hadn't

The word 'hadn't' is incorrectly used in the given sentence is that it follows the word 'none' is negative, which makes a double negative and two negatives neutralize each other's effect. In this case, to pass the intended meaning, one would have to use either 'none' or 'hadn't'. For example, 'All the candidates… none of them had sworn …' or 'All the candidates… they hadn't sworn…'.

(19)   The moment I <u>walked</u> <u>in</u> the room I sensed the place had been <u>abandoned</u> with <u>no-one there.</u>

The correct answer is: (B) in

'Into' makes it clear that the person did not halt at the doorway but continued to the inside. Using 'in' gives the notion of being within, yet 'into' encompasses both ideas – of approaching to make entry and actually getting on the inside. The other underlined words have been used in the sentence correctly.

(20)   "<u>Whose</u> sweater," <u>Mum</u> <u>inquired,</u> "is this? By the way, <u>who's</u> in charge of the sweaters today?"

The correct answer is: No error

'Whose' is a possessive pronoun, and it has been spelled correctly. As for the word 'Mum', it is correctly capitalized because the way it is used in the sentence makes it a proper noun just like 'Tom' and 'Mary'. It is no longer generic the way it is ordinarily used, like in the sentence, 'She ran fast when she learned her mum was home already'.

The verb 'inquired' is correct, and the comma that follows it is correct as well. A comma is always required whenever a quotation has been interrupted, and another comma is used to indicate the ending of that interruption. In fact, it is clear the quotation has resumed when the opening quotation marks are used. 'Who's' is a correct contraction of the two words 'who is'. In this sentence, the common error of confusing the possessive pronoun 'whose' and the contraction 'who's' had not been made.

(21)   The character seen in the leader's administration mirrors his profligate behavior.

Profligate means:

The correct answer is: (D) Immoral

Profligate means degraded, immoral, dissolute, debased, or corrupt. The word comes from a Latin verb 'profligare' which means to destroy, strike down, or overwhelm. In this context, we can use it to say that the leader has a corrupt or immoral character.

(22)   The staff has been charged with expediting the matter by the executive.

Expediting means to:

The correct answer is: (B) Speed up

Expediting means to speed up or to cause a certain process or action happen sooner. In Latin, the word means to set free or to disengage. 'Relieve of' on the other hand means to take responsibility away from someone while 'make easier' means to make a responsibility more manageable. 'Eliminate' means to do away with something altogether.

(23)   The very querulous woman from the ball had dressed beautifully.

Querulous means to be:

The correct answer is: (B) Full of complaints

The word querulous means to complain constantly. Other synonyms that mean querulous include peevish, whiny, petulant, and fretful. The word has its roots from the Latin word 'quer' which means complaining. From this word, other words such as quarrel and quarrelsome which all mean to complain, are also formed.

(24)   She just acquiesced to that whole process.

Acquiesced means to

The correct answer is: (D) Submit to

To acquiesce means to assent to, consent to, submit to, or comply with something without protesting or complaining. It comes from the Latin word acquiescere which means to rest.

(25)   The new land was fecund according to the settlers.

Fecund means to be:

The correct answer is: (B) Fertile

The word fecund is an adjective that means fertile, productive, fruitful, or able to produce offspring, vegetation, or ideas. The word is related to terms like nourishing, produce, or yield.

(26)   Throughout the study, the researchers controlled their data due to participant attrition.

Attrition means:

The correct answer is: (C) Loss

The easiest word that can explain the word attrition is a loss. This means to reduce in size or number. The Latin meaning of this word is wearing out, abrasion, or rubbing away. Participant attrition refers to how participants in a research study that has several levels of research impact findings negatively when they fail to fully participate.

(27)   The contestant abhors many kinds of socialism and that is his stand.

Abhors means:

The correct answer is: (B) Hates

To abhor simply means to loathe, hate, despise, reject, abominate, detest, or find repelling. The Latin meaning of the word is to shudder away or tremble from something.

(28)   Everyone had a viable reason to consider Rita's behavior frugal.

Frugal means:

The correct answer is: (C) Economical

Frugal means to be thrifty or economical. When one has an economical attitude toward food or money, they are said to be frugal. This word comes from a Latin adjective 'frugalis' which means useful, profitable, and economical.

(29)   The treatises written by this philosopher are too esoteric for common readers.

Esoteric means:

The correct answer is: (B) Enigmatic

Esoteric is a word with Greek roots that means inner. Other words that can be used to mean esoteric are enigmatic, arcane, abstruse, or cryptic. This word means that something can only be understood by selected few with special interest or knowledge on that particular subject.

(30)   The bluish color on the patient's lunulae worried the doctor.

Lunulae are found in:

The correct answer is: (A) The beds of the fingernails

Lunulae are those white crescents that you see at the base of your fingernails. The singular form of this word is lunula which means a half-moon. The name is derived from a Latin word 'luna' which means the moon.

(31)   What is the major idea in the passage?

The correct answer is: (B) Several steps are required in the process of developing raisins

Option (B) is correct because there are several different steps explained in the passage regarding the development of raisins. Option (A), it cannot be taken to be the major idea of the passage because it was just a mention in the introductory part of the passage as a minor detail. As for option (C), it cannot also be considered the major idea because shelf fermentation is not mentioned in the passage. Option (D) is also not a suitable answer because although the passage mentions a water bath, it does not give details regarding cleaning in a thorough manner.

(32) What is the major idea in the passage?

The correct answer is: (D) Siv went through a lot of problems in order to reach America and to assist others

In the passage, the main character, Siv, is shown to have undergone very many serious problems beginning in his home country, Cambodia and the passage explains how he managed to overcome these problems. Option (A) is incorrect as the passage does not focus on Siv's global problems and how he persisted with courage. Option (B) is incorrect because the passage does not dwell on how far and wide Siv traveled in his lifetime.

The reason option (C) is unsuitable for an answer is that although Siv did persevere a lot before managing to leave Cambodia, this information is only a small part of the major idea of the passage. This option does not mention anything regarding the very important aspect of Siv's wish to be of help to other people. Option (E) is not suitable for an answer because the main cause of Siv's perseverance was not to gain American citizenship but to escape the grave problems he faced in Cambodia.

(33) What is the major idea in the passage?

The correct answer is: (D) One should fly the flag of America differently according to different situations.

The major idea is about how to treat the US flag at different times according to the respective situations. In ordinary times of hoisting and lowering the flag, it is important to be quick during hoisting but slow when lowering it. It has also been explained in the passage that if the flag needs to be on half-mast, it is important to hoist it fully first before lowering it to half mast. Other explanations pertaining to the handling of the American flag have been given in the passage, and that makes option (D) the best choice for an answer.

Option (A) is incorrect because the passage does not dwell or even mention the symbolism of the flag, and option (B) is an unsuitable answer choice because the passage does not provide information on the number of stars on the flag. Option (C) is an unsuitable answer choice as the passage does not mention what the government would do if the flag of America was badly handled. As for option (E), it is outright wrong because it is said in the passage that the pace at which the flag of America should be lowered is slow while the pace at which it is hoisted should be fast.

(34) What is the major idea in the passage?

The correct answer is: (C) Bamboo is an amazing type of grass with multiple uses

The main focus of the passage is how amazing the bamboo plant is, and how there is a range of uses the plant can be put into. There is no mention of 2,000 as the number of ways bamboo can be made used, which makes option (A) incorrect. Option (B) is incorrect because although Asia was mentioned as a place where bamboo grows very well, the point does not constitute the major idea in the passage. Neither options (D) and (E) are the passage's major idea.

(35) What is the major idea in the passage?

The correct answer is: (A) The race dubbed 'Marathon of the Sands' tests people's endurance limit.

In the passage, the race is described as 'punishing', and this means the people participating are bound to have their endurance limits tested as they run. This explanation makes option (A) a suitable answer. The passage does not indicate the pace at which the participants run, and so (B) is incorrect. Option (C) provides additional information that cannot be considered the main point of the passage. It is true that even the strong runners find the race challenging and the weak runners might not complete the race that goes on for an entire week, but this information only embellishes the major point of how grueling the race is.

As for option (D), the veracity of that information notwithstanding, the important thing is that the issue of which day is toughest is not the major idea of the passage, which makes the option unsuitable as a possible answer. In the passage, it is said that a certain runner disclosed that the reason he runs this harsh marathon is to find his limit, but this may not be a general position. Other participants may have their own reasons for running the race although the passage does not delve into them, so option (E) cannot be correct.

(36) What is the major idea in the passage?

The correct answer is: (C) The Spaniards plundered the Incan empire that can be traced in different cities of ancient times.

The core of the passage is how the Spaniards destroyed a lot of amazing development in the Incan empire. The fact that the Incas once occupied Machu Picchu city is a very small detail compared to the rest of the important information given. As such, option (A) is inappropriate for an answer. Option (B) is also incorrect because although it is said in the passage that Peru is mainly where the Incas lived, this information is too small to be termed the major idea. The passage gives basic information regarding the accomplishments of the Incas including the building of tight walls, and the fact that Peru was one of the places they occupied is minor.

Option (D) is outright wrong because the destruction of the Incan empire happened in the 16th century and not the 13th century. Option (E) is incorrect because the passage mentions impressive things regarding Machu Picchu including how extraordinarily well it was built, but it does not indicate it served as the capital of the Empire of the Incas.

(37)   From the information provided in the passage, it is clear _____ was Piaget's initial discipline in the field of science.

The correct answer is: (A) botany

It is stated clearly at the beginning of the passage that Piaget's original training was in botany, and although he was introduced as an expert in developmental psychology and philosophy, this does not negate the fact that his initial training was in botany. There is also information in the passage that Piaget was a philosopher, yet that does not affect the position that the first trained to be a botanist.

Option (C) is not too farfetched, although not correct because it is said in the passage that the theory he developed pertaining to cognitive development proved to have a great impact in developmental psychology as a field of study.

(38)   Piaget applied the principle of _____ in developing the proposal pertaining to how human beings adapt to their environment.

The correct answer is: (B) the biology he had learned

Toward the end of the passage where the proposal he made regarding people's tendency to adapt is highlighted, it is mentioned that he had noted his observation matched what he had learned in biology so option (B) is correct. As for Freudian psychoanalysis, it is only said to have had some influence on the interests Piaget developed, but it is not said to have had any bearing on his proposal regarding people's manner of adapting to the environment.

The Binet's intelligence test is discussed regarding Piaget's role in helping Binet in scoring as well as the basis for him to determine how differently children think as compared to adults. The test has nothing to do with what this question is about – people's adaptation to the environment. Piaget is said to have applied the method of direct child observation in studying children, but not in relation to the human tendency to adapt to their respective environments.

(39) One of the statements below is true about the experience Piaget had with the tests pertaining to Alfred Binet's intelligence tests.

The correct answer is: (C) According to Piaget, the way children of a younger age thought varied from the way adults thought.

It is stated in the passage that Piaget assisted Binet in the exercise of scoring intelligence tests, but it is not said he assisted in the actual development of those tests. It is also said that Piaget took note of patterns of error in the results recorded after assessing children of a younger age, but it is not indicated the identified patterns caused the tests to become unsuitable for those children. The patterns did not even invalidate the end results.

What is true about those error patterns is that they played a crucial role in helping Piaget design the hypothesis stating that the way children thought was different from the way adults did.

(40) Which one of the following statements concerns Piaget's theory?

The correct answer is: (D) Universal development stages that are progressive, which every human being undergoes

The theory Piaget developed dwelled on the progressive development stages all people go through, and this fact is clearly stated in the passage. This is why option (D) is the best option for an answer.

All the other options are incorrect. This theory had nothing to do with continuous gradual progression since Piaget developed the cognitive development stages as being distinct. If these stages had been gradual and more or less continuous, it would mean they were not separate. The stage progression is said to be universal, and this means it is uniform for everyone as opposed to being unique in each individual.

The passage does not say that children of a younger age made mistakes while adults did not. Rather, the passage indicates there were patterns of particular errors that happened to be consistent and committed by children of a younger age, but which were not noted in adults when Binet's tests were conducted. Hence, Piaget came to the conclusion that younger children have a way of thinking that is different from that of adults.

(41)   There is a theory that holds that people build their knowledge from the interactions they make with their thoughts as well as their experiences. This theory is known as _____.

The correct answer is: (B) constructivism

This theory of constructivism is stated at the end of the passage, where it is said people build knowledge as thoughts and practical encounters. That is the reason option (B) is the best choice for an answer. All the other options are incorrect. For starters, this theory is not called 'biology'. Biology is mentioned as Piaget's initial field of interest, and as the scientific discipline that had a great influence on the theory he created. It is worth noting that it was the knowledge of biology that Piaget applied to establish that people do adapt to their environment by way of assimilation as well as accommodation.

As for cognitive development, it is the focus of the theory Piaget developed, while developmental psychology is that field of study within which the theories of Piaget and others pertaining to cognitive development are grouped.

(42)   Based on the passage, the stage of cognitive development _____ are in according to Piaget is the pre-operational stage.

The correct answer is: (A) toddlers

There is information in the passage explaining that from the age of around two years to the age of seven years, children are within the stage Piaget regarded as 'pre-operational'. As for infants, according to the passage, they are in the cognitive development stage referred to as 'sensorimotor'. It is in the formal operations' stage of Piaget's that teenagers and adults belong.

(43) A child might hold the belief that it was her disobedience that brought about a thunderstorm, a belief that can exemplify what Piaget referred to as _____.

The correct answer is: (B) magical thinking

Magical thinking has been explained as holding the belief that one's own thinking or acting can lead to events that are entirely unrelated or events that are outright external. Hence option (B) is correct. The other options are unsuitable as answers.

Conservation is described in the passage as the capacity to keep in mind properties associated with particular objects in spite of any changes in the way they look, their shape, or how they are arranged. Conservation pertaining to materials of a concrete nature is said to develop during the stage of concrete operations. Magical thinking, egocentrism, and animism all happen in the stage termed 'pre-operational'.

Animism is explained as having the capacity to attribute people's characteristics and behavior to objects that are inanimate. Egocentrism is when individuals think the entire globe revolves around them, and they have an inability to accommodate the viewpoints of other people. Animism and magical thinking are among the characteristics Piaget established were symbolic of the stage referred to as 'pre-occupational', but such characteristics are more specific to magical thinking. As such, egocentrism cannot be the most suitable answer.

(44) Based on the passage, which of the options listed is true regarding the concrete operations stage?

The correct answer is: (C) Children have the capacity to think in a logical manner at this particular stage

It is indicated in the passage that children can initially think in a logical manner at the concrete operations stage, although the kind of logical thinking meant is in reference to objects that are concrete as opposed to abstract. As such option (A), (B) and (D) are definitely incorrect as it refers to children having the tendency to think in a mental, egocentric, and abstract manner respectively.

In the passage, it is explained that the concrete operations stage covers that period when children are able to carry out operations of a mental nature for the very first time, and there is still more information in the passage that indicates that children are incapable of thinking egocentrically during that stage.

(45)   During a typical Piagetian experiment, one researcher poured some liquid in a beaker that was narrow and tall and then transferred that liquid into another beaker that was short and wide, and all that was done before a student who was watching. The researcher then asked that student to identify the beaker that held a larger amount of liquid. The student's reply was that the two beakers held an equal amount of liquid. To which earliest stage among those defined by Piaget does the student belong?

The correct answer is: (C) Concrete operations

The concrete operations stage is clearly identified in the passage as when a person first attains conservation, so long as what is targeted is concrete. As long as a student is already within this stage, it is easy for them to appreciate that liquid remains constant in its volume irrespective of the shape of the container that holds it. It is said in the passage that such a student does not have the capacity to properly perform operations of a mental nature, and such competence would have to wait until the formal operations stage is reached.

However, since the particular experiment makes use of materials that are concrete, the earliest point at which the student would be able to answer the question correctly is obviously the concrete operations stage. The sensorimotor stage is said to cover infancy, while the pre-operational stage is said to cover children whose ages fall within the range of two to seven years; both stages are described as periods when children have not developed logical thinking.

(46)   Choose the answer option that provides the truth regarding the theory by Lawrence Kohlberg according to the information in the passage.

The correct answer is: (D) The theory provides expansion for Piaget's theory of moral development.

As the passage comes to an end, there is information regarding Kohlberg's theory of moral reasoning, and it is said to expand upon the foundations that Piaget established as he formulated his own theory pertaining to moral development. It is important to note that this theory of Kohlberg's is also cognitive, although its basis is the theory by Piaget, which it is not opposed to.

The other options are incorrect and there is a good reason for this. For one, Kohlberg based his theory on the work Piaget did, and so Kohlberg's theory cannot be said to be entirely unrelated to that work. The passage also identifies the theory by Kohlberg as a moral reasoning theory and is focused on the overall and not actually cognitive development.

Science Section of the NLN PAX

(47) From the choices below, which one is a component found under lipids?

The correct answer is: (A) Fatty acids

A lipid is a type of organic compound that is insoluble in water but can dissolve in alcohol. Lipids include oils, fats, waxes, hormones, and vitamins, such as A, E, and D and consist of oxygen, carbon and hydrogen elements.

(48) Which chromosome is affected by Down's syndrome?

The correct answer is: (D) Chromosome 21

Down's syndrome occurs when there is an error in cell division that causes an extra chromosome 21. People with this chromosomal condition tend to have some similarities in physical appearance. Their mental abilities may vary but many of them tend to have moderate reasoning and thinking issues.

(49) Blood gets into the lungs through a certain chamber of the heart. Which one is it?

The correct answer is: (B) Right Ventricle

The heart has four chambers. The two upper chambers that are responsible for receiving blood are called the atria while the lower two chambers that discharge blood are called the ventricles. Oxygen-poor blood goes into the right atrium and it passes through the right ventricle where it is pumped to the lungs and becomes oxygenated.

(50) When you take alcohol excessively over a lengthy period, which organ in the body is likely to be destroyed?

The correct answer is: (A) Liver

One of the roles of the liver is to detoxify the body by getting rid of harmful substances. When a person drinks too much alcohol, the liver is not able to process it properly and the liver becomes overwhelmed. The liver cells become damaged which causes scarring on the liver, a condition called liver cirrhosis.

(51)   There are various types of radiation rays. Which of the following is not one of them?

The correct answer is: (B) Infrared

Radiation refers to the transmission or emission of energy in wave or particle form via space or a material medium. The three main radiation types are Alpha, Beta, and Gamma radiation. An infrared ray is an electromagnetic radiation that cannot be seen with the human eye but can be felt as heat.

(52)   How many oxygen molecules can be held by one hemoglobin molecule to be transported in the blood?

The correct answer is: (C) 4

Red blood cells have a pigment known as hemoglobin. The mammalian hemoglobin molecule is able to carry or bind up to 4 oxygen molecules to be transported to individual cells in the body tissues.

(53)   Which one of the following best explains the process of breathing?

The correct answer is: (D) Pump-handle motion

Pump-handle rib motion refers to the movement of the ribs that causes there to be a change in the front and back diameter of the thorax.

(54)   What do we call animals that consume mostly meat?

The correct answer is: (C) Carnivores

An animal that either exclusively or mainly gets its food from meat is called a carnivore. Arthropods are invertebrates that have jointed legs and an herbivore is an animal whose primary food source is plant material.

(55)   What term is used to refer to the characteristics of genes?

The correct answer is: (B) Phenotype

Phenotype refers to the observable traits or characteristics of an organism as a result of the interaction of its genotype and the environment.

(56) Calculate the acceleration rate of a ball that has a constant velocity is 50m/s over a period of more than 2 minutes.

The correct answer is: (C) 0

If an object is stationary or traveling at a constant speed and in a straight line, then the acceleration speed is always zero. To calculate the velocity of an object, divide the distance over time then add the direction. In this case, a direction is not given.

(57) What term refers to the site where neurons connect?

The correct answer is: (A) Synapse

This is a structure that allows a nerve cell or neuron to pass chemical or electrical signals to other neurons or target effector cells.

(58) What is the kneecap also referred to?

The correct answer is: (C) Patella

The patella is a circular-triangular fat bone that articulates with the thigh bone and protects and covers the front articular surface of the knee joint.

(59) Which one of these terms is used to refer to the joint in the shoulder?

The correct answer is: (B) Ball and socket joint

The ball and socket joint, also known as a spheroid joint, is in the class of synovial joints in which one of the bones with a rounded shaped surface fits into the other bone that has a cup-like depression.

(60)   Which area of the body is the organ of Corti found?

The correct answer is: (A) Ear

The organ of Corti, also known as the spiral organ, is the receptor organ that enables us to hear. It is found in the cochlea located inside the scala media.

(61)   Which vitamin is likely to be lacking in the body if a person is suffering from rickets?

The correct answer is: (A) D

Vitamin D helps to increase the absorption of magnesium, calcium, and phosphate in the body. With a low intake of this vitamin, the body is not able to use the calcium that it needs to make strong bones. Vitamin A deficiency causes conditions like night blindness, Xerophthalmia, and constant infections. Vitamin C deficiency causes connective tissue conditions such as petechiae, gingivitis, internal bleeding, rashes, and non-healing wounds.

(62)   In what group does a steroid fall?

The correct answer is: (D) Lipid

Steroids are in the category of lipids because they do not dissolve in water. They do not look like other lipids because they have 4 fused rings which are composed of one cyclopentane and three cyclohexanes in the molecular structure.

(63)   Cranial nerve X is also referred to as what nerve?

The correct answer is: (A) Vagus

The vagus nerve is the tenth out of a total of twelve cranial nerves that begin from the skull or cranium. It is the longest among the other cranial nerves and takes nerve fibers to the larynx, trachea, pharynx, heart, lungs, and to a large part of the intestinal tract. It also carries sensory information back from the tongue, ears, larynx, and pharynx.

(64)   Which of these PH ranges can you identify as a strong base?

The correct answer is: (C) 11.2 to 12.0

The PH scale ranges from 0 – 14 with most solutions falling within this range. Any solution that falls below the 7.0 range is said to be acidic and any above the 7.0 range is basic or alkaline. The farther away a solution is from the 7.0 mark in its respective class, the stronger it is.

(65)   Which one of the chambers of the heart is responsible for pumping blood in systemic circulation?

The correct answer is: (B) Left Ventricle

Systemic circulation carries arterial blood from the left atrium via the left ventricle and the capillaries to the tissues and organs in the body. The deoxygenated blood that is exchanged in that process is then returned through the systematic veins into the right atrium.

(66)   Newton's second law of motion is represented by which formula?

The correct answer is: (B) F= ma

This law is based on the principle that the increase in the speed of any given object due to the total of all the forces acting on it, is directly proportional to the magnitude of that net force and it is inversely proportional to that objects' mass. The formula F=ma means that (F) which stands for the force that is acting on the object is equivalent to mass (m) of the object multiplied by its acceleration (a).

(67)   In which phase do chromosomes arrange themselves in the mitosis?

The correct answer is (C) Metaphase

During metaphase, chromosomes are aligned beneath the metaphase plate at the center of the cell. Anaphase is incorrect because, during anaphase, chromosomes relocate to opposite sides of the poles to attain the maximum condensation level.

Prophase is incorrect because, during metaphase, chromatin condense and coil up thus formulating the chromosomes with a single DNA that can be easily identified. Telophase is also incorrect because, during telophase, a nuclear membrane that separates the nuclear DNA from the cytoplasm is formed around each set of chromosomes.

(68) Digestive enzymes are contained in which cellular organs?

The correct answer is (B) Lysosomes

Lysosomes are organelle in the cytoplasm capable of breaking down the various types of nutrients, such as proteins, carbohydrates, and lipids. Ribosomes are protein builders of the cell; they connect amino acids one at a time to build a long protein chain.

Golgi apparatus is a packaging organelle that collects simple molecules, assembles them, and makes more complex molecules. A nucleus cannot be the correct answer as well since it serves to control and command the cells.

(69) The process by which organs replace their worn out tissues is called ____.

The correct answer is (B) Mitosis

Mitosis involves the growth and replacement of worn out cells in the body. Transformation takes place when one exogenous cell transfers from one organelle to another organelle that are joined together. Meiosis is when a cell divides into four daughter cells and each only constitutes half the number of chromosomes from the parent cell.

The cellular definition occurs when a cell changes from one type to another type that is more specific as compared to the earlier type.

(70) The model regarded efficient during an enzyme action is called ____.

The correct answer is (A) Lock and Key model

In the Lock and Key model, the enzymes are used as the lock whereas the substrate is the key. Enzymes and substrate perfectly fit into each other thus stabilizing the substrate. Transformation model cannot be used in enzyme functions as it refers to the transfer of DNA cells between microbial cells.

The reason why we can't use Transcription Model is that it focuses on transcription which maps RNA polymerase with DNA on the X-ray structure. This is not compatible with the enzyme action. Enzyme interaction model cannot be used in enzyme function as it focuses on how enzymes and substrates interact to produce a new product.

(71)   Select the statement on enzymes that is false.

The correct answer is (D)

Enzymes are biological catalysts that speed up reactions; they are not destroyed during the process. The statement that enzymes are destroyed during a chemical reaction is false. The answer cannot be (A) as all enzymes are proteins and are referred to as folded chains of amino acids with a particular shape.

The answer is not (B) since due to their reactive nature, it is true that enzymes will require optimum PH to bring the reactants together, reduce their activation energy, and starts the reaction process. Enzymes are biological catalysts hence (C) is also true.

(72)   Select the statement about prostaglandins that is false.

The correct answer is (B)

Prostaglandins are located in every active tissue in humans and animals. The statement that they can only constrict blood vessels is therefore false. Prostaglandins result in response to a particular injury or infection which might lead to inflammation thus causing redness, swelling, pain, or fever. This explains why (A) and (C) are true. (D) is also true; the stimuli that lead to the increase of renal medullary blood flow leading will activate the prostaglandin synthetase thus leading to prostaglandin.

(73)   LDL Cholesterol stands for _____.

The correct is (A) Low-Density Lipoproteins

L.D.L is an abbreviation used to stand for Low-density Lipoproteins Cholesterol.

(74)   What is the process by which arteries harden?

The correct answer is (A) Atherosclerosis

Atherosclerosis refers to the build-up of fats, cholesterol, and other substances inside and on the walls of the arteries thus thickening the arteries and making them harder. Microcirculation refers to the circulation of blood in the small blood vessels and has no effect on the strength of the arteries.

Hypertension refers to a state where the blood force against the artery walls is too high. Venous narrowing also referred to as venous stenosis is manifested through pain, superficial varicosities, and swellings.

(75) The highest blood pressure level shows ____.

The correct answer is (D) Systolic pressure

Systolic pressure refers to the maximum blood pressure during one heartbeat. Optimum pressure is the recommended blood pressure level, hence not the correct answer. Diastolic pressure refers to the minimum blood pressure between two heartbeats, hence not the correct answer. Transient pressure is also not the correct answer since it's the pressure that leads to rapid acceleration.

(76) When subjected to a strong base, a blue litmus paper will turn or stay_____.

The correct answer is (C) Blue

When a blue litmus paper is immersed in a strong base, it stays a blue color. The answer cannot be red since the litmus paper will only turn red if immersed in a strong acidic solution. The answer is not green either since the litmus paper only turns green when immersed in a neutral solution. Orange is also not the answer since the blue litmus paper will only turn orange when immersed in a weak acid of a pH of 5.

(77) Which compound affects alveoli surface tension in the lungs and is necessary during breathing.

The correct answer is (C) Surfactant

Surfactant is the mixture of lipids and proteins secreted in the alveolar space. The surfactant lowers the surface tension at the liquid/air interface within the alveoli of the lungs. Plasma is the colorless fluid part of the blood hence has no effect on the surface tension in the lungs. Sodium chloride is not the correct answer as it is used to reduce sodium loss caused by dehydration or excessive sweating. This does not affect the surface tension in the lungs. Potassium is also not the correct answer since it helps regulate the fluid balance, muscle contraction, and nerve signals; it has no effect on the surface tension of the lungs.

(78) Which function is not regarded as a kidney function?

The correct answer is (C) Transportation

The kidney filters blood before sending it back to the body and it secrets the hormones that help in producing red blood cells. It reabsorbs minerals from blood. The only function that the kidney doesn't perform is transportation.

(79) What is referred to as the kidney's functional unit?

The correct answer is (D) Nephron

A nephron is a functional unit of the kidney, composed of the renal corpuscle and renal tubule which the glomerular filtrate passes through as it turns into urine.

A pyramid is a structural representation that shows the biomass of each tropical level in an ecosystem. The medulla is the part of the brain facilitating respiration and circulation hence has no effect on the kidney. Glomerular is a group of nerve endings or small blood vessels around the end of a kidney tubule, hence not a functional unit of the kidney.

(80) Select the ideal gas law.

The correct answer is (A) PV= knT or PV=RnT

PV= knT or PV=RnT is the formula of the ideal gas law. KTV =PR is incorrect. V=Kt is incorrect as it is the formula for Charles law. PV = k is Bayes law, hence it is not the correct answer.

(81) Select a property that is not a characteristic of a type of gas?

The correct answer is (D) Particles

Gas has 3 main properties: mass, pressure, and volume. Particles are not a property of gas.

(82) 'A particular body that is submerged in a liquid has some upward force act on it that is of similar weight with that of the liquid the body displaced'. This statement describes _____.

The correct answer is (A) Archimedes' principle

The statement describes Archimedes' principle. Boyle's law states that the pressure of a given mass is inversely proportional to its volume at a constant temperature. Anderson's principle states that the vacuum level of semiconductors in an energy band diagram should be aligned.

Charles Darwin stated that at constant pressure, the volume of an ideal gas is directly proportional to the absolute temperature.

(83) What name is given to fluids that easily evaporate?

The correct answer is (B) Volatile fluids

Liquids that easily evaporate even at normal temperatures are known as volatile. Evaporative refers to a liquid that can change from its liquid state to gas. Transient refers to a liquid that lasts for a short while. Viscous refers to a thick and sticky liquid that does not flow easily.

(84) Which of the following is used to describe high-frequency sound waves?

The correct answer is (B) Overtones

High-frequency sound waves are known as overtones. Consonance waves are sweet, pleasant, and acceptable waves. Dissonance waves are unpleasant, unacceptable sound waves. Fundamental waves are the lowest sound frequency of a periodic waveform.

(85) _____ was the first American citizen to be awarded the Nobel Prize for being able to measure how fast light can travel.

The correct answer is (B) Albert Michaelson

Albert Michaelson was the first American physicist to win a Nobel Prize for measuring how fast light can travel. Grimaldi was an Italian who discovered two Paleolithic skeletons. Thomas Young was a British polymath and physician known for his contribution in the light, vision energy among others. Albert Einstein was a German theoretical physicist that invented the theory of relativity.

(86) The anatomical structure connecting the mouth and the stomach is called?

The correct answer is (D) Esophagus

The esophagus is the muscular tube connecting the throat to the stomach. The spinal column is the medulla oblongata in the brainstem to the lumbar region of the vertebral column. Hepatic duct is the tube that carries bile from the liver. The trachea is the tube from the pharynx to the larynx that allows the passage of air to the lungs.

(87) Select the correct statement among the following:

The correct answer is (A): The life of all organism starts as one cell.

In fact, there are even some organisms that remain single-celled, and they are referred to sometimes as being unicellular, a good example is an amoeba. For human beings, it is the sperm from the male and the egg from the female that merge to create one cell known as the zygote, hence bringing about the beginning of greater life. This first stage of embryo development is described as germinal.

(88) According to scientists, _____ has taken place through _____

The correct answer is (B): Natural selection/evolution

According to scientists, evolution takes place through natural selection. There is a difference between natural selection and evolution, as evolution as a form of change is gradual while natural selection means there are specific population members with better chances of surviving and give their genes to their offspring for continuity. Traits passed through generations via evolution takes several generations unlike those passed via natural selection.

(89) Name two science measurement types that very important.

The correct answer is: (D) Qualitative and quantitative

Qualitative and quantitative are very important in scientific measurements. Qualitative methods use description or qualities whereas quantitative method uses numerical results.

(90) A healthy sperm must have:

The correct answer is (C): 23 chromosomes

Healthy sperm will have one chromosome from each pair of chromosomes. Humans have 23 pairs of chromosomes; 22 pairs of chromosomes are autosomal and do not participate in determining gender. The 23rd pair has either X chromosome if it's a girl or Y chromosome if it's a boy. Healthy sperm will have 22 chromosomes that are autosomal and one chromosome that has either an X or Y chromosome and rarely will it have both X and Y chromosomes.

(91) Living things on earth use _____.

The correct answer is (E) A triplet genetic code

Living things use the same triple genetic code with 3 nucleotide sequence known as a codon. A codon has amino acids that are added on a protein. Other living things such as bacteria cannot utilize oxygen as the environment they live in is not properly circulated with oxygen and the only way they release energy is when fermentation takes place. Some living things stay in dark areas such as deep underground and caves. Most living things reproduce through asexual budding or self- fertilization and most developed living things utilize neurotransmitters that exist within their nervous system.

(92) The main reason why sexual reproduction is preferred over asexual form is that:

The correct answer is (B): It leads to diversity.

Through sexual reproduction, genes from the two parents combine creating a new gene. When the two genes combine, they lead to increased diversity in the population thus adapting easily to the changes that may occur in their surroundings.

(93) In an organism scientific name, what do we call the second section of the name?

The correct answer is (A): Species

By the use of binomial nomenclature, the second part of the scientific name of an organism is referred to as a species whereas the first name is called genus. The second section of the name is the most important part as it gives the specific category of the organism. Binomial nomenclature system is used globally and enables scientists to use the same words while referring to a particular species. Species and genus are the last levels of the taxonomy. The categories are arranged from the general level to the specific level: kingdom, phylum, class, order, family, genus, and species. Note that binomial nomenclature focuses on the most specific levels.

(94) When a bacterial cell divides into two new cells, we say the cell has gone through?

The correct answer is (D) Fission

Fission refers to the process of a bacterial cell splitting into new double cells. Being an asexual method of reproduction, the two new cells will grow into different organisms. The replicated duplicate cells are known as daughter cells and mitosis takes place when it's the cell nucleus that replicates. Meiosis leads to a decrease in the number of chromosomes by half in each cell. Replication is when a cell divides into duplicate cells with the same DNA.

(95) Which of the following is not a component of a bacterial cell?

The correct answer is (A): Mitochondria

Mitochondria are not contained in bacterial cells; they are prokaryotes that are built up by single cells. The walls of mitochondria are made up of peptidoglycans. Functions of mitochondria take place within the bacterial cell and the cell membrane. DNA refers to the double helix nucleic acid holding the genetic contents of the organism. It synthesizes

RNA as well as renews itself. Vesicles refer to tiny cavities within cells that contain liquid. A ribosome is a small particle made up of proteins and RNA that construct polypeptides.

(96) Young children are likely to suffer from drastic acute malnutrition defined as:

The correct answer is (C): Age Z height score < -3 or height Z weight score <-3 or edema

Drastic acute malnutrition is not classified using age Z weight score. However, the low age Z height score, or low height Z weight score or the existence of edema can be used to determine whether a child has severe malnutrition.

(97) Children lacking vitamin A are likely to suffer from:

The correct answer is (D): High mortality risk

High risk of mortality and morbidity due to infectious diseases as well as signs in both eyes could be as a result of lack of vitamin A. Goiter is brought about by the lack of iodine. Poor cognitive development is brought about by malnutrition, lack of iodine, or lack of iron. When an individual suffers from generalized malnutrition and lacks calcium, vitamin D, and zinc, the person is likely to suffer from poor bone growth.

(98) Lack of iodine in the body is caused by:

The correct answer is (B): Consuming only central Africa grown foods

Iodine found in most foods is fully dependent on the type of soil where the food grew rather than the specific type of food it is. The iodine content found in the soil varies with geographic location. Central Africa is one of the regions that has soil with low iodine contents; therefore, consumption of food that is only grown in the region is likely to lead to iodine deficiency. Exposure to sunlight will determine your vitamin D status.

(99) Anemia is caused by a lack of which of the following nutrients?

The correct answer is (B): Iron and copper

Anemia is caused mainly by the lack of sufficient iron in the body; red blood cells are manufactured in the bone marrow and need iron. The cells are very important in the structure of hemoglobin. Lack of nutrients, such as riboflavin, folate, copper, and B12 may also contribute to anemia.

(100) Among the following statements, which has not been regarded as a result of kwashiorkor edema?

The correct answer is (D): Lack of iron

According to the research done by Cicely Williams, kwashiorkor is a disease brought about by abrupt weaning of the child. From the 1980s, low consumption of antioxidant and high imbalance levels of oxidative stress have been classified as a result of kwashiorkor. Later in 2013, a change in the components of intestinal bacteria was proposed to be part of the pathogenesis of kwashiorkor.

(101) According to the UNICEF model, malnutrition causes are categorized according to several levels: basic, underlying and immediate. From the following causes, select the one that is not in the underlying category in accordance with the UNICEF model

The correct answer is (A): Inadequate rainfall needed for agricultural purposes

The UNICEF model on malnutrition incorporates an unhealthy environment and lack of proper health services as factors in the UNICEF model. Inadequate rainfall and agriculture are not listed in the model as they are regarded as basic causes. Remember in wealthy regions even during drought people are still able to purchase food hence drought doesn't restrict their access to food.

(102) Which category of people is highly recommended by the World Health Organization to take zinc supplements?

The correct answer is (B): Children suffering from diarrhea or malnutrition.

If detected, zinc deficiency requires daily supplement so as to improve health. In regards to this, WHO does not propose consistent prophylactic supplements to be given to any category of people unless there exists a rare case of acrodermatitisenteropathica. Zinc supplements are therefore only advocated for when a child suffers from severe malnutrition or diarrhea.

(103) What is the core reason a well-nourished individual can suffer from only vitamin D deficiency?

The correct answer is (C): The vitamin D required by our body is not solely dependent on food. Therefore, food isn't a necessary vitamin D determinant.

Vitamin D is mainly absorbed through the skin through exposure to sunlight. It is through the sunlight rays on our skin that our bodies are able to extract vitamin D from cholesterol. Vitamin D is not obtained from most foods hence buying food or obtaining it from agriculture will have a minimal effect on your vitamin D status. It is also important to note that people who are overweight, people with a dark skin tone, those that cover themselves in the sun, and older people do not absorb enough vitamin D from sunlight.

(104) Which of the following is not a reason why elderly people from highly developed countries suffer from mineral or vitamin deficiency?

The correct answer is (D): Renewal of tissues requires high nutritional meals.

Elderly people are most likely to go through a low level of income, cognitive disorder, and social exclusion. This can lead to them consuming low levels of mineral and vitamin-rich meals. The inborn natural factor that is produced by the stomach will also reduce as a person ages resulting in low intakes of vitamin B12. Older people have stopped growing and renewal of tissues is less frequent.

(105) Iron deficiency can lead to an infection as many compounds of iron status are likely to be affected by infections. A person suffering from iron deficiency as well as infection is likely to have which combination of iron status markers?

The correct answer is (A): High serum transferrin receptors, high hepcidin, low hemoglobin, high ferritin

During iron deficiency, serum transferrin receptors increase and are not greatly affected by acute infection. Another factor that may lead to serum transferrin receptors increasing is the case of convalescence where iron is required for tissue synthesis. Serum hepcidin increases whether the iron levels are high or in the case of an infection. In most cases of infection and iron deficiency, hemoglobin tends to be low and not efficient in determining whether it is a result of infection or iron deficiency. Despite being very low during iron deficiency, serum ferritin increases when inflammation occurs.

(106) Which of the following causes discoloration of brass when exposed to air?

The correct answer is (B): Hydrogen sulfide

Hydrogen sulfide is known to corrode most metals, such as brass, iron, steel, and copper.

The effects of hydrogen sulfide on humans include headaches, delirium, nausea, tremors, convulsion, disturbed equilibrium skin, as well as eye irritation and convulsions. Excess exposure to hydrogen sulfide can lead to unconsciousness and even death. It is important to note that hydrogen sulfide liquid gas can easily lead to frostbite-related injury.

(107) Select the non-metal that will stay in its fluid state when exposed to room temperature.

The correct answer is (B): Bromine

Bromine (Br) is one of two gases that will remain in a liquid state at room temperature. With a melting degree of 265.9K, bromine will retain its liquid state as a fuming deep red liquid. When the temperatures are raised, bromine will evaporate forming a gas whose color ranges from red to amber.

(108) The central metal of chlorophyll as a natural chelate compound is:

The correct answer is (B): Magnesium

Magnesium is a very important component during photosynthesis. Located within chlorophyll in plant enzymes, magnesium plays a major role in making the leaves green.

(109) Name the component used to make pencils.

The correct answer is (A): Graphite.

Initially, graphite was considered a type of lead, but over time, it was discovered that graphite mixed with clay will form a strong substance that can easily be placed in rods to work as a pencil as it has a characteristic of leaving gray marks on paper.

(110) Select the metal that when combined with other types of metal it will formulate an amalgam.

The correct answer is (B): Mercury

Amalgam is actually an alloy formed when mercury is combined with another metal. The metal can either be a solid, liquid, or a soft paste. When mercury is mixed with silver it forms a silver-mercury amalgam; this alloy is used in dentistry and is a very important element. To obtain a gold-mercury amalgam that is used to extract gold from ore, mercury is mixed with gold.

(111) State the chemical formula of water.

The correct answer is (B): H2O

Water is composed of two elements: a single oxygen atom and two covalent bonds of hydrogen atoms.

(112) Which gas is often used in filling electric bulbs?

The correct answer is (A): Nitrogen

A bulb is made up of a closed glass that contains an inert gas; this can either be nitrogen gas or argon gas. The reason why nitrogen or argon is used is when the bulb is filled with oxygen or air containing traces of oxygen, the bulb filament will definitely burn.

(113) Washing soda is a name popularly used to refer to:

The correct answer is (A): sodium carbonate

Washing soda is chemically known as sodium carbonate (Na2CO3) and it contains carbonic acid that is a common component of most carbonates. Sodium carbonate in washing powder has the ability to soften hard water making it easier for cleaning detergents to remove dirt from clothes and separate the dirt from water.

Baking soda is scientifically known as sodium bicarbonate. Sodium hydrogen carbonate is known as sodium bicarbonate (NaHCO3) and is a crystal that is white and solid, which can easily be identified as a fine powder. It has various uses thus it has many names including bicarbonate soda, baking soda, bread soda, and cooking soda.

(114) Quartz clocks are made of quartz crystals which are chemically composed of:

The correct answer is (A): silicon dioxide

The quartz crystals used in quartz clocks are made up of silicon dioxide (SiOz). Silicon dioxide is known to be a silicon oxide that is a compound of sand in most regions in the world.

(115) Select the gas commonly known as a greenhouse gas.

The correct answer is (D): hydrogen

Greenhouse gas participates in the role of infrared radiation intake by greenhouses. Gases present in a greenhouse from the one in most abundance to the least abundant include water, carbon dioxide, and methane; ozone and nitrous oxide; and chlorofluorocarbon.

(116) Which of the following statements describe bromine?

The correct answer is (B): red liquid

Bromine is a type of halogen that appears as a fuming red, toxic liquid. It causes choking due to its irritating smell. Bromine in brines and seawater appears as salt. Despite being nonflammable, bromine happens to be a strong oxidizing agent that makes flammable substances explosive and combustible substances flammable.

(117) Which of the following is known as the hardest substance on earth?

The correct answer is (C): Diamond.

Diamond is known to be the hardest substance due to its multiple covalent bonds. A diamond has 4 carbon atoms covalently bonded onto each other. Diamond contains various covalent bonds that make it very strong. Due to this molecular structure, a diamond will require a lot of energy to make it break.

(118) Which type of coal has its deposits containing identifiable marks of the parent plant material?

The correct answer is (D): Peat

When vegetable matter partial decomposes, a substance resembling soil is formed. The substance known as peat is dried and used in gardening or sometimes as fuel. However, peat has various properties, such as acidic pH features, high absorbency, properties to prevent compaction, among others that are very important to gardeners. Note that its absorption levels are higher compared to soil.

(119) Which of the following is the major use of tetraethyl lead?

The correct answer is (D): Petrol additive

The organometallic compound tetraethyl lead is a toxic lead metal that for the better part of the twentieth century was used in the automotive industry as an anti-knocking agent. However, in 1980 it ceased to be used due to its damaging effects on the converter as well as due to its property as a lead metal.

(120) From the following, select the compound that plays the role of a lubricant.

The correct answer is (A): Graphite

Graphite has various carbon atom layers that are weakly attached to each other thus explaining their slippery nature. It is due to the slippery characteristic that enables it to be used in the place of a lubricant.

(121) Which inert gas do deep sea divers use for breathing as a substitute for nitrogen?

The correct answer is (C): helium.

Helium is used to balance the ratio between oxygen and nitrogen. A combination of hydrogen, oxygen, and helium is used in commercial diving by deep sea divers who dive below 130 meters.

(122) Which combination of gas is commonly used in most welding types?

The correct answer is (D): acetylene and oxygen

Acetylene has a characteristic of being the gas that can produce the hottest flame. Due to this property, it does well in cutting metals and welding through a process known as gas cutting or oxy-fuel cutting.

(123) Which name is given to the quality of the substance that absorbs moisture when exposed to air?

The correct answer is (B): Deliquescence

Deliquescence takes place when a substance turns to a solution after it has absorbed moisture within the air. It happens when the partial pressure of the liquid-vapor being absorbed is greater than the vapor pressure of the solution.

(124) Silicon carbide is commonly used for:

The correct answer is (C) Breaking strong substances

Silicon carbide is a combination of silicon and carbon with strong covalent bonds. Due to this property, silicon carbide is regarded as a very strong material that will not easily break or be affected by acid or alkaline conditions.

(125) What is the average saline level of sea water?

The correct answer is (B): 3.5%

The approximate saline level of seawater is 3.5% meaning that every 1000ml of seawater contain 3.5% salt level.

(126) During the rusting of an iron nail, iron oxide is created_____.

The correct answer is (C): with an increased nail weight.

Rust is the name given to the substance formed when iron reacts with oxygen in liquids or air. The iron molecules on the iron nail's surface will mix with oxygen atoms within the air to form a red-brown substance that is commonly known as rust.

(127) The coat used in galvanizing iron sheets is made of:

The correct answer is (C) Zinc

Galvanized iron sheets tend to last longer as compared to non-galvanized iron sheets. This is because the product used in galvanizing is made of zinc that will protect the iron sheets by being the first to corrode before the iron sheet corrodes. To attain better results, most industries have implemented the use of chromate on top of zinc so as to make the sheets last longer.

(128) For most allotropes of carbon, _____.

The correct answer is (C): The softest is graphite while the hardest is diamond.

Graphite has carbon atom layers that have weak covalent bonds thus making graphite a weak carbon. Diamond particles have carbon atoms that are strongly bonded together by strong covalent bonds thus making diamond the strongest carbon alloy.

(129) Fe, Co, Ni are in a category of metals best known as:

The correct answer is (A): Transition metals

Copper, titanium, iron, zinc, among other metals, are known as workhorse metals except for lead, aluminum, and tin that are known as transition metals. They are categorized to be malleable, good conductors of heat electricity, and ductile.

(130) What is described as heavy water?

The correct answer is (A) deuterium

Normal water contains hydrogen-1 isotope. However, heavy water is different from normal water as it contains hydrogen isotope deuterium whose molecules are larger in size than the normal hydrogen isotope.

(131) So as to impart a detectable smell to a gas, ethyl mercaptan and the odorless LPG cooking gas are added together. The chemical ethyl mercaptan is a compound of:

The correct answer is (D) Sulfur

LPG gas is made up of propane as well as butane. Naturally LPG gas is odorless, but to obtain the detectable smell during a leak, LPG gas is mixed with ethyl mercaptan at the storage terminals before released to the market.

(132) What element is found in all acids?

The correct answer is (A): Hydrogen

All acids are made up of hydrogen ions. When an acid that is strong goes through complete ionization, it will split into negatively charged ions and positively charged ions.

(133) Which of the following is used in coating nonstick cooking utensil?

The correct answer is (A): Teflon

Teflon is a type of polytetrafluoroethylene (PTFE) characterized by its lowest friction coefficient on solids. It is also non-reactive due to the strong bonds of carbon-fluorine. Due to these properties, Teflon is used in making containers, such as nonstick cooking pots and other cookware, and pipes for corrosive and reactive chemicals.

(134) Which of the following categorizes monazite as its ore?

The correct answer is (D) Thorium.

Monazite is identified as an ore of thorium due to the decay of thorium and uranium. Monazite will contain a high level of helium that is extracted when the ore is heated. Thorium is used in coating tungsten filaments that are used in electronics such as televisions.

(135) Graphite, carbon, and diamond are categorized as:

The correct answer is (A): Allotropes

Allotropes refer to compounds that are in the same physical state but appear in two or more varying forms. Graphite and diamond are carbon allotropes as they both have carbon atoms.

(136) We use potassium nitrate to make:

The correct answer is: (A) Fertilizer

Potassium nitrate is used as a compound in fertilizers, rocket propellants, fireworks, and to remove tree stumps. Collectively, compounds such as potassium nitrate which contain nitrogen are known as saltpeter.

(137) What can we add to water to remove permanent hardness?

The correct answer is: (C) Sodium carbonate

Hard water usually contains magnesium and calcium which are often called hardness minerals. Softeners are used to remove magnesium and calcium ions from the water. To soften large amounts of water, lime is used which makes calcium precipitate out and carbonate and magnesium to precipitate out as hydroxide. Calcium salts that remain are removed by using sodium carbonate.

(138) Soda water has:

The correct answer is: (B) Carbon dioxide

Carbonated water is simply water that has carbon dioxide infused into it under pressure. This is how bubbly drinks, such as soda water, sparkling water, club soda, fizzy water, and seltzer water are made. The waters are sourced from mineral springs in their natural state and mainly contain sulfur compounds and minerals.

(139) Which is the main ore of the aluminum metal?

The correct answer is: (B) Bauxite

Bauxite is the ore from which aluminum is made. The bauxite is first crushed and then it is purified through the Bayer process. It is washed in hot sodium hydroxide that extracts aluminum from bauxite. It is then taken out of the solution as aluminum hydroxide through the precipitation process.

(140) From the choices below, which one dissolves best in water?

The correct answer is: (B) Sugar

Solubility is measured by how many grams of the substance dissolve at a certain temperature and a certain water volume. Sugar dissolves more than salt and sulfur does not dissolve at all in water. Camphor, a colorless solid obtained from camphor wood, dissolves in water but not as well as sugar.

(141) Which of these was discovered first on the sun's chromospheres layer?

The correct answer is: (C) Helium

The chromosphere is the second layer out of the three layers of the sun that is found right over the photosphere and is red in color.

(142) When at room temperature, which of these is in a liquid state?

The correct answer is: (A) Francium

Francium, formerly called eka-caesium, is a chemical element that has over the years been used in research and to also treat cancers.

(143) In what liquid should sodium metal be kept?

The correct answer is: (C) Kerosene

Due to the reactive nature of sodium, it must be kept away from moisture and oxygen and it should be placed in kerosene. When sodium comes into contact with moisture it turns to sodium hydroxide.

(144) Which mineral gives us radium?

The correct answer is: (C) Pitchblende

Pitchblende, a type of the uraninite mineral which occurs in black or brown masses contains radium and other elements such as lead, helium, and radium which are all radioactive and are formed as a result of the decaying of uranium. There are some actinide elements that can also be found in pitchblende.

(145) What gas is referred to as laughing gas?

The correct answer is: (B) Nitrous oxide

When nitrous oxide and oxygen are combined, it produces a sedative agent that when inhaled through your nose can make you relax. Dentists may also use nitrous oxide when performing certain procedures to ease the patient's tension.

(146) Which atomic numbers represent elements called actinides?

The correct answer is: (D) 89 – 103

Actinides, also known as actinoids, are the 15 chemical elements ranging from actinium with the atomic number 89 to lawrencium with atomic number 103. Actinides are all radioactive.

(147) Which two elements are often used to make transistors?

The correct answer is: (A) Germanium and silicon

Germanium was mostly used long ago to make diodes, transistors, and other electronic components. The semi-metallic element was later replaced by more consistent silicon components in the 1960s. Transistors today are made from geranium or pure silicon but other semiconductors can be used.

(148)   Electric bulbs have filaments that are made of:

The correct answer is: (B) Tungsten

Tungsten light bulbs are incandescent bulbs that work when a filament or metal wire is heated with electricity to a point where it turns white from the heat and glows. The glass contains a gas like argon or sometimes nitrogen and the tungsten filament is located in the center.

(149)   What does LPG mainly consist of?

The correct answer is: (C) Propane, butane, methane

Methane is a powerful greenhouse gas and the main component in natural gases. A single pound of the gas traps heat from the atmosphere 25 times more than an equivalent amount of carbon dioxide. Methane is also captured from landfills and can be used to heat buildings or produce electricity. Butane is mainly used in backyard cooking, camping, and lighters. This gaseous fuel is combined with propane to make LPG which is sold commercially and can be used in heating appliances and vehicles. Propane can be used in furnaces, water heaters, barbecues, laundry driers, portable stoves, and vehicles.

(150)   Which of the choices below best describes air?

The correct answer is: (A) Mixture

Air is made up of many gases and dust particles. It is a mixture because it can easily be separated into its constituents like nitrogen and oxygen through methods such as fractional distillation.

(151)   In case of a fire outbreak associated with petroleum, what category of fire extinguisher from the list below would be appropriate to use?

The correct answer is: (A) The powder type

The powder spreads over the fire and extinguishes it by cutting off the oxygen that feeds the fire. Powder extinguishers also happen to be multi-purpose and can be safely used on three classes of fire – A, B & C. They can also be used on fire that is associated with electrical gadgets and to extinguish fires associated with solids and liquids of an organic nature, like oil, paint, petrol, gas and the like. However, they are not to be used on fires emanating from the frying pan.

Extinguishers that use water plus additives – those used as sprays – are used to put out fires on solid materials of an organic nature, like wood and cloth; paper and plastics; or even coal. The foam type extinguisher is great to use on fires affecting both solids and liquids, petrol, or paint. However, they are not supposed to be used on fires emanating from the frying pan. The soda acid type extinguisher, which comprises mainly sodium bicarbonate and sulfuric acid, normally clears Class A fires.

(152)   Which one of the materials listed below is often referred to as 'polyamide'?

The correct answer is: (B) Nylon

Polyamide is a polymer of the synthetic type made from combining some molecules in the amino group with others from a group of carboxylic acid. Polyamides are strong and resilient and come in handy when strong material is required, not only for clothing but also for carpets, plastics for engineering work, food packaging films, hospital material for sutures, and so on.

(153)   You can use epoxy resins as _____.

The correct answer is: (C) adhesives

The importance of epoxy resins lies mostly in the making of adhesive material and plastics, as well as sealers, primers, coatings, and paints. Sometimes you may hear of epoxy, but that is used in reference to an epoxy resin that has been cured. For that reason, you may find epoxy resin liquefied. As far as epoxy is concerned, you should expect a curing agent to accompany it, and it is the reaction between the two materials that cause hardening.

(154) Many detergents that people use for their laundry and also for cleaning utensils have _____.

The correct answer is: (C) sulphonates

A sulphonate is a kind of salt, and in fact, sodium dodecylbenzene sulfonate is good for cleaning fruit and items used at the table. Some companies even use them in making detergent. As for nitrates, their great use is in making fertilizer. Bicarbonates can be medicinal, with sodium bicarbonate being used as an anti-acid to sort out issues of indigestion and heartburn.

(155) From the list below, choose the one that is a protein.

The correct answer is: (A) Natural rubber

Natural rubber comes from trees, mainly the Ficus and the Hevea, and is a substance of an elastic nature. It is made from tree sap that is latex, and it can also be technically considered a hydrocarbon polymer that is elastic in nature. Cellulose is the major component within the cell of a plant, and it is what ensures the plant remains strong and even stiff. Although people need cellulose in their diet to provide fiber, they do not have the capacity to digest it. Cobalamin is a term used in reference to vitamin B12. Starch falls under polysaccharides and serves to preserve carbohydrates. It is also important as part of people's diet.

(156) When manufacturing _____, wood is the major raw material.

The correct answer is: (B) paper

In order to produce paper from wood, the wood from trees must first be converted into pulp, which is essentially a soup-like liquid that is watery comprising fibers of cellulose and lignin and water.

(157) In the chemical sense, rayon can be considered _____.

The correct answer is: (A) cellulose

305

Rayon is a kind of fiber created from cellulose fiber that has been regenerated. This fiber comes in different varieties, and all in varying grades. The feel, as well as texture, is close to that of natural fiber. Amylase is an enzyme that breaks bonds of glucose molecules within starch. Pectin is a substance present in fruit like apples and berries, and when it is heated and has sugar added, they thicken and form jams or jellies.

(158) Which of the phrases below best describes soap?

The correct answer is: (C) Sodium salts or potassium salts made of heavy fatty acids

The kind of soap produced, whether it is bar soap or liquid soap depends on the salt compound used. Sodium hydroxide or potassium hydroxide (potash) can be used.

(159) From the list below, choose the item that is petroleum wax.

The correct answer is: (A) Paraffin wax

The manner of obtaining paraffin wax from petroleum is the dewaxing of oil that is a lubricant and light. This wax is used in candle making, in the manufacture of paper, and polish material for electrical insulation. The wax also helps in extraction of perfumes from sweet smelling flowers. It also serves as a good base for ointments used as medication and as wood coating with waterproof qualities. In the manufacture of matches of from wood, this wax serves as the material responsible for igniting the matchsticks because it provides hydrocarbon fuel in a vaporized form.

(160) When a barometer reading is dropping, it is a signal of _____.

The correct answer is: (D) rainfall

The function of a barometer is to assess the air pressure within a given environment. Specific changes in the environmental pressure are an indication of weather changes of a short-term nature.

Mathematics Section of the NLN PAX

(161) John has a 4½ yard line. How many parts of 3-inch length can he get from it?

The correct answer is: (C) 54

One yard is three feet while one foot is twelve inches. You need to find the number of feet in the 4.5 yards by multiplying 4.5 x 3 = 13.5 feet. Then find the number of inches in those 13.5 feet by calculating 13.5 x 12 = 162. To establish the number of 3-inch pieces that can be made divide 162 inches ÷ 3 = 54.

(162) A type of dress ordinarily costs $138. If there is a sale and the dress is being sold at a discount of 25%, what would the sale price of the dress?

The correct answer is: (B) $103.50

Calculate the amount of money that is the discount and then subtract it from the original price of the dress. 25% of $138 = $34.50 and $138 - $34.50 = $103.50

(163) At the harbor, there is a raised crane supporting a beam of steel that weighs 3,300 pounds while the beam's other end is on the ground. The weight of the beam borne by the crane is 30%. How many pounds is the crane is supporting?

The correct answer is: (B) 990 pounds

Considering the beam's entire weight is 3,300 pounds, 30% of it is 0.30 x 3300 = 990 pounds. All the other options are different percentages and not 30%.

(164) There is a taxi that charges $5.50 to cover the initial one-fifth of a mile and after that the charge changes to $1.50 per every added fifth of a mile. The waiting charge for the taxi is 20 cents for every minute. Mary rode in the cab starting from her house to a flower store that was a distance of eight miles. There she bought some flowers and then rode to her mother's house that was an additional 3.6 miles away. The driver had had to wait for Mary for 9 minutes as she bought the flowers. How much was Mary supposed to pay the driver?

The correct answer is: (C) $92.80

The first distance covered is 0.2 mile, and the cost was $5.50
For the remaining distance of 8 miles she paid 7.8/0.2 x $1.50 = $58.50
Waiting charges at the flower store = 9min x 20cts = $1.80
For the distance from the store to mother's house was 3.6/0.2 x $1.50 = $27
The total amount of money Mary was supposed to pay for the taxi was $92.80.

(165) Calculate two hundred and thirty-six plus three hundred and one.

The correct answer is: (D) 537

Everything about this problem is simple, and trying to look for hidden meaning would only be misleading. All you need to do is write the figures represented in words and then do simple addition.

236 + 301 = 537

(166) Add four thousand, three hundred and seven to one thousand, eight hundred and sixty-four.

The correct answer is: (B) 6,171

4,307 + 1,864 = 6,171

This problem is simple but it tests your competence and keenness in carrying the right numbers as they graduate in value. Begin adding the tens, meaning the digits in the column on the extreme right, and then you move step by step to the left. In this particular problem, when you add 7+4 you get 11 but you can only write 1 in the tens column and carry the other 1 to the column of hundreds. So now instead of adding 0+6, you will be adding 1+6 on the hundreds column, and that is the reason the answer at the bottom of that column is 7.

(167) Given x = 3 and y = -2, calculate the value of $x^2+3xy-y^2$

The correct answer is: (A) - 13

Substitute the unknown for the values given for x and for y. The equation will become:
$3^2 + 3 \times 3 \times -2 - (-2^2)$

$3^2 + 3 \times 3 \times -2 - (-2^2) = 9 + (9 \times -2) -4 = 9 - 18 - 4 = -13$

(168) Subtract one hundred and sixty-seven from three hundred and fifty-six.

The correct answer is: (B) 189

This is a problem that tests how well you know and remember how to borrow tens from hundreds and hundreds from thousands when the number above is smaller in value than the number below.

356 – 167 = 189

(169) Subtract three thousand four hundred and eighty-seven from five thousand three hundred and six.

The correct answer is (A) 1,819

This is another problem where you need to apply your skills of borrowing, and also to borrow where there is zero.

5,306 – 3,487 = 1,819

You need to begin subtracting from the extreme right. 6 – 7 is impossible so you need to borrow 1 from the next column, but this column has nothing you can borrow from as it is 0. Proceed to the thousands column and borrow 1 from 3 and add it to the hundreds column whose value is now 10 and you borrow 1 from the 10, leaving 9 in the tens place.

You now have 16 – 7 = 9. Next column now has 9 – 8 = 1. Since you borrowed 1 from 3 in the hundreds column it now has 2, and 2 – 3 is not possible. You need to borrow 1 from the thousands column which is 12 – 4 = 8. The column on the extreme left will now be 4 – 3 = 1. Therefore, the answer is 1819.

(170) Write 34 as a percentage of 80.

The correct answer is: (A) 42.5%

Make a fraction of 34 over 80 and multiply by 100 to find the percentage. 34/80 x 100% = 42.5%.

(171) Divide nine hundred and seventeen by seven.

The correct answer is: (D) 131

To calculate 917 ÷ 7, you begin on the extreme left. 9/7 = 1, and so you will be left with 2 because 9 – 7 = 2. You need to carry that 2 to the next column to your right, and as usual, it will become a ten. When you get to the next column you have 20 that you add to the 1 you find and you get 21. 21/7 = 3 and that is what you write down as part of your answer. On the extreme right is 7, and you need to divide that by 7 and the answer is 1. You now need to combine all those digits in the order that you wrote them down to get the correct answer. The result of these calculations is 131, which is the answer provided in option (D).

(172) Multiply seven hundred and seven by seventeen.

The correct answer is: (D) 12,019

This question is testing your skills in long multiplication. Although the numbers are big with numerous digits, to be able to get the correct answer all you require is basic knowledge in simple multiplication, meaning those involving single digits, and keenness where you place every digit of your answer.

707 x 17 = 12,019

Multiply the number above by one digit at a time, and the position you begin putting down your answer – from the right – depends on whether the number you are multiplying by is a ten, a hundreds, etc. When you multiply 7 x 7 and get 49, you are supposed to write down 9 and carry 4 to add onto the next answer you get after multiplying the next number. 9 is supposed to be written right under 7 where the tens belong. Once you are through multiplying by 7 and get 4,949, you need to multiply 707 by 1 and write the answer immediately after the product of 707 x 7. Here you will get 707, but the 7 on the right should be written exactly below 1 because that is where the hundreds begin. After that, you need to add the two products to get the final answer.

(173) Convert 48/100 to a decimal number.

The correct answer is: (A) 0.48

Any time you divide a number by 10, move the presumed decimal point at the end of that number one place to the left. If you are dividing the number by 100, move the decimal point two places to the left. This time the division is by 100 and the decimal is presumed to the right of 8, so move the decimal after the 8 two places to the right, which results in 0.48.

(174)   6.68 + 4.4 + 17.21 + 4

The correct answer is: (D) 32.29

6.68 + 4.40 + 17.24 = 32.29 (note all numbers now have 2 decimal places)

If you want to make your calculations easy and avoid confusing which digit is in the tens place, which one is in the hundreds place, etc., it is a good idea to write all the numbers vertically in a column. Ensure the digits are properly aligned according to the decimal point in each number. If some numbers have fewer numbers following the decimal, it is advisable that you add zeros to ensure the numbers have the same number of decimal places.

(175)   (36.1 + 3.9) * 5.4 * 0 * (13.45 – 9.1)

The correct answer is: (A) 0

Remember * is the same as the multiplication sign x.

In a question like this one, you would normally follow BODMAS, meaning Brackets of Division, Multiplication, Addition, and Subtraction, but you can avoid that and simply do a quick deduction. What you are expected to solve is:

(36.1 + 3.9) * 5.4 * 0 * (13.45 – 9.1)

Whatever is in brackets can be considered one unit. The most significant thing is the presence of zero as a multiplication factor. Irrespective of what you get within the brackets, once you multiply it by zero the result will be zero. That is the same case with the numbers outside the bracket which are 5.4 and 0. That is why option (A) is the correct answer.

(176)   -5 + (-12) + 10

311

The correct answer is: (B) -7

You need to eliminate the brackets first, and the way to do it is working out what needs to be done with the number inside. Here you need to calculate -5 + (-12). When a plus sign is followed by a minus, the minus takes precedent and so, in this case, the equation will be -5 – 12, which becomes -17. So now you have -17 +10 = -7, which is option (B).

(177) 33 – (-28)

The correct answer is: (E) 61

Although it is best to begin your calculations by working out whatever is enclosed in brackets, the most significant point with this question is the use of two minus signs one immediately after the other. (a minus times a minus = a plus) In this case, the question will look like: 33 + 28 = 61.

(178) (30 ÷ 5) + (12 ÷ 3)

The correct answer is: (D) 10

Deal with the brackets first by solving what is inside the brackets. (30 ÷ 5) = 6 and (12 ÷ 3) = 4. Then 6 + 4 = 10.

(179) 1,040 ÷ (-26)

The correct answer is: (A) -40

Dividing a positive number by a negative one is always negative.

(180) (5 + 6) * (8 – 2)

The correct answer is: (C) 66

In questions such as this one, follow the operation order and calculate what is within the brackets first before using the mathematical signs outside the brackets. Begin by adding 5+6 = 11 and then 8 – 2 = 6. Now you can use the multiplication sign outside the brackets: 11 * 6 = 66.

(181) 3 x (-5) x 8 x 2

The correct answer is: (A) -240

Begin calculations from the extreme left. One significant point to note is the multiplication of a positive number with a negative one, the results are always negative.

3 x -5 = -15 and -15 x 8 = -120 and -120 x 2 = -240

(182) 5.791 – 3.81

The correct answer is: (B) 1.981

5.791 – 3.810 = 1.981 (both numbers have 3 decimal places)

The best way to solve a question like this is to arrange the numbers vertically with the decimal points aligned. As you rewrite the numbers, ensure each digit is in its right position – the tenths in their place, the hundredths the same, the thousandths and so on. Add a zero to 3.81 so it is written 3.810. Now both numbers have the same number of decimal places.

(183) $4^6 \div 2^8 =$ _____

The correct answer is: (C) 16

Make the base numbers the same. What has been given as the base are 4 and 2, but then again 4 can be broken down into 2 and that will make the base numbers involved in the division the same. The importance of this uniformity is that when you want to divide numbers of an exponential nature whose base is similar, all you do is subtract the denominator's exponent from the numerator's exponent. To multiply exponential numbers you add their exponents.

This question is: $4^6 \div 2^8$
4 can be written as 2^2. For that reason, $4^6 = (2^2)^6$, which is equal to 2^{12}
Now you have $2^{12} \div 2^8 = 2^4 =$ 2 x 2 x 2 x 2 = 16, which is the correct answer given as option (C).

(184) From the list given below, choose the one whose expression equals X^{mn}

The correct answer is: (A) $(x^m)^n$

Multiply the given exponents. In the case of this question, the exponent m has been multiplied with the exponent n to get mn, with their base remaining as x. This is the same as saying that any exponent product is the same as having one exponent being the power of another power. For example, $2^{2*3} = 2^6 = 64$
It is also equivalent to 4^3 as well as $(2^2)^3$

(185) Tim places a penny on a checkerboard's first square, on the second square, he places two pennies, on the third, he places four, fourth eight and so on till the last square which is the 64th. How many pennies should he have placed on the last square?

The correct answer is: (C) 2^{63}

It is worth noting that the number of coins being placed on every consecutive square doubles – from one to two to four to eight and so on. For example, whereas the 2nd square has 4 pennies, meaning 2^2, the 3rd square has 2^3, which equals 8 coins. That is the criterion you should follow to find the number of coins placed on the 64th square.

The catch here is that the numbering on a checkerboard begins at zero (0), and therefore what is termed the 64th square is actually the 63rd square. As such, the exponent you should use is 63 and not 64. That is why the correct answer is 2^{63}.

(186) Which one of the expressions listed below is equivalent to $x^3 * x^5$?

The correct answer is (D) x^8.

In order to solve multiplication involving exponential numbers if those numbers have a common base, you add their exponents. In this case of $x^3 * x^5$, add 3 + 5 and the exponent will be 8 and then write the base with exponent 8.

(187) After simplifying $50x^{18}t^6w^3z^{20} / 5x^5t^2w^2z^{19}$, the answer is _____.

The correct answer is: (B) $10x^{13}t^4w^z$

First of all, when you have $50x^{18}t^6w^3z^{20}/5x^5t^2w^2z^{19}$, it helps to deal with the regular numbers first, like in this case dividing 50 divided by 5 because they have the same constants, x. The expression now is $10x^{18}t^6w^3z^{20}/x^5t^2w^2z^{19}$. When you divide exponential numbers that have a common base, subtract the exponents. In this case, subtract the powers of the denominator from the powers of the numerator. $x^{18} - x^5 = x^{13}$; $t^6 - t^2 = t^4$; $w^3 - w^2 = w$; and $z^{20} - z^{19} = z$. The answer is, therefore, $10x^{13}t^4wz$ as represented in option (B).

(188) After simplifying the expression, $(3x^2 * 7x^7) + (2y^3 * 9y^{12})$, the answer is ____.

The correct answer is: (D) $21x^9 + 18y^{15}$

First, deal with the brackets. In this case, $(3x^2 * 7x^7) = 21x^9$ and $(2y^3 * 9y^{12}) = 18y^{15}$. What you will have done is multiply the constants (3 x 7) and (2 x 9) in their respective brackets, and then added the exponents of the bases. The answer is $21x^9 + 18y^{15}$.

(189) After simplifying the expression, $(2x^4y^7m^2z) * (5x^2y^3m^8)$, the answer is ____.

The correct answer is: (D) $10x^6y^{10}m^{10}z$

Given the expression $(2x^4y^7m^2z) * (5x^2y^3m^8)$, you need to follow the basic rules of math and the rules of exponents. Deal with the brackets first, but there are no calculations required within either bracket. Therefore, you can open up the brackets and begin doing the calculations across the numbers on either side of the multiplication sign. Remember whenever multiplication is involved and the base numbers are the same, you add the exponents.

You now have $2x^4$ x $5x^2$; y^7 x y^3; m^2 x m^8; and z, which equals $10x^6y^{10}m^{10}z$.

(190) Find the value of x if $2^4 = 4^x$

The correct answer is: (A) 2

This one can be done the long way since the exponent is not very big. It will look like this: 2^4 = 2 x 2 x 2 x 2, and the answer is 16. Since $2^4 = 4^x$, meaning $4^x = 16$, x must be 2.

(191) Find the value of x when $3^4 = 9^x$.

The correct answer is: (A) 2

3^4 is the same as 3 x 3 x 3 x 3, which is 81. It also means 9^x = 81, and so x = 2.

(192) $6^x \div (6^2 + 6^2 + 6^2) = 1/3$. Find x.

The correct answer is: (A) 2

Since the denominator does not have an unknown, you can begin by calculating its value. $(6^2 + 6^2 + 6^2)$ = 36 + 36 + 36 = 108. This means $6^x \div 108$ = 1/3. Proceed to solve this equation like this: $6^x \div 108$ = 1/3; 6^x = 1/3 x 108; 6^x = 36. Then, 6^2 = 36, and that is why x = 2, the value in option (A).

(193) Given the diameter of a circle as 16, what is the area of the circle?

The correct answer is: (C) 64π

The area of a circle is πr^2, and the radius is half of the diameter, or half of 16, which equals 8. $\pi r^2 = \pi \times 8^2$. This is the same as 64π, which is represented in option (C).

(194) With the dimensions provided in the shape below, find the perimeter.

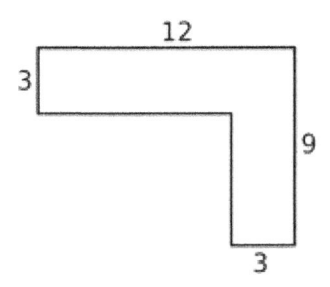

The correct answer is: (D) 42

Calculation of a figure's perimeter involves adding the lengths of all its sides. In this case, it is important that you begin to establish the dimensions not provided. For starters, the segment right opposite 9 can be found by calculating 9 − 3 = 6. To find the length of the segment opposite 12 is found by calculating 12 − 3 = 9. To calculate the perimeter, the lengths to add are: 12 + 9 + 3 + 6 + 9 + 3 = 42.

(195) Given the values of two angles of a triangle as 95° and 35°, find the value of the third angle.

The correct answer is: (D) 50°.

The most important thing to remember is that the values of all the angles of a triangle add up to 180°. In this question, the values of the two angles add up to 95° + 35° = 130°. Hence, the value of the third angle is 180° − 130° = 50°.

(196) Given a circle's circumference to be 30π, calculate the area of that same circle.

The correct answer is: (B) 225π

Considering a circle's conference is πD; it is also 2πr.

30π = 2πr or 30 = 2πr/π. Here π cancels out and you are left with 30 = 2r; r = 15. Since the area of a circle is πr², the area is π15² or 225π.

(197) What do the inner angles of a hexagon add up to?

The correct answer is: (B) 720

A hexagon has 6 sides. Also note that the formula that gives the sum of a polygon's inner angles is: 180° * (n − 2), where n represents the number of sides. Substitute n with 6. The calculation is as follows:

Total angles = 180° * (6 − 2); 180° * (4) = 720°.

(198) A right-angled triangle has two known sides, one 5 centimeters as the height and the other 8 centimeters as the base. What is the area of this triangle?

The correct answer is: (A) 20 cm²

The sides are 5 and 8, and the formula of the area is half base times height or ½bh. With the base being 8 and the height being 5, the calculation is:
½bh = ½ x 8 x 5 = ½ x 40 = 20cm²

317

(199) In a given parallelogram, the 2 inner angles on the right are $(4x + 12)°$ and $(3x + 14)°$ The value of x is _____.

The correct answer is: (D) 22

When you are dealing with a parallelogram, angles that are adjacent are also complimentary, and their sum is 180°. This is the information you should use in calculating the value of x.
$(4x + 12)° + (3x + 14)° = 180°$
$7x + 26 = 180$
$7x = 180 - 26 = 154$
Therefore $x = 154 ÷ 7 = 22$.

(200) Of the options provided below, which one is a set of 3 sides of a right-angled triangle?

The correct answer is: (E) 5, 12, & 13

One of the important things to remember is the principle that every right-angled triangle must satisfy $a^2 + b^2 = c^2$ as per the Pythagorean Theorem.
Use this principle to test the validity of each of the answer choices provided.
Is $4^2 + 5^2 = 6^2$ or $16 + 25 = 36$? No, $4^2 + 5^2 = 36$
Is $5^2 + 10^2 = 15^2$ or $25 + 100 = 225$? No, $5^2 + 10^2 = 125$
Is $3^2 + 13^2 = 14^2$ or $9 + 169 = 196$? No, $3^2 + 13^2 = 178$
Is $4^2 + 9^2 = 10^2$ or $16 + 81 = 100$? No, $4^2 + 9^2 = 97$
Is $5^2 + 12^2 = 13^2$ or $25 + 144 = 169$? Yes, it is. Clearly, the set of measurements matching those of a right-angled triangle is option (E) with 5, 12, & 13.

Made in the USA
Middletown, DE
09 August 2019